I'm Sleeping With the Pastor!

Success Kit for Pastors' wives and those who love us

Dr. Sena Whitaker

With chapter to Pastors by Pastor Earl Whitaker

EARSEN Publishing Company
Cypress, TX

Copyright Page

First printing 2013

ISBN-10: 0-9789953-0-9
ISBN-13: 978-0-9789953-0-0

Library of Congress Catalog Card Number: 2006908763

EARSEN Publishing Company Houston, TEXAS

Cover Design by Eric Chinn

A bold, personal collection of a pastor's wife's experience and advice.

"Marriage is under siege," warns Whitaker in her debut self-help guide—and people need to be prepared to "live beyond fairy tales." Whitaker strings together anecdotes, advice and axioms in this guide... She writes about America's rising divorce rate, and in a section titled "Waterproof Matches: Enhancing Intimacy," she details the numerous ways readers can bring passion back into their marriages, as well as steps they can take to prevent conflict. Helpful reminders, such as having a "win-win" approach to arguments, stand alongside apt advice, such as avoiding turning everything into a spiritual discussion. In "Life Vests," the author urges that readers eat right and exercise and discusses how it's crucial to care for one's body as well as one's soul. Citing Benjamin Franklin's adage, "To lengthen thy life, lessen thy meals," she writes about the psychological impact of good health while owning up to her own struggle with her weight. She also takes on topics such as finances, infidelity and grief, offering practical advice intermingled with personal stories and colorful examples. This candid, relatable book dishes out honesty and humor on every page.
----Kirkus Review

About the Author

Sena Whitaker, Ph.D., Th.M., has twenty one years' experience as a pastor's wife. She is the Founding President of Ministers of the Heart, Inc., Interdenominational Fellowship of Female Ministers, and the Omar Jamal Aycox Foundation, Inc. She is also an ordained Minister, and has certifications in Christian Counseling, and Expository Preaching. Dr. Whitaker was born in Chester, Pennsylvania, and was raised in Philadelphia. She is married to Pastor Earl Whitaker Sr. They are the parents of five sons and a daughter.

Dedication

I dedicate this book to the triune only true and living God: Father, Son, and Holy Spirit; my Sustainer, Savior, and Sanctifier. How I adore You and bless Your glorious and awesome name! You are almighty, sovereign, infinite, most holy, and faithful. To You be the praise, honor, and glory for all the things You have done to make this book possible. Human language could never express how eternally grateful I am to You for loving me beyond measure, entrusting me with this project, guiding me through every word, staying by my side every step of the way, and for doing far above more than I could ask or think in all areas of my life. Thank You!

Acknowledgments

Many persons contributed to the development of this book, and if you are one of them, then thank you for helping me bring my experiences in written form. I could never have written it without your support and encouragement. I am especially indebted to:

Earl, the love of my life—for being my hero and champion, giving me the inspiration and courage for writing this book, writing a chapter to pastors, posing for the cover, propelling me to fulfill my God-ordained purpose, and for choosing to spend the rest of your life with me.

My parents, the late Abraham and Mary Jackson—for instilling in me the desire to pursue my dreams.

My beautiful sister and best friend Elyse Wayns—for understanding my passion to write this book, our deep conversations, and for loving me more.

My sensational sisters and brother, Martha Brooking, Bertha Jackson, Anthony Jackson—for your love, support, and for being there for me during the good times and the bad times.

My beloved son Joseph Aycox Jr. (Jay)—for having a huge chunk of my heart and for being a huge part of this journey.

My lovely daughter Tammie Mask—for your inquisitiveness, posing for the cover, laughing with me when the creative juices weren't flowing and listening as I read my rough manuscripts without murmuring and complaining.

Dr. Amanda Bowie—for inspiring me with your tenacious spirit and for enriching this book by providing psychological expertise to issues that have an impact on the body and soul.

Eric Chinn, for catching the vision, expecting great things from me, and designing the cover.

Bishop Dr. Victor S. Couzens—for prodding me to stop procrastinating and keep moving until I finished.

Pastor Dan Goodman—for being a dear brother and insightful accountability partner.

Bishop Anthony Flowers—for prophetical utterance and unwavering interest in my progress.

Mike Lange—for eagerly and patiently waiting to purchase the first copy.

The Church of the Living God Culverhouse, Inc—for being my second family and for your love and understanding in permitting me to miss numerous weekly services so I could complete this book.

Thirty pastors' wives, eleven pastors, and fifty-nine congregants—for adding depth to the book by completing surveys and allowing me to quote your responses.

I am also grateful for other women of God who have paved the way for me to write this book and for those who have demonstrated the qualities of being a successful pastor's wife.

Contents

A Letter To The Reader xiii
Introduction xv

TOUR 1: FROM SENA TO SISTERS

Relationship with God

Chapter 1
GPS: Gods Providential System 1

Chapter 2
Bread & Water: Communion with God 13

Relationship with Our Pastor Husbands

Chapter 3
Waterproof Matches: Enhancing Intimacy 31

Chapter 4
Knife: Tension Between Marriage & Ministry 49

Chapter 5
Tube Tent: Living in the Parsonage 59

Chapter 6
Work Gloves: Chores & Activities Around the Church 63

Relationship with Others

Chapter 7
Earthquake Wax: Parenting 71

Chapter 8
Thermal Blankets: Friends & Acquaintances 81

Chapter 9
Anti-Terrorism Supplies: Destructive Criticism & Disrespect 91

Relationship with Ourselves

Chapter 10
Compass: Our Identity 99

Chapter 11
Life Vest: Caring for our Body & Soul 109

Chapter 12
Rechargeable Flashlights: Stress, Anger, and Time Management 127

Chapter 13
Gas Mask: To Prevent Haughtiness 143

Chapter 14
Duct Tape: Guarding Our Tongues 149

Chapter 15
Cold Weather Gear: Dress Codes 161

Chapter 16
Medication: Cheerfulness 169

Chapter 17
Backpacks: Financial Management 175

Chapter 18
Bandages & Dressings: Infidelity 185

Chapter 19
Storm Shelter: Contrary Winds 193

Chapter 20
Tissue Packs: Grief Protection 199

Chapter 21
Signaling Mirror: Attracting Help 209

Chapter 22
The Recovery Room: Altar Call 219

TOUR 2: FROM PASTOR TO PASTORS
Chapter 23
Letter from Earl to Pastors 233

EPILOGUE
A Pastors Wife by Gods Design 239

APPENDIX
a) From Sister to Sister 245
b) From Female Pastors to First Lady 275
c) From Congregation to First Lady 285
d) Prayers & Affirmations 303
e) Additional Resources 317

WORKS CITED 319

A Letter to the Reader

Peace be unto you!

"I'm Sleeping with the Pastor!" is written for pastors' wives and for all who love us and desire to pull back the curtain to get a microscopic view of life as a pastor's wife. I am honored that you chose to add my book to your collection. The subject of clergy wives is fascinating and informative. Several good books have been written on this subject, many of which I referred to in this book. My most important goal in writing is to present clear and practical advice to help women in the pastoral wife ministry thrive in their high calling. At the same time, my desire is that all who read this book will be awakened and motivated by the challenges and opportunities pastors' wives face. May God bless you richly for sowing into my ministry.

The format of the book is written in such a way to include essential items found in emergency survival kits. It is not meant to be a philosophical treatise, a collection of personal opinions, or a book that downs our pastor husbands. It is my sharing with you, in everyday language, what I have learned from personal experience, feedback from other pastors' wives, research, picking my pastor husband's brain, seeking the Lord with all my heart, and praying continuously for guidance and wisdom.

Before we move to the introduction, let me describe my motivation for writing *"I'm Sleeping with the Pastor."*

I have twenty one years' experience of being married to a pastor. As a pastor's wife I have encountered pleasant and not so pleasant realities. Admittedly, there were times when the demands were so daunting I didn't think I could survive. Through the years I've found that I could live with joy and victory in the midst of upheaval as I leaned and depended on God to work His marvelous will through me.

The book was conceived in bed as I lay next to my husband, Pastor Earl Whitaker. We were conversing about his schedule for the week. After a few minutes of discussion, I grew somewhat unnerved that most of what he said centered on his activities at the church and little mention was made of our personal schedule. It dawned on me that this man next to me was not only my husband Earl but also the pastor of our church. I looked at him and exclaimed with great revelation and insight, "I'm sleeping with the pastor!"

Earl and I began to reflect on what it means to be married to the pastor and its many challenges and opportunities. During the conversation, and many conversations following, it became apparent that while we agreed on many points, we were not always in sync. More often than not, I felt as though we lived in two different worlds in our roles as pastor and pastor's wife, even though our lives were co-mingled.

I pray you will be open to what the Lord is saying to you through this book, and that you will enjoy reading it as much as Earl and I enjoyed writing it.

Your fellow servant,

Sena

Introduction

The *Merriam-Webster 11th Collegiate Dictionary* defines survival as "the act or fact of living or continuing longer than another person or thing." A survival kit is a package of basic tools and supplies prepared in advance as an aid to survival in an emergency; in other words, a survival kit greatly increases our chances to survive. The term "survival kit" also refers to larger, portable survival kits prepared by survivalists, called "bug-out bags" (BOBs), "Personal Emergency Relocation Kits" (PERKs) or "Get Out of Dodge" (GOOD) kits, which are packed into backpacks or duffel bags. These kits are designed specifically to be more easily carried by the individual in case alternate forms of transportation are unavailable or impossible to use.

Generally speaking, when survival situations are discussed, images such as plane crashes and getting lost in the woods typically come to mind. Survival is not limited to just these kinds of incidents. A great many other situations might arise that will place you in a position where you must survive—such as being a pastor's wife.

Few ministries compare with your unique calling as a pastor's wife. You are blessed and highly favored. Your ministry is so unique that you are often referred to as the "first lady," although "first lady" does not imply that other women are second, it is a term of respect given to you as the pastor's wife to distinguish you from other women in the church.

Dr. Gregory Stock, author of *The Book of Questions* asked a question: "Which would you prefer: a wild, turbulent life filled with joy, sorrow, passion, and adventure—intoxicating successes and stunning setbacks; or a happy, secure, predictable life surrounded by family and friends without such wide swings of fortune and mood?" (*The Book of Questions*, 116). Undoubtedly, you may long for the latter; in reality, the world of a pastor's wife is much like the former. You encounter survival situations on a daily basis as you fulfill your commission to live victoriously and pleasing to God, your husband, your local church, and yourself.

Life as a pastor's wife can be a fearful place if you do not have the proper knowledge and skills to safely get through each day. To remove the challenge is to remove the joy, so you don't merely want to survive, you want to be successful. You need a success kit. That is the goal of *"I'm Sleeping with the Pastor!"*

The book is divided into two tours:

Tour 1: From Sena To Sisters

I am your guide for this tour. During the tour we will look at our relationship with God, our husbands, others and ourselves. That's fine if you don't agree with me on every point; each of us has our own opinions. Judge what I say for yourself and from your own experiences. Earl has also given us his reflections at the end of chapters three and four. While the book is a success kit for pastors' wives, most of what I've written is equally important to every Christian woman, so women of God please join us on our journey. Pastors and other men of faith will find several notes worth taking. I welcome you to grab a ringside seat and keep an eye on us as we travel.

Tour 2: From Pastor To Pastor

This tour is guided by Earl. It is a chapter written to our pastor husbands to address their relationship with us. I didn't edit it; I presented it just as Earl wrote it. Everyone reading this book will find Earl's commentary intriguing.

Appendix

The appendix includes a compilation of words of encouragement and advice from other pastors' wives, female pastors, and perspectives from members of the congregation toward pastors' wives. I've also included prayers and affirmations to strengthen you when the road is rough and the hills are hard to climb, and a list of valuable resources.

Now for the journey before us…

Tour 1

From Sena To Sisters

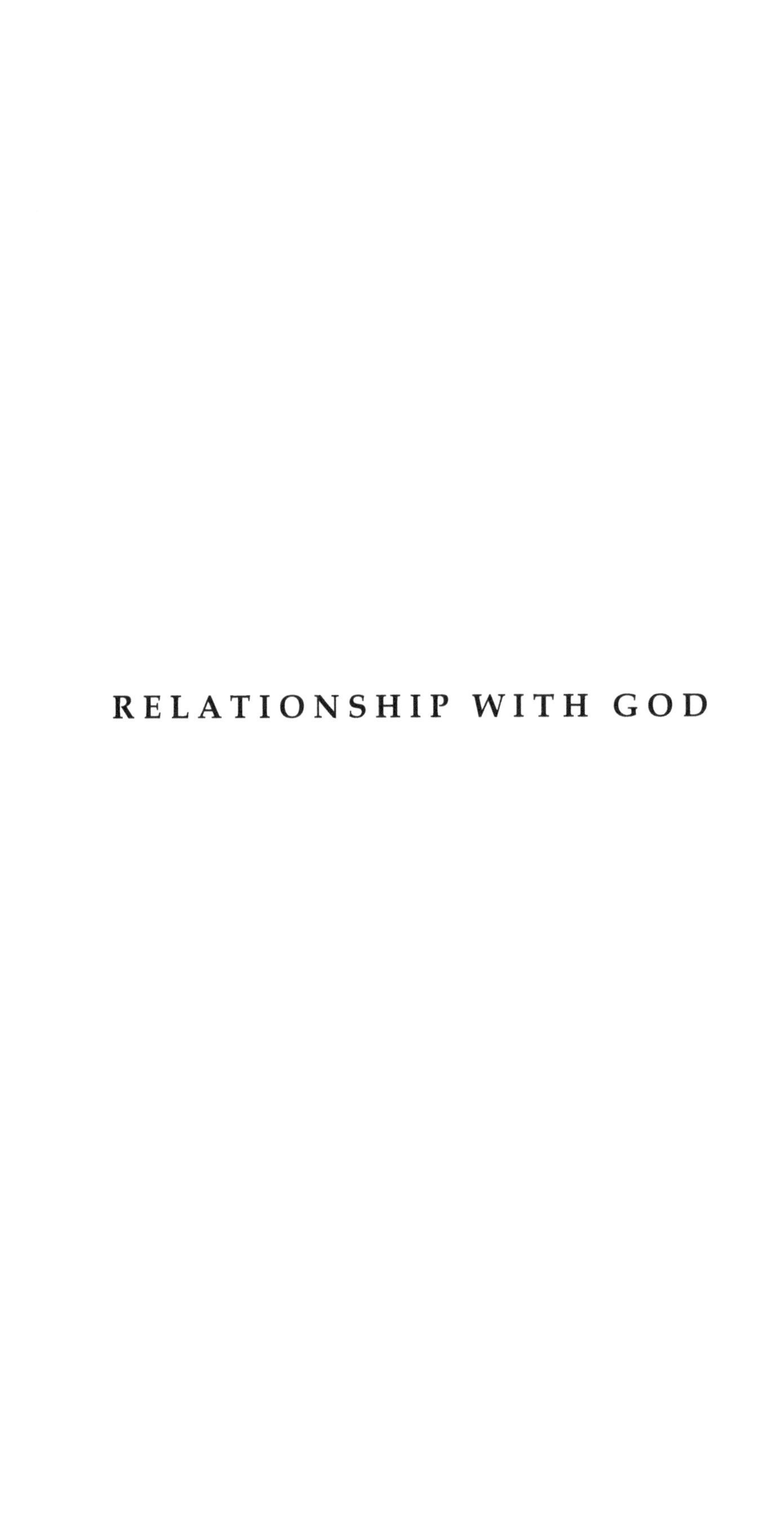

RELATIONSHIP WITH GOD

1

God's Providential System

For you are my rock and my fortress; therefore, for Your name's sake, lead me and guide me.

—Psalm 31:3

I will instruct you and teach you in the way you should go; I will guide you with My eye.

—Psalm 32:8.

There are no shortcuts for any place worth going.

—Beverly Sills

> *Success seems to be largely a matter of hanging on when others have let go.*
>
> —William Feather

There is a starting point for everything, even with surviving. The starting point is choosing a destination. Where do you want to go? How do you get there? When do you need a guide? Without this information, you cannot end up where you want to go. A Global Positioning System (GPS) can be indispensable in this case. A standard GPS receiver will not only place you on a map at any particular location, but will also trace your path across a map as you move. In this chapter we will discuss how to have a marriage according to God's directions. Read on, and I'll show you what I mean.

Once Upon A Time...

I've always liked fairy tales—especially tales of princes and princesses. They usually start with "Once upon a time" and end with "And they lived happily ever after." One of my favorite fairy tales is *Sleeping Beauty*. You may know the story. Here's a summary from my grandson, Kelsey:

"Once there was a royal family who had a baby daughter. After she was born, everyone came to see her, even three fairies. An evil witch also came. The evil witch put a spell on her that when she became sixteen she would prick her finger on a sewing needle and she would fall into a deep sleep. On her sixteenth birthday, she did exactly what the witch had spelled her to do. A few years later, while she was still asleep, a handsome prince came to the castle and saw the princess and kissed her, and she came back from the deep sleep. The prince and princess got married, and they lived happily ever after."

I wouldn't want to have an evil witch cast a spell on me so that I fell asleep for years, but I do like the part of the story about the handsome prince kissing her, reviving her, and living happily ever after.

Your Love Story

How does your love story read, sisters? Does it read like *Sleeping Beauty*? Why do I ask? I ask because marriage is under siege. Marriage is not a fairy tale; one day, as Janet and Sarah Parshall have written in *When the Fairy Dust Settles*, the reality of marriage sets in. Problems and emergencies can flare up without notice. When we are faced with these disasters, they can be psychologically and physically traumatizing if we are not prepared to live beyond fairy tales.

The Barna Group's September 8, 2004 article, *Born Again Christians Are Just As Likely to Divorce as are Non-Christians* tells us that marriage is more than a fairy tale, and Christians are not exempt from the pain of marriage break-ups. The researchers interviewed a nationally representative sample of 3614 adults over 18 years old and found that more than one-third of them had called it quits. This research confirmed a finding by the Barna Group 10 years prior that the divorce rate was the same among born-again and non-born again Christians: 35%.—*barna.org, Barna Update*

This is devastating, sisters. God is making a clarion call for this divorce trend to come to a halt! Pastoral couples are also vulnerable to becoming divorce statistics:

> *Among the hundreds of pastors Leadership editors meet, interview, or correspond with each year, the specter of a marital meltdown is usually their greatest fear. No other tragedy in the ministry holds such a threat. Virtually every month seems to include news of more personal pain, aborted pastorates, alienated offspring, and individuals called of God now trying to get through the long days and longer nights doing something else for a living.*
>
> —*Merrill, 8*

Indisputably, we need God's Providential System to maximize our chance of surviving the marriage meltdown that is attacking clergy couples. Pursuing this further, we can't fall into the trap of reading secular marriage manuals or looking to the world for a marriage template.

Infallible Directions

> *The traditional family and marriage as defined from the dawn of time are among the few institutions that have, in fact, stood the test of time. If we now choose to stand idly by while these institutions are overthrown, the family as it has been known for millennia will be gone. And with its demise will come chaos such as the world has never seen before.*
>
> — Dobson, Marriage Under Fire, 24-25

Those of you who own a standard GPS know how helpful it is for keeping you on the right road. Earl bought me a GPS several years ago, since I am directionally dysfunctional and get lost all of the time. It gives me a map of where I am and the roads ahead, when the next turn is, when I make a wrong turn, when I need to make a U-turn, and the number of miles to my destination. It is a blessing from heaven.

Even so, as helpful as a man-made GPS is it is not infallible. GPS satellites transmit signals to GPS receivers on the ground, and a GPS receiver "knows" the location of the satellite, because that information is included in satellite transmissions. Conditions such as heavy tree cover, clouds, and tall buildings interfere with transmissions. I've gone for miles with my GPS flashing the message, "Searching for better accuracy." It then flashes a message, "Are you outside?" because it doesn't have a clue where I am. There are times that I simply have to turn it off and fend for myself.

With God's GPS we don't have to search for better accuracy for our marriages to survive. His GPS is the Holy Spirit. The Holy Spirit leads us and guides us into all truth so that our marriages will be God honoring rather than patterned after myths, lies, and fairy tales the world has conjured up about marriage. It is not uncommon to hear of two women marrying or two men marrying—or to know couples who are cohabitating without the benefit of a marriage license.

This is a little off subject, but I remember what Bishop Jerry Maiden said: "People get a license for a dog, for a gun, for a boat, a car, and everything else. But they don't want to get one to marry someone. That should tell them that the person they are living with thinks more of their dog than they do you." Earl uses a phrase periodically when he preaches on this subject: "If you are shacking, start packing."

I just thought I'd throw that in for a little humor. Cohabitating should not be an issue for pastors' wives, although I do know of pastors who have shacked. Our duty is to embrace God's infallible directions for our marriage. Without His directions our marriages have little chance of survival and no chance of thriving, for if we don't have the right directions we can never find our way.

God's directions are infallible because He ordained marriage and designed the way marriage is to function. God ordained three institutions: marriage, government, and church. Marriage was the first institution God ordained, even before the church. There are three purposes for marriage: (1) for two people to complete each other; (2) to demonstrate the love that Christ has for His church, and the reverence that the church has for Christ; (3) to reproduce godly seed.

Following God's GPS will teach us how to live happily here and after. Let's look briefly at His directions for marriage.

A Covenant, Not a Contract

God is the only third party in marriage that can make it work.

—*Anonymous*

Marriage is not a contract; it is a covenant between two believers, for Psalm 89:34 tells us that God is a God of covenants. A contract has an expiration date, a covenant is forever. Your husband and you established your covenant the day you were married.

Do you remember your wedding day? The fairy dust was sprinkled all around you, and you were on cloud nine. You may not remember all that transpired on your wedding day, but one thing you can't forget is that you promised to stay with your husband until death do you part—that meant even when the fairy dust settled and you were able to see clearly.

You can't plead insanity, sisters. You were in your right mind when you strutted down the aisle with all of those witnesses watching.

God was watching you too. Folk may let you off the hook, but God doesn't. When the minister said, "Dearly beloved, we are gathered together here in the sight of God, and in the presence of these witnesses, to join together this man and this woman in holy matrimony," and you said, "I Do," you were entering into a covenant relationship with God and your husband, where God is the greatest partner.

Your pledge lasts a lifetime not because of the paper you have in your safety deposit box, or because both of your names are on the deed, or you have fifteen children together, but because you made an unbreakable, unconditional covenant. The marriage is sustained because God will bless based on the covenant He has with your husband and you.

Leave and Cleave

In Genesis 2:24 three commands are given to us concerning the marriage covenant. These commands are clear, concise, and to the point: "leave your father and mother, cleave to your spouse, and become one flesh."

In Hebrew, "cleave" means, "to adhere to, to stick, to be strongly attached by a bond, to pursue, to overtake." In Greek it means, "to stick like glue," thus implying an inseparable union.

If we want to be technical, we can say that God is talking to our husbands in Genesis 2:24, but we know that is not going to fly. God would never tell our husbands to leave, cleave, and become one flesh and we take the whole family with us. We are in this together. The bottom line: marriage requires a lifetime commitment for both husband and wife. Look before we leap.

How can we leave, cleave, and become one flesh? God answered this question: love and respect. When the world looks at our marriages it should see how a man loves his wife and how a wife responds to her husband's love.

> *Nevertheless let each one of you in particular so love his own wife as himself, and let the wife see that she respects her husband.*
>
> —Ephesians 5:33

Love and Respect

If you have to think about whether you love someone or not then the answer is no. When you love someone, you just know.
—*Janice Markowitz*

In *Love and Respect*, Dr. Emerson Eggerichs tells us that there is a strong link between love and respect. He calls this the "Love and Respect Connection." He goes on to state what he calls the "Crazy Cycle": when a husband feels disrespected he acts in unloving ways towards his wife; when she feels unloved she acts in unloving ways towards her husband. Furthermore, Dr. Eggerichs writes that husbands need respect and wives need love as much as they need air to breathe. — *p. 38-40.*

Sisters, God made us nurturers, and He made us to be loved. It stands to reason if we want our husbands to breathe and love us we have to respect them.

What does that look like in action? Each of us probably has our own viewpoint of respect. Whatever our view we cannot have respect for our husbands without submission. Yes, we have to talk about it.

Submission

Fewer marriages would skid, if more who said, "I do," did.
—*Old Codger's Wisdom*

A passage that many women loath, and many men love, is Ephesians 5:22—23:

Wives, submit to your own husbands, as to the Lord. For the husband is head of the wife, as also Christ is head of the church; and He is the Savior of the Body.

It doesn't matter that Ephesians 5:21 tells us to be subject to one another in the fear of the Lord, there is something about these two verses that make many sisters cringe. I've seen this reaction in the faces of women when I officiate at a marriage ceremony, and I still almost choke when I read them. Why? Because of that big "S" word in verse 22. Yes, let's say it all together—Submit.

Bette Midler sings so beautifully about submission in action in "Wind Beneath My Wings."

It is a song about someone willing to take a back seat to let another shine. I like the song, and it often gives me a warm fuzzy to know that I am the "wind beneath Earl's wings"—whether or not he realizes it, but I'm still trying to raise my submission tolerance level. One reason is that submission is often used in a negative connotation to mean slavery or inferiority. I am repulsed by this description. If that's submission, I don't want to touch it with a ten-foot pole; it is demeaning, demoralizing, and degrading to women.

In short, slavery and inferiority to our husbands is not God's design for marriage. His design is that there would be mutual submission in marriage based on love (Ephesians 6; 1 Peter 3:1–2; Philippians 2:7–8). We are our husband's helpmate (Genesis 2:18). Being a helpmate is not a putdown; it is someone who helps. God identifies Himself as a Helper in Hebrews 13:6 so there is nothing derogatory about the term. Submission is even present in the Godhead, for God is a God of order. Jesus is submissive to the Father; the Holy Spirit is submissive to the Son.

Hannah Whitall Smith explains what mutual submission based on love is like in a letter she wrote in 1883 to Frank Costelloe, a young man her daughter Mary Smith fell in love with, to confront Costelloe on his commitment to equality between the sexes and the authority only of love:

> *Whatever submission one may render to the other, must be voluntary and from love, otherwise it is the most degrading bondage. Woman is man's equal, the other half of the human being; and to usurp authority over her is so to dislocate the divine order and to cause loss of harmony in all the relations between the sexes.*
>
> — Smith and Dieter, December 18.

P. B. Wilson, author of *Liberated Through Submission* provides an explanation of submission that may help us to further understand what it looks like in practice: "Submission means what the dictionary says it means. It means to yield—yield to people, precepts and principles that have been placed in our lives as authorities." —*WILSON, 26*

Earl's definition of submission is: "Submission is honoring, respecting, and acting in accordance with God ordained authority." Correspondingly, as Pastor Anthony White stated, "In order for us to walk in authority, we must first be under authority. We are only qualified to lead to the degree that we are willing to serve."—*Epitome Magazine, August, 2009, 17 (*He was speaking to men, but it applies to us as well).

Personally, I prefer to think of submission as riding in the second chariot. Second chair isn't bad, particularly in marriage. Granted, the scenery never changes when you are in that position, and you are always reminded that there is someone else in authority. But it also reminds you of the importance of your position. When your husband needs help and he looks back, who does he see? You, taking up the rear.

Sisters, I hope co-joining submission with authority is not a bee in your bonnet, because whether or not we admit it, we will always be under someone's authority. When we were children, we were under our parents' authority. We went to school, and we were under the teacher's authority. We went to work and were under our bosses' authority.

Some of us rebelled, for it is inherent in us to rebel against authority. To illustrate: We often get an attitude when a police officer pulls us over. We were on our way to do something totally different than sitting on the side of the road with a police officer, right?

You know how embarrassing it is. Everyone knows you have broken the law. It doesn't matter what those other perpetrators were doing when he caught you—if you indeed were driving 80 in a 60 mph speed zone. What comes to mind? Why did he pull me over? Doesn't he have anything better to do with his time? Go and catch real crooks. The only reason you keep your thoughts to yourself and submit to his authority is for fear that you may get socked with four or five tickets or spend a night in jail. When you drive off you really let him have it, don't you? Yes, I've been there.

Examples of Submission

Do you want a real live example of a woman who submitted to her husband? Sarah. The Bible tells me that she even called him Lord. Now, I'm not suggesting that you call your husband Lord; I'm just saying that Sarah humbled herself under Abraham—even to the point where he lied not once but twice to put her in jeopardy. What happened both times? God got her out of the mess that Abraham put her in. Look how God blessed her for her obedience: He gave her a child when she was ninety years old. I know, some of us had other kinds of blessings in mind.

If you want an example of a woman who habitually did not submit to her husband's authority I have one for you. I'm not talking about Eve, either, for it's debatable where Adam was when she ate the fruit. I'm talking about me. Am I alone? No.

Let me tell on myself:

My late former spouse and I had a close and jovial marriage, though we were notorious for disagreeing with one another. If he said up, I'd say down. If he said left, I'd say right. This worked for us the majority of the time. Occasionally he and I would disagree and it was not a laughing matter. I balked when he attempted to assert his authority. I felt that I knew as much (or more) about things as he did, so I wasn't going to submit. If I had a better way of doing it I did it my way—to each his own.

My rebellion lasted a number of years until I submitted to the Holy Spirit. He reminded me that I was to revere and respect my husband's authority out of obedience and love for God, not based on my criteria; God would not hear my prayers if I continued to walk in iniquity; and I was going to have to give an account of everything I did in this life whether it was good or evil.

Needless to say, that was enough to make me come to myself, repent, and submit. Although it was monstrous at times to let my spouse have the deciding vote, I found out that it was far better to be in God's will than in God's way. It is in His will that blessings abound.

Sisters, I want to caution you that there is a difference in being submissive and just "going along to get along." To me, when I submit I'm loving and kind. When I "go along" it's with grumbling and sarcasm. Let me give you an example: I like dogs and Earl does also, but we disagree about where a dog should stay. Earl's opinion is that a dog should stay outdoors; mine is that it's okay to have an indoor pet. Since we can't come to an agreement we still don't have a dog. I've frequently told Earl in no uncertain terms that I was going along with him but I was unhappy about it. The last time we talked about dogs I was so livid that I saw stars and couldn't say another word until I got my second wind. Trust me; it took more than ten minutes. This is as best as I can describe it, but do you see the difference?

Our Husbands Aren't Off the Hook

When it's hard to respect and submit, we can remember what our husbands are required to do: they are required to love us as their own bodies. Even when we are unlovable—PMS and all. They also have to love those of us who are past the PMS stage but have a seamy side ensnared by episodes of grumpiness. They have to take care of us, too. Look at what God said:

> *Husbands, love your wives, just as Christ loved the church and gave himself up for her to make her holy, cleansing her by the washing with water through the word, and to present her to himself as a radiant church, without stain or wrinkle or any other blemish, but holy and blameless. In this same way, husbands ought to love their wives as their own bodies. He who loves his wife loves himself. After all, no one ever hated his own body, but he feeds and cares for it, just as Christ does the church—for we are members of his body. For this reason a man will leave his father and mother and be united to his wife, and the two will become one flesh."*
>
> —*Ephesians 5:25–31, NIV*

Don't think loving us this way is a snap. Listen to what Rainier Maria Rilke said:

> *For one human being to love another that is perhaps the most difficult task of all our tasks; the ultimate, the last test and proof, the work for which all other work is but preparation.*
>
> — *brainyquote.com, Ranier Maria Rilke Quotes*

I certainly agree. Look at God's description of love and what love does:

> *Love is patient and kind. Love is not jealous or boastful or proud or rude. It does not demand its own way. It is not irritable, and it keeps no record of being wronged. It does not rejoice about injustice but rejoices whenever the truth wins out. Love never gives up, never loses faith, is always hopeful, and endures through every circumstance.*
>
> —*1 Corinthians 13:4–7, NLT*

Don't run to store and have a big neon sign made with these verses to remind your husband of his love responsibilities. God requires you to love him the same way. Ouch, but it is what it is!

The Reward of Marriage God's Way

Sisters, I have to admit that my marriage is not a fairy tale by a long haul, and Earl and I do not ride off into the sunset every day. Your marriage may not be the pick of the litter either. Hang in there. If you let God have His awesome way your marriage will be the best human relationship there is—to death do you part.

Let's Pray…

Be a blessing!

2

Bread & Water: Communion With God

We can live about three weeks without food (bread), so be sure to keep some around if you want to survive—and it doesn't have to be fried chicken and biscuits. It is estimated that a person can live only three days without water. According to Byron Dalyrmple, survival expert: "Water is the most important factor in survival, regardless of where you are. It is estimated that at 110-degree temperature, an inactive person lives for five days if he has available two quarts of water per day, a total of ten quarts. At about seventy-five degrees he has a chance of quadrupling his life expectancy on the same ten quarts. But these are bare minimums, and this is also a substantial quantity of water. At a moderate temperature a person ever mildly active needs an average of two quarts of water per day. That's three and a half gallons per week."

—*Dalyrmple, 12.*

Communion with God is as essential to a successful marriage as are bread and water to the body. Before we continue on our journey and discuss our relationship with our husbands, others, and ourselves, let's make a parenthetical stop to discuss the importance of spending time in God's presence.

In His Presence

When we love earthly friends we are not satisfied with only a few minutes together at a time, nor can we learn to know their real character, or appreciate the depths of their nature, if we only have a few passing words with them as we go about our daily routine, even if those passing words should occur every few minutes. Neither can we know God in this way.

—Smith and Dieter, January 18.

Spending time in God's presence is an act of personal worship, and is a sacred love affair that is reserved only for God. As we commune with Him through quiet meditation, prayer, and Bible study we experience "fullness of joy, and pleasures forevermore" (Psalm 16:11). David compared his longing to spend time in God's presence with a deer longing for water (Psalm 42:11). Job treasured God's Word more than his daily bread (Job 23:12, NIV). When the Holy Spirit led Jesus into the wilderness to be tempted by the devil, Jesus reminded Satan that man shall not live by bread alone, but by every word of God (Luke 4:4).

John and Archie Parrish aptly point out the essentialness of personal worship:

Personal worship is the primary source of power in your life. The more consistent you are at this point, the more strength you will have to accomplish God's will. As you worship God, you demonstrate your love to Him and fulfill the first and greatest commandment. This pleases God and He discloses Himself to you more intimately as you obey Him in this specific manner.

—Parish, 42

The July 13 *Fresh Word for Today* also drives the point home well of the value of spending quality time in God's presence. The meditation is titled, "Basic Survival Skills." In this meditation, author Bob Gass tells the story of Jeremiah Denton, a high-ranking American who was subjected to grueling torture as a prisoner of war in North Vietnam. Mr. Denton was able to survive and overcome what he had been through. When he returned home he was elected to the United States Senate. When asked how he did it, he said, one of his "basic survival skills" was quoting passages of Scripture he had memorized from the Bible. He used these Scriptures to build a wall of protection around him as these Scriptures literally became his prayers.—*Gass, 194*

My sisters, spending time in God's presence builds a wall of protection around us, too. To this end, we must make prayer and Bible study an important part of our daily lives.

Prayer

> *Living a life without prayer is like building a house without nails.*
>
> —Anonymous

> *For Christians prayer is like breathing. You don't have to think to breathe because the atmosphere exerts pressure on your lungs and forces you to breathe. That's why it is more difficult to hold your breath than it is to breathe. Similarly, when you're born into the family of God, you enter into a spiritual atmosphere wherein God's presence and grace exert pressure, or influence, on your life. Prayer is the normal response to that pressure.*
>
> —MacArthur, 13

What Is Prayer?

There are many definitions of prayer. The simplest ones I know are:

- Prayer is calling home to talk with our Father.
- Prayer is talking to God as you would a beloved friend—without pretense or shame.

- Prayer is like quietly opening a door and slipping into the very presence of God.
- Prayer is asking God to do what we cannot do ourselves.

Why Should We Pray?

Someone asked the question, "If God knows what we need already, then why pray?" Here are a few reasons:

- *Prayerlessness is sin.* We are commanded in 1 Thessalonians 5:17 to pray without ceasing. When we don't pray we are defiantly and arrogantly telling God we don't need His help. How foolish, knowing that "it is in Him that we live, move, and have our being."—*Acts* 17:28
- *Prayer gets God's will done on earth as it is in heaven (Matthew 6:9–13).* It also allows God to work on us and adjust us to His will. First John 5:14–15 tells us when we ask according to God's will we receive what we have asked for.
- *Prayer brings peace.* Philippians 4:6–7 tells us to be anxious for nothing, but in everything by prayer and supplication, with thanksgiving, let your requests be made known to God; and the peace of God, which surpasses all understanding, will guard your hearts and minds through Christ Jesus.
- *We claim our rights as children of God through prayer.* If you are like me, there is some "stuff" you need to talk to your Daddy about that is for His ears only, and there is some "stuff" you need Him to change. Is there a witness in the house?
- *Prayer works!* We can't do anything without God's help. Prayer has rescued more than one couple, and it will rescue us, too. Spending time in prayer is akin to matriculating through Knee-bone University, for God answers knee-mail. As Pastor Joseph Mitcham says, "Prayer goes where you can't."

I heard Dr. C. E. Glover expand on the effectiveness of prayer in his sermon, *The Power of Prayer*:

> *Prayer will go over the head of the president. Prayer will go over the head of the board of directors. Even over the deacon board and*

auxiliaries. In fact, prayer has the power to transform lives, change circumstances, give us perseverance in the midst of trials, alter the course of nations, and change men and women for Christ... Prayer spans three worlds, heaven, earth, and hell simultaneously. It influences God like no other endeavor. It influences the devil more than any human enterprise. The devil hates prayer because it throws the battle to God, and pits God against the enemy with all His power.

—*Preached at EK Bailey International Expository Preaching Conference, July 2007*

What Should We Pray?

Pray about everyone and everything that concerns us. God wants to be included in every area of our lives. However, you have to accept Jesus Christ as Savior and make him Lord of your life to approach God as Father. Therefore, before you pray any other prayer you must be sure of your salvation. If you have any doubt, please pray this prayer from Christian Word Ministries (CWM) out loud:

Heavenly Father I come to You now in the name of Your Son Jesus Christ. I confess that I am a sinner and that I have sinned against You. I ask You to forgive me for all of my sins and I repent for my sins and I choose to follow and obey and accept Your Son Jesus Christ as my Lord and Savior. I believe in my heart that You sent Your Son Jesus Christ to die for my sins on the cross of Calvary. I believe that Your Son Jesus Christ was born of the Virgin Mary, was crucified and died on the cross at Calvary for me and the sins of all others. I believe that after 3 days He was raised from the dead, ascended into heaven, and is alive today. I ask You Jesus Christ to be the Lord of my life and to be my Savior. I receive You now as my Lord and Savior with all my heart. I believe that Jesus Christ is my King and my God and the Lord of my life. I believe that Jesus Christ is alive in me, and I declare that Jesus Christ is the Lord of my life.

—*Prayers, 117-18*

On the authority of God's Word in Romans 10:9-10 and John 5:24, if you prayed this prayer from your heart the Holy Spirit will give you assurance of salvation. Romans 8:16 tells us that He bears witness with our spirit that we are the children of God. Other prayers and affirmations by CWM are included in Appendix D. Each of you has their permission to copy any of these prayers and redistribute them in any way.

When Should We Pray?

Anytime. Psalm 55:17 prompts us to pray with these words: "Evening and morning and at noon I will pray, and cry aloud, and He shall hear my voice." That tells me you can pray under any circumstance, in any attire, and in any posture. You can even have your "best days" as you pray in your old flannel "I just can't part with this" nightgown that you should have put in the trash years ago (does anyone know what I'm talking about?). *A Book of Prayer* by Stormie Omartian may also help you stay on the prayer track. It contains 365 prayers for victorious living—one for every day of the year.

How Should We Pray?

This is between God and you. Three patterns I enjoy are: the Model Prayer that Jesus gave us in Matthew 6:9–13, A.C.T.S (Adoration, Confession, Thanksgiving, Supplication) and P.A.C.E. (Praise, Acceptance of God's Acceptance of me, Giving God Control of my life, and Expecting great things from God).

Just Pray!

> *Satan can't keep God from answering our prayers, but he will keep us from asking.*
>
> —*Dr. Adrian Rogers,* Adrianisms, *Vol 2, 33*

Sisters, whatever the definition or the reason you are most easeful with, pray and watch God change things. Don't be like the little boy in this illustration:

> *A cartoon pictured a little boy kneeling in prayer. Obviously disgruntled with God, he was saying, "Aunt Harriet hasn't gotten married, Uncle Hubert hasn't any work, and Daddy's hair is still falling out...I'm getting tired of praying for this family without getting any results."*
>
> —*Jones, 293*

Also, ask in Jesus' name, for Jesus' name is the stamp that sends your prayer. Jesus told us in John 16:23 that God would give us whatever we ask in His name. When you ask in Jesus' name it means you ask what Jesus would ask. When you don't get it, there's a reason, for God's answers are yes, no, and wait. God will answer no if you pray with the wrong motives (James 4:3). If you know your motives are right wait to see what God will do. His delays are not denials, so just pray and leave the rest to him. He will work it out.

The old cliché, "He may not come when you want Him, but He's always on time" is not a fact. God is omnipresent, so there is no place that He cannot be at all times. He may not answer according to your timeframe, but He will always answer according to His. When He does, it's what's best for you. I did hear something that we can stake our claim on: "I don't know how He's going to do it, I don't know when He's going to fix it, but I know God will make a way for me." Psalm 4:3 tells us that He has set apart for Himself those who are godly, and will hear when we call to Him.

You don't have to pray loud; God can hear your faintest cry. John MacArthur told the story of little boy who softly prayed to God. All of a sudden, he said, "and God, please bless me with a bicycle" very loudly. His mother told him, "God is not deaf". The little boy said, "Yes I know, but Grandma's in the other room and she's hard of hearing."

I thank God He's not like Grandma. You can be confident that God hears you even when you go through seasons when all you can say is "Ump ump ump," for you have divine prayer partners: Jesus never ceases to pray for you (Hebrew 7:25), and the Holy Spirit intercedes for you in groaning that cannot be uttered (Romans 8:26); so pray, pray, pray!

Take Time to Pray

I woke up early one morning and rushed into the day;
I had so much to accomplish that I did not have time to pray.
Problems just tumbled about me, and heavier came each task.
"Why doesn't God help me? I wondered. He answered, "You didn't ask."
I wanted to see joy and beauty, but the day toiled on, gray and bleak;
I wondered why God did not show me. He said, "But you did not seek."
I tried to come into God's presence; I used all my keys at the lock.
God gently and lovingly chided, "My child, you did not knock."
I woke up early this morning and paused before entering the day;
I had so much to accomplish that I had to take time to pray.

—Author Unknown

Bible Study

Nobody ever outgrows Scripture; the book widens and deepens with our years.

—*Charles H. Spurgeon*

An unnamed woman in a crowd called out to Jesus, "Blessed is the mother who gave You birth and nursed you." Jesus answered, "Yea, rather, blessed are those that hear the Word of God and obey it" (Luke 11:27–28, NIV). This passage teaches us that nothing we do can be compared to the blessedness of hearing and obeying the Word of God.

Someone said the Bible is "basic instructions before leaving Earth" because everything we need is in the Word of God. It has also been said that the Bible is bleach in our dirty laundry, since the Word of God cleans us up. I like to think of the Bible as God's love letter to us. If you are like me, you need a love letter every now and then to stay encouraged. You can read God's love letter any time you want to be reminded of how precious you are to Him, and how much He loves you.

Above all, the Bible guarantees that heaven and Earth will pass away before one letter of God's Word fails. If God said it that settles it—whether or not we believe it! Listen to the Scriptures:

> *God is not a man, that He should lie, nor a son of man, that He should repent. Has He said, and will He not do? Or has He spoken, and will He not make it good?*
>
> —*Numbers 23:19*

Distractions

Your relationship with God is the most vital romance you have, so you must covet and guard your communion with Him. To do this you must be aware of distractions and overcome reasons and excuses for being distracted.

Dr. Adrian Rogers puts it this way:

> *Anything that distracts us from vital prayer in our lives is a treacherous thing. It steals from us the blessings the Father wants to bestow, and it takes from the Father the glory he so richly deserves.*
>
> —*Rogers, Vol. 1, 39*

Busyness, Procrastination, Laziness

You can't build a reputation on what you are going to do.

—Henry Ford

Well, sisters, what excuses do you have? We all have our culprits. I can narrow mine down to three: busyness, procrastination, and laziness.

"Busyness is the archenemy of every marriage." These words were written by Drs. Les and Leslie Parrot in *Your Time-Starved Marriage.* The Parrots tell us:

> *In a national survey of married couples, researchers found that, on average, we spend less than three minutes of meaningful conversation together in a typical day.*
>
> —Parrot, 28

Thankfully, Earl and I spend more than three minutes a day conversing. Still, busyness is the archenemy of my relationship with God. I spend half of the day putting out fires and the other half starting fires. When I do get on my knees, my mind wanders so much that I might as well get up because I'm not really talking to God; I'm distracted thinking about everything I have to do that day. The same thing happens when I read the Bible. All I have to do is come across a name that I can't pronounce or a word I don't quite understand, and my mind takes me back to my "To Do" list.

Often my busyness is a cover-up for procrastination. Yes, I know I shouldn't put off for tomorrow what I can do today, so I try not to make a habit of doing that. What I find myself doing is putting off until later what I should be doing right now. Often I put off spending quality time with God. My senseless rationale is, when I pray I need to have more time to talk to God like I want to. Or I'll study later, because it wouldn't be "fair" to God to rush through a passage, knowing that I'm not going to have much time to devote to it. Oh, am I the only one who has done this? No!

I overheard a conversation in which a man said to his child, "Don't put off for tomorrow what you can do the day after tomorrow." I chuckled, but it's really not that funny, and it's not funny at all when it comes to spending time with God.

Then, there's just plain laziness. I'm guilty of this at times too, and there is no excuse. For those of you who are looking for one, here's a joke about laziness:

> *A man went to the doctor because he was having trouble concentrating. The doctor told him there was nothing wrong with him, he was just lazy. The man asked the doctor for the medical term so he could tell his wife so she wouldn't ask him to do anything.*
>
> —*Anonymous*

This joke may be laughable, but there is nothing amusing about anything that can keep us from spending time with God and studying His Word.

What Helps Me

Sisters, you may be interested in implementing all or some of what helps me intensify my time with God:

Prayer

- *Set your clock an hour earlier, and get up when the alarm goes off—no snoozing.* If an hour is too much, start with fifteen minutes. It's not how much time you pray, it is how effective and fervent you pray.
- *Find a quiet place.* I assure you I know this is emphatically easier said than done for those of us who have small children or grandchildren. The patter of little feet can follow you like a shadow. I'm at the grandparent stage, and it's not as easy to get away as I thought it would be. More often than not,

my quiet place is in the restroom (I know I'm not by myself, either).

- *Consecrate yourself before God.* Use Romans 12:1–2 to present each member of your body to Him before proceeding in prayer. Remember to bring your thoughts into subjection, too (2 Corinthians 10:4–5).
- *Say "good morning" to God before you say one word to anyone else.*
- *Silently wait on God.* Psalm 46:10 tells us to be still before Him and know that He is God. I read somewhere that we are to be still before God at least ten minutes before we say anything. Let Him talk first. This is rather painstaking for me because I don't do well with silence. Unconsciously I habitually wait about two minutes before I start babbling. Sometimes I hear God speak and sometimes I don't hear Him say a thing. Your experience may be analogous to mine, but don't despond. Wait longer next time. If you can't hear Him in the wind, earthquake, or fire; you'll hear Him in a still small voice (1 Kings 19:12).
- *Search Paul's writings for Scriptures containing the word "prayer" and pray these Scriptures.*
- *Pray for something different each day.* For example, Monday: pray for family; Tuesday: government; Wednesday: lost souls, etc.
- *Keep a prayer journal.* Include your prayer request, date of the request, and the date God answered your prayer.
- *Sing to God.* He enjoys it. I think He's the only one who can really appreciate my singing.
- *Play soft worship music as you pray.*
- *Find a prayer partner and pray together.*
- *Read books about prayer.*
- *Memorize the promises of God*, and bring them to your remembrance throughout the day.
- *Fast and pray regularly.*
- *Enjoy your time with God.* It is not a chore; it's a wonderful privilege to commune with the God of the universe—our Father, and our Abba (Papa).

Bible Study

- *Read passages the Holy Spirit prompts you to read.* Often when I pray, the Holy Spirit will speak to me about a passage, and I'll study it following my time of prayer. You may find *Bible Study Made Easy* by Mark Water helpful. If you like a question and answer approach to studying the Bible, a good resource is *4000 Questions & Answers on the Bible* (A. Dana Adams).
- *Write down what the Holy Spirit reveals to you during your study time.*
- *Use a good devotional.* We all have our favorites.
- *Memorize Scripture.* Write the Scripture on an index card and refer to it throughout the day. You may not be able to memorize a hundred Scriptures a year, but ten isn't bad at all.
- *Invest in a good concordance or Bible software.* Two of my favorite software developers are Logos and Biblesoft.
- *Recognize that sermon preparation is not spending quality time with God.* I had to throw this in for preachers and teachers like myself. We love the Bible, but we must resist the temptation to study the Bible for a message only. We must study it to hear from God. The Holy Spirit will give us a message as we study, but that should not be our main motivation during our quiet time with God.

Choosing the Best Part

It isn't that the doing doesn't need doing, it's that the being must come first, and then we will find that the necessary part of the doing will get done!

—*Jill Briscoe,* in Women's Devotional Bible, *1119*

Sisters, as I bring this chapter to a close I want to encourage you again to put first things first and keep the main thing the main thing: spending quality time in God's presence daily. You can't knuckle under to busyness, procrastination, laziness, or let anything else get in the way of spending time with God. There is nothing like sitting at the Master's feet. When Jesus visited Mary and Martha, Mary sat at his feet while Martha busied herself with serving. Martha complained to Jesus that Mary wasn't helping her. Jesus reminded Martha that Mary had chosen the best part, and it would not be taken away from her (Luke 10:38-42).

If you want the best part you too must guard your time with God. Without this your daily devotion does not have a fighting chance. Communion with God is so vital that the enemy will do everything possible to make you stop praying and reading the Bible effectively and consistently. Jesus was able to thwart enemy plots because He prayed and knew the Word of God, and you can too. Spend as much time with God as is necessary to cultivate the best relationship possible with the One who loves you like no other. "Seek first the kingdom of God, and His righteousness, and all of these things will be added unto you" (Matthew 6:33).

I end with this story:

> *A little girl went to the store with her mother and was very polite and mannerly while in the store, so much so that the store keeper wanted to give her a gift. He told her to put her hands in the candy jar and pull out a handful. She didn't do it. The owner wondered what was wrong, so he asked her to do it again.*
>
> *She didn't do it. Finally, he asked her what was wrong. She said, "I'll take it, if you reach your hand in the jar for me." He reached his hands into the jar and pulled out a handful of candy and gave it to the little girl, to which she replied, "thank you, sir." When she and her mother left the store, the mother told her she was confused. She asked her if she wanted the candy, and she said, yes she did, very much so. So the mother said, "then why didn't you put your hand into the jar and take some?" She said, "Mother, I wanted him to put his hand into the jar, because his hand is much bigger than mine."*
>
> —Anonymous

Likewise, God's hand is much bigger than yours. Knowing this, give Him first place in your life. By the way, God's telephone number is Jeremiah 33:3. I heard Him say, "Call to me and I will answer you and tell you great and unsearchable things you do not know." You don't have to have a BlackBerry or iPhone to reach him, either.

Let's Pray...

Be a blessing!

Now that we've ensured that our most important relationship has top priority in our lives, we can continue on our journey...

RELATIONSHIP WITH OUR PASTOR HUSBANDS

3

Waterproof Matches: Enhancing Intimacy

Fire building is a valuable and important skill for survival. In many instances it is necessary for water purification, additional warmth, cooking, and even signaling. The best matches for fire-building are waterproof because you can strike them anywhere, they ignite easily, and they burn long enough to get a fire going. In this chapter we will discuss how to enhance intimacy with our pastor husbands by building and keeping our matrimonial fires sizzling, as Dr. Ed Young says in his book "10 Commandments of Marriage." Without sizzle, our marriages will be limp along 'dis-a-do' arrangements. Like Judge Lynn Toler of TV's Divorce Court once commented, "Rings don't make a marriage."

Hard Work

How can we keep our matrimonial fires burning? By working hard, harder and hardest. Author Bob Barnes says in "*What Makes a Man Feel Loved:*"

> *Somewhere between the thrill of the engagement, the hectic preparation for the wedding, and the joy of The Big Day—and often despite excellent pre-marital counseling—the message gets lost, overlooked, or silenced. That message? Marriage is hard work!—p. 11*

Mrs. Norman Vincent Peale adds:

> *...Any woman might have other stimulating jobs, but none is so difficult and demanding, so exciting and potentially rewarding as the job of living with a man, studying him, supporting him, liberating his strength, compensating for his weaknesses, making his whole being sing and soar the way it was designed to do.*
>
> —*Peale*, 2

I agree with Mr. Barnes and Mrs. Peale. I think marriage is especially difficult when we are married to men who are what Paul and Sandy Coughlin call Christian Nice Guys, or CNG (*Coughlin, p. 11-12*). Of course every pastor should be a Christian and nice, but these men have emotionally checked-out. They are consistently passive, and their emotions and will (choices) have been disengaged.

We may also be consigned to husbands who are as inviting as ditchwater or as wooing as a tooth extraction. These will require overtime plus. Albeit, whatever the situation, we can't cut and run; we can extend our honeymoon. The benefits far outweigh the labor involved.

Extending the Honeymoon

The bonds of matrimony are a good investment only when the interest is kept up.

—*Anonymous*

Sisters, if we are extend our honeymoons the first thing we must do is to tear down any walls we've built between our husbands and ourselves:

Walls

Their wedding picture mocked them from the table,
these two whose minds no longer touched each other.
They lived with such a heavy barricade between them that
neither battering ram of words nor artilleries of touch
could break it down.
Somewhere, between the oldest child's first tooth and the
youngest daughter's graduation, they lost each other.
Throughout the years, each slowly unraveled that tangled ball
of string called self, and as they tugged at stubborn
knots each hid his searching from the other.
Sometimes she cried at night and begged the whispering darkness
to tell her who she was.
He lay beside her, snoring like a hibernating bear,
unaware of her winter.
Once, after they had made love, he wanted to tell her how
afraid he was of dying, but fearing to show his naked
soul, he spoke instead about the beauty of her breasts.
She took a course in modern art, trying to find herself in
colors splashed upon a canvas, and complaining to other women
about men who were insensitive.
He climbed a tomb called "the office," wrapped his mind in
a shroud of paper figures and buried himself in customers.

Slowly, the wall between them rose, cemented by the mortar of indifference.
One day, reaching out to touch each other, they found a barrier they could not penetrate, and recoiling from the coldness of the stone, each retreated from the stranger on the other side.
For when love dies, it is not in a moment of angry battle, nor when fiery bodies lose their heat.
It lies panting, exhausted, expiring at the bottom of a wall it could not scale.

—*Source unknown, in Gillogly, 123-24*

Some of you may be able to identify with the couple in this reading. If so, it's no use crying over spilt milk; you can begin again with a clean slate. Start by turning a deaf ear to the jokes you've heard about the honeymoon being over when the fantasy stops and reality kicks in. Why can't your fantasy be a reality?

In Strike The Original Match, Dr. Charles Swindoll asks the question, "The Honeymoon: Why Can't It Begin...Again?" He writes:

I find that the honeymoon sometimes ends simply because habits become set in concrete. For no special reason, couples just become disinterested and frigid. God planned intimacy to be warm, exciting, healthy, and growing. Break with the routine.

—*p. 80-81*

One way to break with the routine is to rehearse some of those fantasies you had before you married your husband. I don't know what they were. More than likely you pinned your hopes on believing that marriage to the man you call "husband" was going to be a field day.

Can you remember the first time you saw your husband? Or your first date? I do. The first time I saw Earl was at church. He was ministering, and I was impressed by his extraordinary giftedness as a preacher and singer. Little did I know he and I would date years later after being widowed from wonderful spouses.

Our first date was on Valentine's Day; we went to Outback Steak House. I remember sitting across the table from him and enjoying being in his company. He had everything that I had ever admired in a man: good looks, intelligence, kindness; and his conversation reinforced my assessment that he was Spirit-filled. He did have a hobby that I, being from the east coast did not embrace: hunting; but this didn't stop my enjoying his company immensely and knowing that I wanted to see him again. When he asked if he could see me, of course the answer was yes.

We didn't have a courtship; we just fused. I enjoyed being with him, and he enjoyed being with me. Not that we have similar personalities. Earl is tranquil and contemplative, I'm vivacious and impulsive. I felt this was a good blend. Certainly, I didn't want to marry anyone who was just like me; identicalness is good for twins, but I'm told if your husband is just like you, one of you is unnecessary. Don't shoot the messenger—I'm just telling you what I've been told.

As the months went by I started envisioning what life would be like as Earl's wife. Guess what? He proposed to me on a warm July evening, and you know what I said: Yes! Seven months later, in one of the most magnificent churches in Cleveland, Texas, on the first day of February 2003, as the clock struck 3:00 p.m. (okay, it was a "little" after three), surrounded by those who knew and loved me—marry him I did. God's special wedding gift to us was an 80 degrees picture perfect day.

Earl and I had a fantastic honeymoon in Greece, and I found out that I loved him more than I did when I said, "I Do."

You have a story to tell about your first date and your wedding. I'm sure you also had a great time on your honeymoon, whether near or far. But, sisters, are any of you like me? After the honeymoon, Earl and I had to learn to become one as God had ordained. Someone said this isn't hard; the hard thing is to determine which one the two will become. This is true even with clergy couples. However, your honeymoon doesn't have to end, and your matrimonial fires don't have to dim.

Here are a few fire starters to make your marriage sizzle:

Communicate

Communication is to love what blood is to life.

—*Wright and Roberts*, After You Say I Do, 56

If a man has enough horse sense to treat his wife like a thoroughbred, she will never turn into an old nag.
—*Old Codger Wisdom*

In our marriage class, Earl and I emphasize that the three most important words for intimacy are communication, communication, and communication. You must have communication if you want to keep the home fires lit. You can't have intimacy without communication. It is key. True communication is sharing and listening as your husband and you inform, investigate, and understand each other.

In spite of this, it's surprising how little couples really communicate—including pastors' wives. Oh, we talk, but we can talk without communicating.

Components of Communication

There are three components of communication: content, tone, and nonverbal. Content: what you say, is only 7 percent of the message; tone is 38 percent; and nonverbal is 55 percent. Therefore, you must watch not only what you say, but how you say it. That means keeping those hands off of those hips and keeping that neck still when you want to get your point across.

Silent treatment is communication, but it does not foster intimacy. You are on one side of the bed hugging the pillow and mattress for all it's worth, murmuring under your breath, "He'd better not put his hands on me!" Yes, I've been there.

If you're anything like me, you do this even though you may want your husband to touch you. But you want an apology first. When you receive the apology, in your mind, he should have a better apology. I see you smiling. I think it's a sister-thing. At the same time, when you do this, you are just making it harder on yourself. In what way, I don't know, but believe me, our husbands have a plan for the "silent treatment." They know that most of us like to talk, and we do. I think God has given us 10,000 words a day and our husbands a thousand. They don't have any problem keeping their mouths closed, while we want to use the rest of our words for the day. In fact, they probably welcome our silence. I I think Earl welcomes mine, especially if we are in the car driving from church to home.

That doesn't mean you have to let your husband bait you into being silent when you want to talk. Time is out for walking around the house with your mouth poked out, giving your husband the silent treatment, and expecting him to read your mind. Time is also out for burying your head in books, newspapers, or the television. It's okay to do this if both of you agree to it, but your head has to come out of the books sometime. If you don't, all you'll find yourself talking about is what you've read and what he hasn't read. Isn't that exciting? No.

Levels of Communication

If communication is to be rewarding, you must be willing to deepen your level of interaction with your husband.

H. Norman Wright tells us there are five levels of communication that correspond to degrees of intimacy in a marriage relationship. The levels are similar to peeling back the layers of an onion to get to the core. Mr. Wright lists these levels as (1) sharing facts, explanations, or information; (2) sharing the ideas and opinions of other people; (3) sharing your own ideas and opinions; (4) sharing personal preferences, beliefs, concerns, some of your own personal experiences; (5) sharing inner feelings and preferences, likes and dislikes (*Wright,* Communication: Key To Your Marriage, *33-35*).

Dr. Susan Campbell also writes about the importance of communicating your feelings in *Saying What's Real, 7 Keys to Authentic Communication and Relationship Success*. She tells us we can heal childhood wounds and greatly enhance our relationships with our husbands by practicing the language of feelings. For example, instead of masking your real feelings and deal with unconscious negative reactions when your husband communicates to you in a manner you feel is inappropriate, you can use "hearing you say that, I feel":

> *Using "Hearing you say that, I feel..." to frame your response keeps your communications responsible. You're taking responsibility for what you feel, not telling others how they should be. You're*

> *"staying on your own side of the net"—a metaphor for speaking only about what you experience rather than telling others how they feel or what they should be doing differently.—p. 24-25.*

Listening

> *The most important thing in communication is to hear what isn't being said.*
>
> —PETER F. DRUCKER

Listening is also part of communication, but it has become a lost art. What is listening? It is holding your peace and piece—tongue that is. In our society, it is often felt that talking is better than listening. It's obvious that God doesn't think so, because He gave us one mouth and two ears. Does that tell us anything?

I'm not going to insult your intelligence by telling you why you should listen. You know why: so you can hear what the other person is saying. I pray I'll master listening before I go to heaven. Is there anyone other than me who cuts off folk in the middle of their sentences when they are saying something you don't want to hear, or you think you know what they are going to say? After all, what I have to say is important. What does that say about what they have to say—save your breath? Uhm. If this hits you, you don't have to say anything, just look straight ahead. Now doesn't that sound "churchy?"

What's the remedy? Stephen Covey advises us to develop the habit of seeking first to understand then to be understood. Covey refers to this habit as Principles of Empathetic Communication. He describes this principle as listening emphatically with the goal of clearly understanding the other person before you attempt to get them to understand your view. This creates an atmosphere of care and respect (*Covey, p. 235-261*). James 1:19 also give us good advice: "So then, my beloved brethren, let every man be swift to hear, slow to speak, slow to wrath."

Paul and Sandy Coughlin tell us listening with empathy is essential if we are to build intimacy with our husbands:

Expressing yourself in a truthful, concise, non-shaming, and gracious manner builds intimacy. Conversely, many of us expect our spouse to somehow read our hearts and minds to discover how we feel or think...However, expressing yourself well is only half the undertaking. Listening with empathy is also foundational, especially since most of us have not experienced (regularly or ever) true empathetic listening. Most of us have been highly exposed to passive and selective listening that focuses or tunes in on what relates to us.

—*Coughlin, 170.*

You know when you are listening with empathy when you are able to repeat back to others what they have said. Let's try this on our husbands and send them into orbit for a couple of hours. Only kidding. But I'm not kidding now: Learn the art of using love starters to change the subject when your husband doesn't talk about anything but church-related topics.

A love talk starter from Les and Leslie Parrot is:

Matthew Porter, the writer, said to his wife: "You do something to me—something that simply mystifies me." What does your spouse do to mystify you?—Parrot, Love Talk Starters, 126

Resolve Conflict

Marital conflict is created one of two ways: (1) couples fail to make each other happy, or (2) couples make each other unhappy. In the first case, couples are frustrated because their emotional needs are not being met. In the second case, they're deliberately hurting each other. The first cause of conflict is failure to care, and the second, failure to protect."

—*William F. Harley,* His Needs, Her Needs, *15*

Sisters, every marriage will have conflict. But conflict doesn't have to be mortal; it can even be fun, if it doesn't get out of hand.

Here are a few tips:

- *Stop having major flare-ups over minor disagreements.* Ouch, Sena.
- *Enter conflict situations with a win-win attitude.* Who wants to lose?
- *Remove "someday" from your calendar.* Discuss things that need to be settled promptly, and drop things that don't need to be settled ever. I can't remember where I heard this, but it's good advice.
- *One size does not fit all.* That's why Cinderella's sisters didn't get the prince. The shoes didn't fit. Handle conflict in the way that best fits your husband's and your personality.
- *Don't spiritualize everything.* While you know that our amazing Father is a problem solver, and can do anything but lie, fail, and deny Himself, you must also realize that He gave you wisdom to do things for yourself, so don't hide behind Bible verses to avoid necessary confrontations.
- *Recognize that there are three ways to communicate: adult, parent and child.* Talk to your husband as an adult. Adults reason together (Isaiah 1:18). When you are in the parent mode you tell him what he should or should not do; he's not going to do anything. Children holler and scream. You know this isn't going to get you anywhere.
- *Watch your volume.* Loud does not mean right. If possible, stay cool, calm and collected, and stay focused on the subject under discussion. I know this may be a stretch, but try.
- *Crocodile tears get old after a while.* So learn to turn off the faucet every now and then. Ask yourself: "How would I feel if my husband cried every time he didn't get his way?"

P.S. The favorite part of marriage can be making up.

Be Into him

What signs are you giving your husband that you are into him? In his book *What Makes a Man Feel Loved?*, Bob Barnes lists several ways for you to express to your husband that that you enjoy being in his world, such as: listening to his dreams, reading a book out loud to each other and giving him a certificate for a foot rub (p. 34).

Ponder this: When was the last time you whispered in your husband's ear, "I Love You?" Right now, or as soon as you see him again, is as good a time as any.

Date

Being married doesn't stop us from wanting to date. Still, a pastor's wife has to accept this truth: "The ministry never has been and never will be a nine-to-five job." As a consequence, you have to make the most out of every second that you have.

Here are some dating suggestions:

- *Establish a "Date Day"*. Earl and I have set aside Friday to date. We aren't able to do something together every Friday but we keep our date day on the calendar.
- *Plan one-day vacations if you can't take a few days or a week.* You don't have to spend a lot of money. Earl and I toured Blue Bell Ice Creamery for a few dollars and received ice cream at the end of the tour. Not bad for a day of fun.
- *Don't be selfish.* Do something you like to do and something your husband likes to do. I went hunting with Earl a couple of times. To my surprise I really had fun. I even rode on the four-wheeler with him. He still doesn't like shopping with me, but I have a plan.
- *Be spontaneous; don't get stuck in a rut.* Have fun and enjoy one another. Earl and I went to New Orleans on the spur of the moment. We had to stop by Wal-Mart to buy clothes, but that was one of the best three days I have ever spent with him.
- *Send your husband flowers.* I sent Earl flowers twice and he was on cloud nine. I need to send him some again soon.
- *If you need to, make a standing appointment with your husband so he can give you the same TLC (tender loving care) he gives so freely to others.* I read somewhere that some pastors' wives have called their husband's office and, using a pseudonym, made an appointment to see him. That's rather drastic, but I think it's worthy of consideration.

Meet Your Husband's Emotional Needs

What are your husband's emotional needs? It would do you well to know the answer to this question. Much research has been done about needs of men and women. It doesn't take a rocket scientist to know that men and women are different. Knowing your husband's emotional needs will allow you to minister to your husband. If he doesn't open up to you, you have to be willing to open up to him.

Avoid Love Busters

Love busters are habits that destroy romantic love. Williard F. Harley, Jr. wrote about them in his book, *Love Busters.* He lists love busters that we need to be aware of and avoid such as selfish demands and independent behavior.

In her book, *What's It Like Being Married to Me?*, Linda Dillow discusses another love buster: sophisticated venting. She says that some wives are unaware they are gold-medal gripers about their husbands (p. 33). Ouch!

Learn Your Husband's Love Language

Let me see you raise your hand. How many of you know your husband's love language? Well, if you want to increase intimacy, you'll do well to find out. In *The Five Love Languages*, Gary Chapman outlines five ways you and your husband want to be loved. Learn to love him the right way. Teach him to love you like you want to be loved.

Don't Be a Change Agent

God never intended for us to become clones of each other, for we are uniquely made. He has given us each talents, gifts, and abilities, and He wants us to use them for his glory. God never intended for us to be change agents, either. As Bishop Dr. Mable Berry has said, "You can't change what you didn't make." As much as we would like, your husband is not the exception to the rule. Your responsibility is to honor him. The Holy Spirit has to change him and change you too.

I found this out the hard way. I tried to change Earl many times to conform to my image instead of God's image. He let me know in no uncertain terms that I wasn't God, and that my responsibility was to let God change him and me. I took his advice.

Welcome Sexual Intimacy

Sisters, sex is not a bad word; it is a good word. God designed marriage and He wants you to have a fulfilling sex life.

Dr. Willard Harley tells us very candidly that the first thing our husbands can't do without is sexual fulfillment. Listen to what Dr. Harley says:

> *When a man chooses a wife, he promises to remain faithful to her for life. This means that he believes his wife will be his only sexual partner "until death do us part." He makes this commitment because he trusts her to be as sexually interested in him as he is in her. He trusts her to be sexually available to him whenever he needs to make love and to meet all his sexual needs, just as she trust him to meet her emotionally.*
>
> *Unfortunately in many marriages the man finds that putting his trust in this woman has turned into one of the biggest mistakes of his life. He has agreed to limit his sexual experience to a wife who is unwilling to meet that vital need. He finds himself up the proverbial creek without a paddle. If his religious or moral convictions are strong, he may try to make the best of it. Some husbands tough it out, but many cannot. They find sex elsewhere.—*Harley, *His Needs Her Needs*, 49-50

That's tight, but it's right. Like me, you may have flinched when you read those last words. We will discuss infidelity in chapter eighteen but we clearly don't even want to think of giving our husbands any reasons for straying. We must do everything we can to ensure their most important need is met.

Our husbands aren't the only benefactor of satisfying sexual intimacy. God made us sexual creatures too, and a good love life sweetens a lot of bitter things. Remember, we can be saintly and sexy. I know we are saved, sanctified, and filled with the Holy Spirit, but the bedroom is not the place to be a cold fish or a church mouse. The marriage bed is undefiled, and it is the place to give your husband everything you've got. There may even be an occasion or two where a good "hallelujah" is in order.

If you still want to keep the strait jacket on, read what the Bible has to say about sexual intimacy. God told us in 1 Corinthians 7:4 that the wife does not have authority over her own body, but the husband does. Likewise the husband does not have authority over his own body, but the wife does.

Do we need to go into details here, sisters? You know what that means.

Your body belongs to him, and his body belongs to you. When he wants your body, what are you supposed to do? Give him your body. I'm not being coarse here, I'm talking about husband and wife. That's what we are commanded to do. We cannot rebuff our husbands or be sexually frigid. If so, they will become resentful at being rejected. That's not good!

Here are a few ideas to digest:

- *Reconsider going to bed wearing that old flannel nightgown that's not conducive to love-making.* Be truthful, don't you have one, or know someone who does? I have a gray flannel nightgown with a picture of one of the Seven Dwarfs on the front and another one of them on the back. That's good when I'm home alone, but Earl isn't too thrilled about it.

  He's also not seduced by my eighth wonder of the world two-piece yellow flannel pajamas that have bacon and eggs imprinted all over them; or by my blue cotton nightgown with a picture of a lady with her hair in rollers, and the words "I don't do breakfast" in big bold letters across the front. The fact that it matches my big black rollers doesn't seem to change his opinion, either. I just have to change into something more suitable—until he goes to sleep.

- *Good perfume always works, as long as you don't overdo it.* Spray some of it on the sheets; he'll like it.
- *Romantic Christian music also helps.* It's old, but T. D. Jakes' *Sacred Love Songs* CD is always a hit in the bedroom.
- *Read the Song of Solomon together.* I believe God put that in the Bible especially as a fire starter for clergy couples. It is a love song between a king and a Shulamite maiden falling madly in love with one another. The song covers the events preceding the wedding, the events accompanying the wedding, and the events after the wedding. In each stage, both the bride and the groom express how the other light up their life. The song will light up your life, too.
- *Don't let the fire die down even if you've been married for a long time.* In the late stages of marriage sex can be exciting and sizzling. Studies of marital satisfaction show that the highest scores occur during the middle years, as kids leave home.
- *Don't fall victim to what Dr. Laura Schlessinger describes as the White Rabbit Syndrome*—the retort that the white rabbit gave in *Alice in Wonderland*—"I'm late, I'm late for a very important date." According to Dr. Schlessinger, sadly this is the same retort many wives give their husbands, who are eager to make an intimate connection (*Schlessinger, 15.)*
- *If necessary, set a sexual appointment with your husband.* In their book, *The Great Marriage Q & A Book,* in response to the question, "Our sex life has become boring. What kinds of appropriate things can we do to make sex more exciting?" Dr. Gary and Barbara Rosberg advise two things: spontaneity and intentionality. Spontaneity means doing something creative and different in order to bring romance and spark back into your physical relationship. Surprise your husband or catch him off-guard and let him know what you want—now! Intentionality means to be purposeful. Some couples will literally perk up their sex life by scheduling it. The fact that it's on the calendar will reduce stress for your husband (*p. 110*).
- *Don't assume that your husband wants sexual intimacy* if he rubs your back, brings you roses, or makes you breakfast in

bed. He may just be trying to be romantic, affectionate, and warm.

- *Do everything to the glory of God.* If God doesn't smile at what you are doing, prayerfully reconsider changing how your husband and you express your love physically to one another.

Remarry Him Almost Every Day

Given the remote possibility that the above fire starters do not ignite your marriage as you desire, you can always do what I heard an elderly lady say she does: She marries her husband all over again almost every day. The reason why she has to remarry him is that he's changed quite a bit over the years, and every day she finds something out about him that she didn't know when they first married. Because she's willing to marry him all over again almost every day, her marriage is full of life and vitality.

This may be a stretch for some of you, but when you think about it, it makes a lot of sense. If you marry your husband all over again almost every day then you are always a new bride. You know how exhilarating it is to be new bride. Okay, use your imagination. Now, take a couple of minutes to put your old flannel nightgowns in the trash and strike those matches. Did I hear you say something?

Let's Pray…

Be a blessing!

Reflections from Earl:

- Honor one another.
- Make each other feel special.
- Keep yourself attractive. Make him feel good. Do not let yourself go. He is still a man before anything else. Personal hygiene is important.
- Fulfill him sexually. If you are not having good experiences out of the bedroom, it will not be good inside.

- Marital sex is the ultimate expression of covenant keeping, communion, and surrender. When we get married we cut the marriage covenant. And from that point forward, we have communion together. The coming together of husband and wife should symbolize the love and communion that Christ has with his church.
- Don't accept disrespect from your husband. Address it when he makes off-colored remarks about other women. Voice your discomfort appropriately, e.g., "How would you feel if it were opposite?"

4

Knife: Tension Between Marriage and Ministry

Sisters, you need a knife in survival situations. If you are on a camping trip or in the wilderness, you will need a good cutting tool. You also need a good cutting tool when you have to cut through the tension between marriage and ministry. This chapter centers on how this plays out in relating to your husband as pastor. If you are not a pastor's wife you may want to skip this chapter, as I'm revealing some "behind the scene" business that you really may not want to know. Just kidding.

Bipolar Psychological Disorder

Bipolar is having two diametrically or opposed natures or views. The term is also is used to characterize a psychological disorder that affects millions of Americans. My eldest son, Jay, has been diagnosed as being bipolar.

Persons with a bipolar psychological disorder (sudden change in moods, going from severe highs to deep dark lows) are in a constant state of tension, and find themselves almost living in two bodies. They seem to have a split personality. You can be interacting with one of their personalities, but while you are getting used to that, like a car on a wet street coming to a screeching halt, before you know it, they've taken on an entirely different personality. If you've ever lived with someone with this disorder, you know it can be trying—much like that which was portrayed in *The Three Faces of Eve*, a story of a woman with multiple personalities.

There is medication to treat this disorder, but the road is hard. If you don't mind, sisters, let's stop here right now and pray for all who are victimized by this disease. Thank you.

The Great Divide

Happiness is a function of accepting what is.

—*Werner Erhard*

Arguably, pastors' wives are bipolar when we relate to our husbands as pastors. The tension between marriage and ministry often pull us in two competing directions. We value our pastoral husbands' ministry, but our marriages often suffer because of his ministry. That's because the dynamics of church relationships are different from those of the husband/wife relationship. I call this the great divide.

Diane Langberg writes:

> *All clergy marriages must deal with tension between ministry and family. Ministry couples must also learn to live with a job that is never done; no matter what is accomplished, new needs arise and must be met. They struggle with living up to others' expectations, with having the church determine their income, and with having their house belong to others and used as an extension of the church. These issues all contribute to the strain on pastoral marriages and result in frightening divorce statistics.*

More men are leaving the ministry due to discouragement and more ministry couples are divorcing than ever before.

—LANGBERG, 14

Operating in the Great Divide

Life's under no obligation to give us what we expect.

—MARGARET MITCHELL

Sisters, you can operate successfully in the great divide although it is splintered. Recognizably, you can't stealthily wiggle your nose and make the tension between marriage and ministry disappear. It comes with the territory. Still, you can significantly reduce the strain on your marriage by: 1) evaluating your expectations for your marriage, 2) finding your place in your husband's ministry, and 3) encouraging your husband in his ministry.

1. *Your Expectations.* Are your expectations for your marriage realistic? Remember, you married a pastor. A pastor is on call 24 hours every day, and is completely devoted to ministry. Caring for two families is not a piece of cake. He may not have a whole lot of time left for you after ministering to God and others. I have to constantly re-evaluate the expectations I have for Earl. Sometimes they are realistic and sometimes they aren't, so I have to adjust accordingly. We'll discuss this in more detail in other chapters.
2. *Finding your place in your husband's ministry.* This is not all cookies and cream. It will require laying aside your wifely privileges as you relate to your husband as pastor. You may also have to put some of your personal ministerial ambitions on hold as you fulfill your pastoral wife ministry requirements. Therefore, it is imperative that hard questions be answered.

Specifically, what do you do when your husband and you both have an assortment of strengths and gifts in the ministry? Because he's the pastor, should your gifts lie dormant? I'm talking about when you've both been called to a teaching and preaching ministry or called to exercise your gifts in some other way in the Body of Christ. How do you know when to step forward? When to step back? How do you minister effectively and still be in subjection to your husband? Should you decline opportunities to minister that conflict with your husband's schedule, or the church calendar?

The book club answer is to learn how to supplement one another and discover where we can work together smoothly and where we are better off taking separate tracks. The more you contribute to your joint ministry, the less chance there is of derailing your husband's career.

I agree with the book club answer, but I'll be frank with you. Putting it in practice is not a cinch for Earl and me. One of the stoniest terrains he and I are traversing as pastor and wife is discovering how I can contribute to his ministry while I grow and flourish in mine. I was a pastor before Earl and I married, and chose to leave the church to join him at the church he is called to pastor. Although Earl has given me a place in his ministry, opportunities to preach and teach the Word of God are considerably less than I had anticipated, and it is a great source of tension. The last thing I want to do is derail his career. Yet, I want to exercise my gifts. Often, because of the tension, I am Jolly Rancher at church, but when the coast is clear, I don't grin like a Cheshire cat, and I'm not Mrs. Congeniality.

Now that I've admitted my waywardness, I don't want to give you the impression that I'm being asked to make bricks without straw, or have gone completely off the deep end when relating to Earl as pastor. Even with the tension, I'm so thankful to God for being Earl's wife. I pray you feel the same way about your marriage. My prayer is that your ministry will flourish and grow as you find your place in your husband's ministry.

Encourage your husband in his ministry. There are several ways you can encourage your husband. Allow me to share a few:

- Honor Him

  Don't get common with your husband; give him the honor he is due. You are a pastor's wife but you are also a member of the congregation and God has entrusted your husband to watch over your soul. I refer to Earl as Pastor Whitaker when I'm addressing him in church, and outside the church when I'm in the company of members of our congregation.

- Maintain Confidentiality

When a wife runs her fingers in his hair, he should be careful—she may be after his scalp.

—ANONYMOUS

Certainly, as a pastor's wife, you want your husband to share his life and his days with you. When he does, keep what your husband tells you to yourself unless he gives you approval to share with others.

When your husband chooses not to share with you, don't lay his head in your lap to get the scoop. You are not Delilah! We'll talk about her later, but let me tell you this: Samson's problem was not Delilah's lap. His problem was being tired and worn out with all of her pestering. When he put his head in Delilah's lap he just wanted to rest. She bothered him so much that he told her everything in order to get some peace.

I'm not taking up for Samson as he disobeyed God, but let your husband rest when he's tired. Question him to no end after he wakes up (just kidding!).

Nuff said.

- Stay in His Corner

Most marital problems are caused by the marriage of two people who are in love with themselves.

—ANONYMOUS

Always be best friends with your husband, even if you have to struggle to do so. A friend of mine, Peggy Young, gave me advice that convicts me when I want to act up: "If you want to be treated like a queen, treat your husband like a king." The best way to treat your husband like a king is to stay in his corner—to be his cheerleader; his best support system.

How many times have you seen a boxer look as though he is down and out, but he hangs on until the bell rings, for he knows if he can make it to the corner, everything will be all right? Often the one who seems to teeter-totter on his last legs returns to win the fight. Why? He had someone in his corner.

Now, a boxer doesn't want to fight his opponent, barely make it to his corner, and get knocked out. No, he wants tender loving care, salve for his bruised eye, tape those broken ribs, do a quick fix on those broken teeth if the opponent knocked out the mouthpiece. After getting a little TLC, he's ready to fight the next round.

That's the way it should be with your pastor husband. He gets beat up all day long in the world, just like a boxer. When he comes home, he needs to know incontestably that you care, that you are his biggest fan, and that you think the world of him.

This is no picnic to stomach, but I'll say it straight. Another reason why you need to be in your husband's corner is that if you don't, someone else will. He may not be much in your eyes, but your "trash" may be someone else's treasure. What I'm trying to say is that your marriage may not be ideal, and you may have "big issues" with being married to your husband, but everyone else doesn't necessarily see it that way.

Some women find it easy to see your husband as a hero. When that happens, your husband can begin to operate according to Willie Sutton's Law: "I rob banks 'cause that's where the money is." Show your husband without reservation that he is your hero, and you are where the money is—not Ms. Daisy down the pew.

David's wife Michal is a prime example of a wife not in her husband's corner. The Bible tells us when David brought the Ark of the Covenant back to Israel he danced with all of his might before God. David danced so much that he danced out of his clothes. Michal saw all of this as she looked out the window. Instead of joining him in the dance she despised him in her heart. In no uncertain terms she let David know how ashamed she was of him, the king of Israel, for acting uncouthly. The Bible says because of what she did God closed up her womb, and she was barren all of the days of her life (2 Samuel 6:16, 23).

I'm not insinuating that God will close up your womb if you have an attitude toward your husband; I'm trying to convey that you must visibly demonstrate that you are in his corner. Eliminate "he knows I'm in his corner" stuff. Let him know today and always how much you appreciate him. He may be a great man, but he is not a mind reader. He wants to know that you are there for him.

Here are a few ways to show your husband you care:

- *Pack a small suitcase with items he will need:*
  Change of shirt
  Underwear
  Handkerchiefs
  Water, juice, tea
  A nice card or love letter
- *Be his armor bearer if he'll let you.*
- *Never say anything about your husband that you can't say to his face.*
- *Attend as many church events as possible*—especially funeral services where your husband is officiating or delivering the eulogy. Most likely, he's grieving also. He needs your support.
- *Show your husband respect by rising when he comes to the pulpit.* Say amen once in a while, except when he's using you as a negative example.
- *Shake his hand after the message and let him know how you were helped.*
- *When you are tired, tell him you'd prefer to stay home.* I've traveled tired with Earl on many occasions, and I believe he would have been better off without me. I yawned throughout the service, had little pep in my step, and could only muster a few sluggish amens between yawns. I'm sure those sitting next to me thought I didn't like the message or the messenger. Wrong. Now I stay home when I'm drained unless it's absolutely necessary to travel with him. I'm sure Earl can appreciate that more than having his wife acting like a zombie.
- *Pray for him.* Remember, prayer changes things. Two model prayers are found in Colossians 4:3–4 and 1 Thessalonians 3:1–2.

Let's Pray…

Be a blessing!

Reflections from Earl

- Encourage him.
- Study to find your husband's purpose. What is his giftedness? What is he about? Help him recognize that God has given him a purpose. Don't do it for his benefit only. The only way you can be fulfilled is by your husband walking in his creative purpose.
- Hold up before him what God has said about his role in the marriage. Don't assume that your husband knows it.
- Don't dishonor him. A man is all about ego and fulfilling his role. When his role is threatened, he will not function at his best. He may resort to attacking, withdrawal, or other negative behaviors.
- One of the worst ways you can dishonor your husband is by embarrassing him in public. If he is somewhere and you disagree with him, don't openly and blatantly attack him. He is your leader. Think about it: you wouldn't attack your boss openly would you? Your husband may not respond back to you openly, but may start doing things on his own without involving you.
- Meet his emotional needs.
- Learn his love language.
- Show him consistently that you honor his thoughts as a leader.
- Females are strong, and culturally this may be a problem especially for those of us who may have been single for a while. You must resist the temptation to take over. Even if he fails, support him.
- If he is indecisive, learn the technique of teaching him how to come to a decision.
- Take an interest in what concerns him, not fix the problem, but just to show him that you care.
- Maintain confidentiality. If you have a problem with confidentiality, tell him not to tell you anything, or if he does, ask him not to name names.
- Let him vent until he gets things off of his chest.
- Don't compare your husband's approach to including you in his ministry with that of other pastors.

- Have realistic expectations as to how you are to be used in your husband's ministry. Each church has a different setting, and because of personality differences, or ministries that are not cohesive, you and your husband may not be able to work well together. If this is your case, admit it, do what God has called you to do, and support him in what God has called him to do.

5

Tube Tent: Living In the Parsonage

Shelter is a must in survival situations. Even if you are in a wilderness perhaps the most important part of your trip will be to ensure you have suitable shelter. You need a good night's rest to handle the challenges of the next day. You can survive longer in the wilderness when you have shelter suited to your needs. The first component to sleeping well is a good tent. It's not home, but will work for a few days until you get home. In this chapter we will focus on living in the parsonage, and how we can live successfully when a house is not a home.

When a House Is Not a Home

A house becomes a home when you can write, "I love you" on the furniture.

— *Anonymous*

I can't remember everything, but thank God, I do remember a song titled, "A House is Not a Home." Parts of the lyrics are, *"a house is not a home when you aren't there..."*

That's a good song, sisters. It's been my experience that a house doesn't have to be a home even sitting there with your pastor husband. What am I talking about? I'm talking about the parsonage. There is something about the parsonage. Is it home or not home?

The September/October 2009 issue of *Preaching Magazine* (p. 28-29) featured an article by Janet T. and Philip D. Jamieson titled, "Using Pastoral Housing Strategically." The authors state, "It is almost always better to own your own home that to live in a church-owned residence ...for some, living in a parsonage is a true gift...for others it is a death sentence." *—preaching .com*

Many of you are living in a parsonage, have lived in a parsonage, or will live in a parsonage some day. How do you see the parsonage? As a gift or as a death sentence?

Some say they find no warmth in a parsonage. Others are not interested in a parsonage and don't want to invest money fixing it up or remodeling and making it "livable" to their tastes. What about all of the nightmares you hear about living in the parsonage, such as people who come bounding by the parsonage for visits at inopportune moments? Or the pastor goes to his study, and the sight of his car outside the church becomes an invitation for drop-ins? We wives don't talk much about these kinds of problems, but they can be real.

Earl and I lived in the church parsonage for eight years. Many questions ran through my mind when he and I elected to stay there while away from home. Earl pastors 127 miles from home, or 254 miles round trip. Before we moved into the parsonage, he and I stayed in hotel rooms. This got old quick, especially for me. How long can you gleefully stay in a hotel room packed like sardines with not enough room to swing a cat? We transitioned to the church parsonage seventeen months after we were married.

For me, our move to the parsonage was approving and disapproving. On the approving side, the parsonage was much more spacious than a hotel room and the church members respected our privacy.

On the disapproving side, I had a bad case of homesickness. The parsonage was nice but its neutral décor was not as gratifying to me as our home. I like our home. It's bright and cozy, with royal blue carpets, antique white furnishings, forest green kitchen, and colorful bathrooms. As a consequence I found myself staying at home more often than Earl would like me to stay at home. I was able to use the "price of gas" excuse on many occasions—and who can argue about the price of gas these days? I tried a myriad of other excuses that wore thin fast. Thus once a week I reluctantly packed the car to the hilt and drove 127 miles to the parsonage, glaring at every mileage sign. My scowl didn't fade when Earl drove; it just gave me another opportunity to bellow within myself, "I don't want to live my entire life at the parsonage."

Learning To Be Content

Are you ready for a bolt from the blue? After I lived in the parsonage for a few years I learned to be content and to have an attitude of gratitude. It was much more desirable than the Day's Inn. Furthermore, I realized that not every church respects the office of pastor enough to provide a place for the man or woman of God to dwell.

I even had occasional bouts of "homey" feelings when I drove on to the parking lot, grateful for being blessed with somewhere to lay my head other than concrete. Look at Jesus, the Son of God. I heard Jesus say, "Foxes have holes, and birds have nests, but the Son of Man has nowhere to lay His head." It wasn't because He was poor; it was His choice. Second Corinthians 8:9 tells us, "…though He was rich, yet for our sakes He became poor, that we through His poverty might become rich." I also appreciated our home more than before we moved into the parsonage. Isn't it strange what a change of attitude can do?

Sisters, I don't know your attitude toward living in a parsonage. If you are living in one now, or will be living in a parsonage in the future, my prayer is that you will make that house your home. A home is not where you have your mailing address, but a home is where you have your heart. Further, may the parsonage serve as a reminder to you that this old world is not your home, anyway. I heard Jesus say in John 14 that He was going away to prepare a mansion for us. That's living large!

Let's Pray…

Be a blessing!

6

Work Gloves: Chores & Activities Around the Church

Pastors' wives have to be prepared for emergencies at church as well as home. Work gloves provide heavy-duty hand protection and prevent hand injuries when you handle material and perform chores around the church. They're in our success kit.

Calling Mollie Maid

He who wants to change the world should already begin by cleaning the dishes.

—*Paul Carvel*

I hope someone out there can read my lips:

"I don't like to do housework." "I really don't like to do housework." "I hate doing housework." "The only reason I do housework is because I like a clean house."

Sisters, do you hear me? "I don't like to clean!" I even have an old scraggly nightgown that I wear every once in a while that says, "I don't do housework!" I believe there is at least one person reading this book who doesn't like to clean, either. Good; misery likes company. Yet, that doesn't amount to a hill of beans. We pastors' wives are going to get grime under our fingernails sometimes. Yes, you too.

Helping your husband clean his office is a great opportunity. This is only upon invitation, my sisters. It may torment you to see the piles of out-of-date paraphernalia. Yet, you have to remember that it is his office, not yours. His untidiness is not a reflection of your character.

That being said, when he asks, help him, okay? Don't remind him that you are not his mama. Every office needs a feminine touch—yours, not Sister So & So, for some sisters don't mind cleaning. If he asks you to help him decorate, go light on the lace. The office should reflect him, not you. He's the pastor.

If Earl had given me decorating carte blanche at our church's prior location, there would have had more flowers and more frills in his office. Instead, he had eagles on his desk and bookcase, a painting with a portrait of the woods on one wall, and the mounted head of a deer that he killed on another wall. Now you know this isn't me, but it wasn't my office. Honestly, I'm glad Earl's office reflected him not me. He's all man, and I thank God for it.

Thank God for your husband, too. There are still bonuses attached to cleaning his office, even though he may not let you put plush teddy bears on the desk. It may give you fleeting glimpses of your sweetie. You have to catch him when you can.

Mrs. Bubbles

Law of Window Cleaning: It's on the other side.

—*Anonymous*

While we are on the subject of cleaning, let me throw this in. Cleaning the other areas of the church is not just for everyone else; it's for the pastor's wife, too. The cleanliness of the church is a reflection of us. We can pick up the broom and even clean out a toilet or two. I would venture to say that at least 90 percent of you are already sweeping and cleaning toilets. Thank God for you. For the other 10 percent, if you haven't tried it, you may want to try it. Will you like it? I doubt it. But think of the joy you will feel knowing that you had a part in keeping God's sanctuary clean.

Our church had several cleanup crews before we relocated. I attached myself to the Cleo and Carolyn Brooks' crew, but regrettably my schedule didn't allow me to help as often as I would have liked. Currently, we do not have crews at our present location, but that doesn't prevent me from picking up paper and cleaning dirty surfaces when I see them. If your schedule is tight you can pick up a few pieces of paper, too, whether or not your church has crews. Don't give me that look; you know you can.

To Scrub or Not to Scrub

Oh, you probably know what I'm going to talk about here before you read any further. I'm talking about visitations—home, hospital, and other places. This comes with the territory. Being a pastor's wife is not all it's cracked up to be.

What other vocation do you know of that the wife accompanies her husband as much as a pastor's wife? I can't think of any. Doctors' wives don't go with them when they have to visit a patient, and plumbers' wives aren't expected to help their husband fix commodes. But guess what, sisters? We've drawn the straw that says, "When you can go, go."

So, start getting used to the smell of hospitals, nursing homes, prisons, or whatever place God may use you to minister with your husband. Don't be too good to help someone who can't help themselves. Go for sure when you husband has to visit a sick sister. It's also okay to help with a bedpan or change a senior female saint's clothes. There are some things a female is not going to ask a man to do.

If you'd rather stay home, always remember—you may be up today, but tomorrow someone may have to change your Depends. So scrub your hands, suck it up, and keep smiling. Ask for special grace and strength when emptying the bedpan. I've done many things when visiting persons in hospitals and nursing homes that I thought I'd never have the guts to do, and I'm still here. Not the bedpan yet—Thank God!

Let me take a station break to say this: when you visit someone you didn't come to stay. Make your visits short and sweet, so they'll want to see you again.

Church Meetings

This section is not a shot in the dark. I stuck this here because I couldn't find a better place.

Sisters, I believe the jury is still deliberating about whether pastors' wives should attend church meetings. Some of my pastoral wife friends believe that the pastor's wife should attend church meetings so she can stay abreast of what is going on in the church and also make her vote count. Others believe that a pastor's wife should stay home so she will not be subjected to censure of her husband in the midst of church politics or conflict. The argument is that the woman is the weaker vessel (1 Peter 3:7). If things get too heated, she is going to get in a huff and want to defend her husband—even to the point of fighting for him. Do we really do that? Sometimes.

I'm sure most of you reading this book have found yourselves in the midst of church politics and conflict at one time or the other. We've all been in meetings when insults and demeaning remarks were hurled at our husbands. When he hurts, you hurt. It's tempting to climb on your bandwagon and give everyone a sanctified straightening out. You can't. Therefore, my suggestion is, "to thy own self be true." If your temperament is such that you know you can handle what goes on in the meeting, by all means go; if you know you could be a detriment to your husband, stay at home. Remember that your husband and you are a team. Your negative behavior could put his and your ministry on the shelf one day.

Sometimes you may find yourself at odds with your pastor husband. Oh, I forgot—the first lady is not to disagree with her husband—ouch. Rather than getting in the middle of the conflict, it is best to talk to him at home about it. With God's help, your husband and you can commit to give each other latitude to have differences of opinions and different approaches to resolving problems. However, you must never forget that God called him to be the pastor and holds him, not you, responsible for governing the church. As much as you may like to, God did not appoint you to mind the store, either. Trust me on this one my sisters. I have the hat, tee-shirt, bumper sticker and everything else associated with breaking this tip—and the stories behind them are not pretty.

That doesn't mean you shouldn't share your ideas if you decide to go to meetings. They may not be good to others, but they're good to you, so express them. Some pastors' wives don't express their ideas for fear they will be rejected or ridiculed or shot down. As a result, many creative ideas go down the drain. Speak up. Who knows, your ideas may be accepted—even if you are the pastor's wife.

One more bit of advice: Before you say, "I second the motion," take a refresher course in Roberts Rules of Order. Just kidding.

Let's pray…

Be a blessing!

RELATIONSHIP WITH OTHERS

7

Earthquake Wax: Parenting

Earthquake wax is used to protect our homes against damage or injury during an earthquake and should be included in emergency survival kits. According to Brynne Chandler, "Earthquake wax is the best thing since sliced bread. You scoop a little bit of soft, waxy stuff out of a fat, little pot, roll it into balls or strips and attach it to the bottom of your precious breakables. Set them in place and they will stay there through just about anything—including earthquakes."—ehow.com.—How to Remove Earthquake Wax", February 6, 2010.

Sisters, we must safeguard our relationship with our children. They are far more precious than any breakable we possess. If this relationship is not secure, it can be just as damaging as being caught unprepared in an earthquake. We will find ways to use our own earthquake wax to "quake-proof" our homes to protect against damage or injury to our relationship with our children in this chapter.

PKs (Preacher's Kids)

Making the decision to have a child is momentous. It is to decide forever to have your heart go walking around outside your body.
—*Elizabeth Stone*

Children are the hands by which we take hold of heaven.
—*Henry Ward Beecher*

As I stood over the silvery blue casket and pronounced the words, "Earth to earth, ashes to ashes and dust to dust," a million memories rushed through my head like a powerful water stream about the young man whose body we were laying to rest.

Memories of the times I lay on the bed with him listening to his dreams before and after he graduated from Morehouse College in Atlanta, Georgia. Or just talking about his day, and what he and his girlfriend Olivia were planning to do. Or laughing at one of the jokes that he always seemed to have ready for those who needed something to cheer their day. I even thought back to his simultaneous first and last recital. I wanted him to play the piano; he wanted to play the sax. I thought about how he wanted to be a comedian and a lawyer; I wanted him to be a lawyer first and then a comedian.

As my thoughts raced on like a skier going downhill, I thought about his first steps and his first words. I even thought about the nine months I had carried him in my womb, and the joy he brought to my life and to the life of others in so many ways. What was I doing at his gravesite after only twenty-two years of life?

When I said goodbye to him on December 10, 1996, I couldn't have known that that was the last time I would lay eyes on him. He was killed on his job by armed robbers. Shot four times in the back. The coroner was called to the scene, and at 1:14 a.m. he was pronounced "Dead On Arrival." So here I was saying, "Earth to earth, dust to dust, ashes to ashes."

Sisters, why do I tell you this story?

Because it is about my youngest son, Omar Jamal, a preacher's kid (a.k.a. PK). My intention is to accent the importance of your relationship with your children. In a billion years I would not want a mother to have to go through what I went through—losing a child who had just begun to live. I pray that none of you reading this book will ever have to experience the death of a child. In the hope that you haven't had that faith-testing experience, you still face incredible challenges raising PKs.

Let's talk about the good, the bad, and the ugly.

Good, Bad, and the Ugly

> *When was the last time you heard someone say, 'If parents learned to get along better with each other and their kids, then many of our social problems could be successfully addressed?' Is this opinion just wishful thinking? I don't think so.*
>
> — *Korem*, 85

The Good

The good is that our children are a heritage from the Lord, and blessed is the man who has a quiver full (Psalm 127:5). Notice, it said, blessed is the man. Did anyone ask us how we feel about it? Let's take a minute to remember just one of the contractions. But PK's are indeed a blessing from the Lord. God has entrusted us with His most precious asset: life.

The Bad

There is the bad, too. I believe the bad is that we parents forget that while PK's are an astounding group, they are still just ordinary children. Yes, still children. Not miniature adults. Not super kids. Just our kids.

I'm convinced that God has given PKs special grace. Frequently they have to put up with an awful lot of stress and abuse from congregations as well as neglect from their clergy parents. Because we forget they are just children we sometimes make unnatural demands. The most compelling evidence for this is our tendency to drag our PK's to church every time the door opens. I'm aware that talking about church attendance is a hot potato. Some of you may think it is heresy for me to suggest that we require our children to go to church too much. I'm going to jump this broom anyway.

Now don't get me wrong. I'm a minister and a strong advocate for going to church. In my opinion, everyone in the family needs to attend worship services regularly. The Bible tells us not to forsake the assembling of ourselves together (Hebrews 10:25). Most assuredly that includes our children, too. Still, many of our children can't do anything other than go to church and school due to the number of weekly services we ride herd on them to attend. I believe they need quality time alone with our husbands and us—just to bond and do family things. We already talked about the demands on our husbands, so in many cases, you are the one who will have to provide this outlet for your child.

Since we're at this bridge, let's talk about letting the church raise our children. God never gave that assignment to the church—He gave it to our husbands and us. You can expect a lot of scrutiny and unwanted input, because for some reason many folk expect PK's to be little angels while their kids can be little devils. It's the pot calling the kettle black. Having said that, some of our children could use a little extra input from the congregation and we know it. So don't get an attitude when a member or two helps you out. It's not necessarily a putdown of your parental skills, but if it is, hone up to it and make the needed changes.

The Ugly

Let's talk about the ugly. There are many but I'll discuss five:

First, one of the ugliest things PKs face is parental favoritism. Please avoid this at all cost; favoritism is sure to cause a quake and a rift. Look at favoritism in the Bible, and you'll know what I mean: Isaac favored Essau and Rebekah favored Jacob, causing dysfunction in the family. In another biblical story Jacob favored Joseph and gave him status and privileges that his brothers didn't have. This caused jealousy and envy among his brothers because they knew Jacob loved Joseph more that he loved them.

Second, it's ugly when we try to re-mold our children in a way God did not intend. Yes, we quote "Train up..." (Proverbs 11:6), and we sometimes wring our hands, "I don't know why he or she turned out that way." We have to realize that no two children have the same personalities. God gave our children a natural bent, and the way we want to bend them may not be the way God wanted them to grow. Round pegs are not meant for square holes and square holes are not meant for round pegs.

My children Jay and Omar have very different personalities. Jay, my special gift from God, has a Type-A personality like me. Jay's a lot of fun: He's very intense, likes trying new things, is the life of the party, and is always on the go.

On the other hand, Omar was laid back—too laid back for me. I called him unconcerned, he called me frenetic. I couldn't prod Omar, he just took his good old time. Showing my frustration didn't work, either. He just wasn't me. He took his time to smell the roses. I wanted someone to send me a bouquet so I could look at them as I ran out of the door.

Your children may be very different too. In light of this, you don't have to try to reinvent the wheel to make them into someone they are not. Esteem the diversity, and keep feeding and clothing them. Soon you'll find that formula or breast milk won't do. You'll also find that they don't stay two years old forever. One day they will grow up; some even move out. We empty nesters may be able to say amen to that, but the truth is we still miss them. I didn't hear you say anything.

Third, it's ugly when we do everything we can for our children, raise them in the love and admonition of God, pray for them night and day, and they still go astray. Let me release you here, my sisters. If this is your narrative, tell yourself, "It's not my fault" and let God work things out. He told you to bring your children up, not to be their conscience. You cannot change what you didn't make—even your children. Additionally, you cannot worry yourself to death about choices they've made. Does it hurt? Of course it hurts. In any event, you have to realize that your children are still in God's hands and that your prayers are covering them. No matter how far they stray, please don't refer to your children as "Black Sheep" of the family. This suggests that they're scoundrels. What does this say about you? You had them.

We will all do well to take Jeremiah 31:16–17 to heart.

> *Thus says the Lord: "Refrain your voice from weeping, and your eyes from tears; for your work shall be rewarded, says the Lord. And they shall come back from the land of the enemy. There is hope in your future, says the Lord, that your children shall come back to their own border."*

Fourth, it's ugly when we are not positive role models for our children. The Bible says, "Honor your father and mother." We have the crucial responsibility of making it effortless for our children to obey this command by living honorable, God-fearing lives. Children don't want to live with doubt and uncertainty about their relationship with us and they don't want to live with doubt and uncertainty about our relationship with God.

Fifth, it's ugly when we use the children as a weapon against our spouse. A woman who did explains why:

> *I used the children. I had no other weapon. I never confided in them, but on occasion, when I felt I was being ripped to shreds, I would say to them in his (husband's) presence, "If you only knew what a hypocrite your daddy is...." Instead of convicting him, my words would infuriate him. Sometimes he would leave the house, slamming the door behind him. When that happened I knew I had driven him into the arms of another woman, but the pain was so deep I seemed unable to keep from lashing out.*
>
> — *Michele Buckingham quoted by Michelle Obleton in Carter: Women to Women, 155*

Discipline

> *Discipline doesn't break a child's spirit half as often as the lack of it breaks a parent's heart.*
>
> —*Anonymous*

> *"Unconditional love; loves your kids for who they are, not for what they do; it isn't something you will achieve every minute of every day. But it is the thought we must hold in our hearts every day."*
>
> —*Stephanie Marston*

Sisters, be tenderhearted to your children. Discipline in love. God chastens us—but it's in love and for our good (Hebrews 12:6-13). Forgive them when they make mistakes. I didn't say to condone what they've done, but when they are godly sorrowful be caring and compassionate like the prodigal son's father (Luke 15:18–24). It doesn't hurt to kill the fatted calf every now and then.

Treasure the times your children come to you to talk. Always leave the light on, and keep a seat at the table for them. They need to know that you are there for them, that they can come to you any time day or night and tell you their deepest secrets.

Omar discussed some things with me that I never would have discussed with my mother. How I treasure those times! Jay and I talk a lot too. I can't understand everything he says because of his disability. I still treasure every moment we share—especially when he's praying, singing, and testifying.

Blended Families

> *A family stitched together with love seldom unravels.*
>
> —*Denny Davis*

A blended family is comprised of a couple and their children from a previous marriage. Living in a blended family is challenging. According to *The Blender*:

> *By 2010 blended families will be the most common type of family in America, most families don't make it to their fifth anniversary, and statistically, 60 percent of second marriages, and 73 percent*

of third marriages end in divorce (U.S. Bureau of the Census, 2006).

—THE BLENDER, *HELP FOR STEPFAMILIES WITH A CHRISTIAN TWIST, WWW.ADVICEFROMTHEBLENDER.COM*

Sisters with blended families: Your family may not be the pot of gold at the end of the rainbow, but your marriage does not have to be a divorce statistic. Remember, we live our marriages God's way.

Earl and I have a blended family. When we married I gained three sons: Earl Jr, Torrance, and Jeffrey. The best advice I can give from experience is to love them, don't ever put them before your husband, don't try to change them, don't try to replace their biological parent, and pray for them. In time, God will develop a good relationship between you; if not, He still works all things together for the good of them that love Him and are called according to His purposes (Romans 8:28). Discipline: your home, your rules.

GRANDCHILDREN

Grandchildren are God's reward for not killing your children.

—*ANONYMOUS*

I thank God for grandchildren, and am blessed to have many. My advice for caring for grandchildren is rather simple: love them, spoil them, and discipline them gently. Never let them or their parents forget that you are Grandmom, not Mom, so set limits for the duration of their visits. For those of you who have the responsibility of caring for grandchildren full-time: I applaud all you are doing to invest in the life God has entrusted to you. If it were possible I'd send you a box of chocolate hearts everyday in celebration of your love.

Childlessness

> *Faith goes up the stairs that love has built and looks out the window which hope has opened.*
>
> —*Anonymous*

Some of you have read this chapter with difficulty, as you desire to have children or grandchildren, but in His sovereignty God has chosen otherwise.

I can't say I know how you feel as this has not been my experience, but I have secondhand knowledge about infertility. My mother was married ten years before she had a child. She told me how dispirited she was when others had children and the doctor repeatedly told her that she could not conceive. Miraculously God opened her womb, and she birthed six children, with me being the third child.

I have also observed firsthand the attempts that friends of mine went through to conceive. In some cases they were successful, and in some cases, they failed. I am not in a position to say why this is; only God knows why. God does seem to give an extra helping of love to those of whom He has chosen to close their womb. I have seen this repeatedly. A case in point is Ramona Logan, our long-term former Youth Director. She has not birthed children of her own, but God uses her mightily in ministry to our youth. She has become a surrogate mother to the children, and is a witness to all who know her of the boundless love of God.

If you yearn constantly for a child, and your husband concurs, you may want to consider adoption. There are so many children who have never felt the warmth of a mother's care and long for the love God has poured into your heart.

Pray for our Children

As I close this chapter, let us join our hearts in prayer for our children and our relationship with them. We don't know what each other is going through, but we do know in times like these we have to saturate our children with prayer. May we pray that God will save, heal, deliver, and set them free to be all He purposed them to be for His glory. With God's help, they will emerge committed to Christ and understanding the importance of being godly men and women.

Let's Pray…

Be a blessing!

8

Thermal Blankets: Friends & Acquaintances

Survival experts recommend having a blanket to keep you warm in an emergency. I keep a blanket in the trunk of my car. I never know when the car is going to break down and the temperature drops. It's even better to have friends to warm your heart and soul. They're in our success kit.

Selecting Fruit

I love fruit. Two of my favorites are bananas and peaches. You will never guess how long it takes me to select the right banana or peach. I look at the bananas to see if they are too green, hold them in my hand to see if they are too firm, turn them over to see if there are any spots on them. With the peaches, I go through the same ritual, but I want to see if they are soft, and I even smell them to see if they are sweet. I got this one from Earl, I really can't tell the difference, but it gives the impression that I know what I'm doing. Eighty percent of the time when I get home I have the fruit that I thought I had selected. The other 20 percent of the time? I am disappointed because I made a bad selection. Ignorance is not bliss.

Selecting Your Friends

> *Even the Lone Ranger didn't do it alone.*
>
> —*Harvey Mackay*

> *Friendship is one of the things women do best. We are better at making friends than many of the things we put our minds to because it comes naturally*
>
> —*Hunter, 109*

Well, sisters, what about selecting your friends? There is a saying, "Diamonds are a girl's best friend, and a dog is a man's best friend." I don't know about this, but one thing I do know, all women, including pastors' wives need friends. In fact, Proverbs 18 tells us, "He who would have friends must show himself to be friendly."

However, one of the best kept secrets among pastors' wives is loneliness. We don't talk about it much, but many of us are lonely. I don't believe God wants us to sit around friendless because we are pastors' wives. You can ask Him for wisdom to choose your friends wisely. If you are not discerning you can be drawn into ungodly, dangerous relationships. When you choose a friend, it opens you up for transparency, heartache, and other heart issues. Hanging with the wrong crowd can also stop the flow of God's will and God's best for your life.

Let's look at four classes of people we need to discern: tried and true friends, frenemies, Peninnahs, and males.

Tried and True Friends

> *A friend leaves footprints on your heart like you leave them on sand, they get washed away, but best friends leave footprints on your heart like you leave them on the moon, those stay forever.*
>
> —*Victoria Elise Shakespeare*

I thank God for true friends. True friends pass the test of time and prove themselves to be faithful time and time again. We will take our love for them into eternity. Unless you have a valid reason for doing so, don't limit your selection of friends based on size, shape, ethnicity, age, or gender. You need Naomi's, Ruth's, and Priscilla's in your life. Naomi's are older women that you can look to for motherly advice, Ruth's are younger women who can come to you for motherly advice, and Priscilla's are friends close to your own age who walk this road of life with you.

Several Scriptures point to the value of true friends. One of my favorites is Ecclesiastes 4:9–12:

> *Two are better than one,*
> *Because they have a good reward for their labor.*
> *For if they fall, one will lift up his companion.*
> *But woe to him who is alone when he falls,*
> *For he has no one to help him up.*
> *Again, if two lie down together, they will keep warm;*
> *But how can one be warm alone?*
> *Though one may be overpowered by another, two can withstand him.*
> *And a threefold cord is not quickly broken.*

If you have true friends, please pray for them. A great prayer is found in Colossians 1:3–14.

Frenemies

> *Best friends are like diamonds, precious and rare; fake friends are like leaves, found everywhere.*
>
> —Unknown

If you are lost in the wilderness, depending on where you are wandering, it is possible you will encounter a snake or alligator. It is believed that swamps are full of slithering poisonous serpents, waiting to feed on anyone who crosses their paths. The major rattlesnakes found in North America swamps are Cottonmouth, Maswsasauga, Eastern Diamondback, Canebrake. When bitten, it is essential that you treat the bite properly or you will die.

Frenemies, or fake friends, are enemies who pretend to be friends. They are as slithering and poisonous as the most deadly snake. Take their names off of your mutual admiration society list; their hearts do not bleed for you when they bite.

You are in good company when you have frenemies. David's familiar friend turned his back on him (Psalm 41:9). Jesus had frenemies, most notably Judas. He was with Jesus for three years, but betrayed him. Yet, Jesus called him friend (Matthew 26:50). I've never been betrayed with a kiss, but I have personal experiences with frenemies who have double-crossed me. It is doubtful they are reading this book so it does no good to give them any more space than I already have.

Since you may have some out there somewhere here's good advice to heed from David Cottrell, author of *Monday Morning Choices*:

> *If you have done everything you can to allow the enemies to choose to be allies and they still choose to be enemies, move forward. Chasing after a poisonous snake that has bitten you will not solve the problem. It is far better to move in a direction away from the snake and allow the snake to go its own way*
>
> —Cottrell, 32

Peninnahs

> *In order to have an enemy, one must be somebody. One must be a force before he can be resisted by another force. A malicious enemy is better than a clumsy friend.*
>
> —*Anonymous*

No matter where you are you will come up against attacks from flying or crawling pests such as mosquitoes, ticks, chiggers, and spiders, so be prepared for them. If you are properly prepared, you can live with these pests under most conditions. Crawling pests have a lot in common with those sisters we know don't care for us and have no problem letting us know. For want of a better phrase, let's refer to these sisters as Peninnahs. It's not that our male friends couldn't be a Peninnah, but let's make it another sister-thing.

The story of Peninnah is found in 1 Samuel 1. Hannah and Peninnah were both married to Elkanah. Peninnah was an irritant to Hannah: she bugged Hannah; she ridiculed Hannah; she despised Hannah; and she made life hell for Hannah. Why? Because she had children and Hannah was barren. It may also have been because Elkanah loved Hannah. Love comes with a cost, you know.

If you can find anything wonderful about Peninnah it is that she was Hannah's best enemy. She brought Hannah to her knees, caused her to fast and pray, and to cry out to God for a child. You may know the end of the story. God blessed Hannah with Samuel—Israel's first judge, and a mighty man of God. God also blessed her with six more children. I told you God answers prayer.

Now, what pastor's wife can't relate to this woman? You may not call her Peninnah, but I believe every one of us had or has a Peninnah. She is the shackle around your ankle that goes overboard to gore your last nerve. Her primary objective is to upset your apple cart. You try your level best to get along with her, but she turns up her nose at whatever you do. She may not even speak to you when you come into the sanctuary. She may not support your ministry. She may smile in your face and act like a real goody-goody while stabbing you in the back. Up to now, every time you see her you want to dodge, for she is intent on barring the way to your success as a pastor's wife.

Oh, but from this moment on, you don't have to avoid Peninnah; you can covertly tell her, "Be my guest." When she gets on your last nerve (by the way, how many last nerves do we have?), get on your knees and start thanking God for using her to take you to the next level. Peninnah may make you work twice as hard the next time you are on a committee, make you teach that class with all of the vigor and vim that you have, or make you lose those twenty pounds that you have been trying to shed for two years—just so you can show her what you are made of.

Males

Should married women have male friends? I do. I have several godly male friends that I've adopted as brothers. This may not work for you. If it does, as with female friends, choose your friends wisely. In addition, always make sure your husband is aware of, and endorses the relationship. Keep it holy and friendly.

Sharing Personal Information

> *Confidentiality is a virtue of the loyal, as loyalty is the virtue of faithfulness.*
>
> —Edwin Louis Cole

Sisters, keep the safety chain on. While it's good to have someone to confide in, be careful with the information you share with your friends. Everyone can't handle your insecurities. Don't be conned by cross my heart and scouts honor hype, either. Too many pastors' wives have been hurt because they've shared information lock, stock, and barrel, only to have it come back to haunt them.

My sister Elyse is my female best friend. I can confide in her with just about everything. It's the same way with my daughter Tammie; we've solved every problem together except world peace. Nonetheless, I set boundaries with both Elyse and Tammie—not because they can't be trusted. There are just some things they don't need to know, and others they can't handle. Because of their love for me they may want to read the riot act to someone or rake them over the coals. That could be hazardous for them or for me.

Chirlanda Richardson is my spiritual daughter and hairstylist. Our conversations range from soup to nuts—you know how it is when you are in the stylist's chair; yet we both limit what we share. Word of caution: please don't dog your husband every time you sit in the hair stylists' chair. You wouldn't want him to dog you out every time he went to the barber.

Whether you have many friends or few, there is a friend who sticks closer than a brother. You can share all of your secrets with Him, for He loves you like none other. His name is Jesus, and you know He loves you because He gave His life for you. Greater love has no man than this that He lay down His life for a friend (John 15:13). You can call Him in the morning, evening, or midnight. I heard someone say, "The more I call Him, the better I feel." I believe there is a witness in the house today!

Let's pray…

Be a blessing!

Extra Credit

In addition to Earl and my late parents, Abraham and Mary Jackson, following is a list of names I would include in my obituary if there was ample space. The list is not all-inclusive, as God has blessed me with a bundle of relatives, friends and colleagues whom I love dearly. The purpose of the list is to reveal the depth of love and support that I have in my life to enable me to do the work God has purposed me to do.

"Siblings by another mother" are my dearest and closest sister-friends. "By Choice" mothers, children, sisters and brothers are members of my non-biological extended family. Spiritual daughters are those who give me an opportunity to assist in their spiritual development. The prefix "Lady" denotes those who are first ladies. Church families are congregations who have exhibited unimaginable fondness and warmth to me over the years.

You may be tempted to skip reading this list, but if you read it now you won't have to wait 150 years until I die to read it:

- *Sons by birth and Daughter by adoption:* Joseph Aycox Jr, Omar Jamal Aycox*, Tammie Mask (Stephon).
- *Children (by marriage):* Earl Whitaker Jr, Torrance Whitaker, Jeffrey Whitaker, Navarro Thompson, Yolanda Thompson, Andre Thompson, Greg Thompson, Jerry Thompson, Jeanine Thompson.
- *Siblings:* Ernest Jackson, Edward Jackson, Lillian Jackson, Elyse Jackson-Wayns (Tez Foster), Martha Brooking, Anthony Jackson, Benjamin Jackson*, Bert Jackson.
- *Siblings (by another mother):* Marian Easley, Thelma Kennedy-Malveaux (Jerome), Julie Johnson (Vince), Evangelist Bernadine Ware, Gladys Walker (Huey), Pastor Valetta Shaw, Rita Loudd (Ernest)
- *Sisters and Brothers in Love (not in-law):* Evangelist Lillian Windom, Vernell Whitaker, Fayetta Jackson (Michael), Evangelist Nancy Boone (Alvis), Beverly Whitaker, Pastor Deborah Whitaker, Juanita Whitaker.
- *Favorite Aunt:* Mary Jackson-Wilson.
- *Nieces and Nephews:* Joseph Brooking (Sherry Grant), Andrez Brooking (Kim), Gina Wayns, Gia Wayns, Shannon Wayns, Icie Allen (Marlon), Corliss Jackson, Shanine Jackson, Ebony Jackson (Aaron), Rosalyn Jackson, Michael Jackson, Julian Johnson, Dominic Johnson, Phaziah Malveaux, Qadera Malveaux, Clinten Kegler, Elder Chester Whitaker, Grace Windom, Patricia Gage, Truscenia Garrett, Cathy Campbell, Brenda Rison, Sheila Lyons, Benita Whitaker Cleveland, Tilford Earl Whitaker, Anthony Whitaker, Brandon Whitaker, Anita Drummond, Ronnie Matthews, Sandra Driver, Roy Whitaker, Marquetta Tilley, Trudy Green, Judy Jackson (Louis), Remon Green (Kenya), Marlon Ware.
- *Grandchildren and Great-Grandchildren:* Raven Whitaker, Stephen Mask, Kelsey Walker, Brianna Mask, Kennedy Hinton, Jordan Whitaker; and many others from children by marriage and love-related, including Jade Jenkins (Jason), Cameron Jones (Monica), Shawnique Jones, Shnea Jones, Cecilia Edwards, Moniqua Shaw, Ryleigh Whitaker, and a bushel full of other lovely grands and great-grands as well as grand-nephews and grand-nieces that are very dear to me.

- *Godchildren:* Demetra Baxter-Smith, Justin Walker, Brittany Wallace, Dr. Wesley Thomas, Roxanne Washington, RoShawn Lee.
- *Mothers (by choice):* Lenora Blair, Wilhelmenia Hardy, Lillie Mae Brown, Bernice Mitchell.
- *Children (by choice):* Dr. Amanda Bowie, Evangelist Lori Blanton, Sandra Jones, Rhonda Sparks, Henry "Scooter" Credit, Jr.
- *Sisters (by choice):* Bonnie Mask, Wanda Davis, Missionary Sherri Levine, Evangelist May Dessa Thomas, Carla Scurlock, Evangelist Lady Barbara Lacy, Pastor Diana Culberson, Evangelist Tina Goodman Pope, Evangelist Danita Goodman, Stephanie Goodman.
- *Brothers (by choice):* Bishop Jerry Burley (Sandra), Pastor Dan Goodman Jr. (Penny), Elder Larry Goodman, Vince Johnson, Ernest Loudd, Jerome Malveaux, Pastor Ray A. Riley, Huey Walker.
- *Spiritual Daughters:* Evangelist Alva Taylor, Minister Erica Cole, Minister Donna Christwell, Chirlanda Richardson, Sharla Dirden, Qutaria Thomas, Minister Domenece Harlan, Mitzi Garrett, Lady Barbara Jones, Shalonda Guillory, Tycia Rodgers, Evangelist Tenelle Hines, Evangelist Media Cole.
- *Fathers in the Ministry:* Reverend Robert E. Price*, Bishop C. C. Berry Jr., Bishop Ural F. Ware*.
- *Mentors:* Pastor Earl Whitaker, Dr. Wheeler Jones, Dr. R. L. Thornton, Pastor Anthony Gaskill
- *Role Models:* Pastor Mary Henderson, Apostle Gwendolyn Hollins, Bishop Annell Haney, Bishop Dolores Blackmon, Bishop Dr. Mable Berry, Pastor Barbara Linton, Lady Billie Berry, Katherine Tima, Mary Porter, Melba Goodman, Dr. Sheila Bailey, Bishop Leroy Shankle Sr. & State Supervisor Lady Verdia Shankle, Dr. & Mrs. Samuel J. Gilbert Sr.
- *Other Special Friends and Colleagues:* Overseer Kenneth Morgan, Lady Evelyn Morgan, Dr. Nile Smith, Bishop Cedric Kenebrew & Pastor Lady Erika Kenebrew, Bishop Robert E. Tyler & Lady Missionary Carolyn Tyler, Bishop Harry Hendricks & Lady Barbara Hendricks, Missionary Beverly Russell, Mrs. Jean Dominguez, Myrlene King, Mary Louis, Mattie Mitchell, Ann Blair, Carlene Wyrick, Bill & Peggy Dermott, Danley Gibbs, Sally

Conley, Pastor T. C. Collins & Evangelist Lady Veronica Collins, Overseer Obie Lacy, Overseer Joseph Mitcham & Lady Lisa Mitcham, Bishop Lawrence White & First Lady Audrey White, Pastor Perry Dixon, Pastor Oscar Dixon & Evangelist Lady Peggy Dixon, Pastor Daniel Patterson & Lady Jean Patterson, Lady Minnie Gaskill, Evangelist Sandy Shaw, Eric Chinn, Deacon Robert Blunt, Albert & Mae Jackson, Melvin Lewis & Evangelist Ruby Lewis, Evangelist Annie Deams, Ola Johnson*, Lady Mary Brown*, Evangelist Renee' Walker, Missionary Joi Booty, Lady Linda Maiden, Minister Elizabeth Brickle, Amelia Peggy Young, Shermicker Money, Dorothy Wesley, Sandra Coley, Mother Velmer Jackson, Ethelyn Farmer, Eldress Dr. Gloria Collins, Missionary Pearly Blunt, Evangelist Cathy Thompson, Evangelist Agnes Taylor, Mollie Hardesty, Ministers of the Heart Inc. Sisterhood, Devereux 619 Featherbed Staff.

- *Church Families:*

  Under Earl's Care: Church of the Living God Culverhouse, Inc., Lufkin, TX.

  Home Churches: New Mt. Zion Baptist Church, Dallas, TX (Dr. R. E. Price, Pastor*); Church of the Living God, Temple #18, Houston, TX (Elder Jaap Richardson, Pastor).

  Others: Churches in The General Assembly Church of the Living God, PGT, Headquartered in Tyler, TX (Presiding Bishop, C. C. Berry, Jr).; Church of the Living God, PGT, Temple #1, Houston, TX (Elder Dan E. Goodman Jr., Pastor); Church of the Living God, PGT, Shreveport, LA (Bishop Jerry Maiden, Pastor; and National PGT President); Church of the Living God Ministries, Oklahoma City, OK (Overseer Kenneth Morgan, Pastor); Church of the Living God, CWFF, Laneville, TX (Evangelist Valetta Shaw, Pastor); Fontaine First Baptist Church, Houston, TX, (Rev. John Henry Brown, Pastor); Friendship Baptist Church, Sugarland, TX, (Rev. Amos Jones, Pastor).

*Deceased.

9

Anti-Terrorism Supplies: Destructive Criticism & Disrespect

There are several definitions of terrorism. For our purpose, terrorism is the calculated use of violence (or the threat of violence) against civilians in order to attain goals that are political or religious or ideological in nature; this is done through intimidation or coercion or instilling fear. It is no mystery that terrorism is on the rise. In 1968 the United States Department of State (DOS) reported one hundred and fifty incidents of international terrorism, resulting in 124 fatalities and 224 injuries. The figures for 2010 (domestic and international) were 11,632 attacks, resulting in 13,191 fatalities, and 30,868 injuries. (Source: Johnstonsarchives.net, Statistics on Terrorism).

Gratefully, though it may not result in fatalities and injuries, terrorism toward pastors' wives also is on the rise. Few situations are as terrorizing as is destructive criticism and disrespect. Therefore, it is essential that our success kit contain preparedness supplies specifically designed to combat these terrorist attacks.

Nagging Problem

The LORD is on my side; I will not fear. What can man do to me?
—*Psalm 118:6*

Don't let the littleness of others bring out the littleness in you.
—*Old Codger Wisdom*

Nobody can make you feel inferior without your consent.
—*Eleanor Roosevelt*

Dr. Wheeler Jones of Tyler, Texas, preached a message at Earl's 2006 pastoral anniversary services titled, "What to do with a Nagging Problem." His text was taken from Second Corinthians 12:7–9. His four points were:

1. Take it to Jesus.
2. Tell it to Jesus.
3. Turn it over to Jesus.
4. Trust Jesus.

I am so glad that we can do just that, sisters. Two nagging problems that many pastors' wives face are destructive criticism and disrespect. We discussed Peninnahs in the last chapter and certainly much of the contempt we receive comes from that group of women. Another group we have to contend with as pastors' wives is those that Marshall Shelley call Well-Intentioned Dragons. Mr. Shelley says:

Dragons are best known for what comes out of their mouths. At times their mouths are flame-throwers; other times, the heat and smoke are not apparent, but the noxious gas does the damage.

—*Shelley, 11*

Let's discuss how we can counteract destructive criticism and disrespect from these dragons:

Destructive Criticism: "Are You Talking to Me?"

The trouble with most of us is that we would rather be ruined by praise than saved by criticism.

—*Norman Vincent Peale*

He has the right to criticize who has the heart to help.

—*Abraham Lincoln*

Criticism is advantageous when it is constructive. Constructive criticism turns the high beams on our blind spots so we can see things as they really are and correct those that need changing. Destructive criticism is injurious. The purpose of destructive criticism is to berate and belittle us. Every successful pastor's wife has to know how to annul destructive criticism or it will get the best of you. It comes with the job; in fact, it comes with being human.

The bottom line is that you can't take things too personally when someone destructively criticizes you. Weigh the source, "know when to hold them, and know when to fold them." You also have to have orange-peel skin—thick!—or you will find yourself on the loony farm counting ants. Resist the temptation to read and believe your own press reports that everything is okay, when it's not. Beware of folk who are always praising and complimenting you.

A good rule of thumb when dealing with criticism is:

If one person tells you that you have a problem, you may not have one, that's just their opinion. If two people tell you, you still may not have a problem, but it's suspect. If three people tell you that you have a problem, more than likely, you have a problem; so face the bugger and fix it.

I have buggers that people criticize me about; such as, I don't return phone calls promptly and I'm always late. These criticisms are constructive because they're on target in varying degrees, and I'm trying to mend my character flaws. I am also the recipient of destructive criticism from folk who are off-base in their assessment of my character. I could lie and say that what they say doesn't bother me, but it does. Nevertheless, their comments are not show-stoppers, and I'm not going to let them get my goat. Don't let folk get the best of you, either. Address what needs to be addressed and go on.

Disrespect: "Oh No You Didn't!"

> *You have heard their reproach, O Lord, all their schemes against me, the lips of my enemies and their whispering against me all the day. Look at their sitting down and their rising up; I am their taunting song.*
>
> —*Lamentations 3:61–63*

Disrespect is so nagging that I've mentioned it several times thus far in the book. Before moving to the next chapter I felt it was needful to dive a little deeper as disrespect is a blaring problem for pastor's wives (see Appendix A).

Disrespect hits in the groin. The purpose of disrespect is to devalue you and make you feel like a Neanderthal. Some people have the unmitigated gall to get joy out of seeing you squirm; pleasure out of bringing you down. Who do you think you are anyway, Mrs. First Lady?

If you want to keep the faith when being assaulted by their dastardly distain, realize that we all have lovers, haters, and tweeners.

Lovers will love you regardless of what you do. Haters will hate you no matter what you do, and "tweeners" can go either way—depending on the issue. Your responsibility is to love them all. "Do not repay evil with evil, or insult with insult, but with blessing, because to this you were called" (1 Peter 3:9).

Above all, don't get vexed if dragons take your kindness for weakness and spew their contemptible venom all the more. You are called to be a thermostat, not a thermometer. A thermometer registers the temperature; a thermostat regulates the temperature. Sit tight; in the end you win. Isaiah 54:17 tells us "No weapon formed against you shall prosper, and every tongue that rises against you in judgment you shall condemn. This is the heritage of the servants of the Lord."

I close this chapter with words from Beth Moore:

> *There is so much I don't know. So much I'm uncertain of. So much that makes me wonder. But sister, I'm certain of this. I promise you based on the authority of God himself and centuries of witnesses to his faithfulness, if you will place your trust in him, he will always—I said always—make sure that in the end you will look upon your foes in triumph.*
>
> —*Moore,* So Long Insecurity *226*

Let's Pray…

Be a blessing!

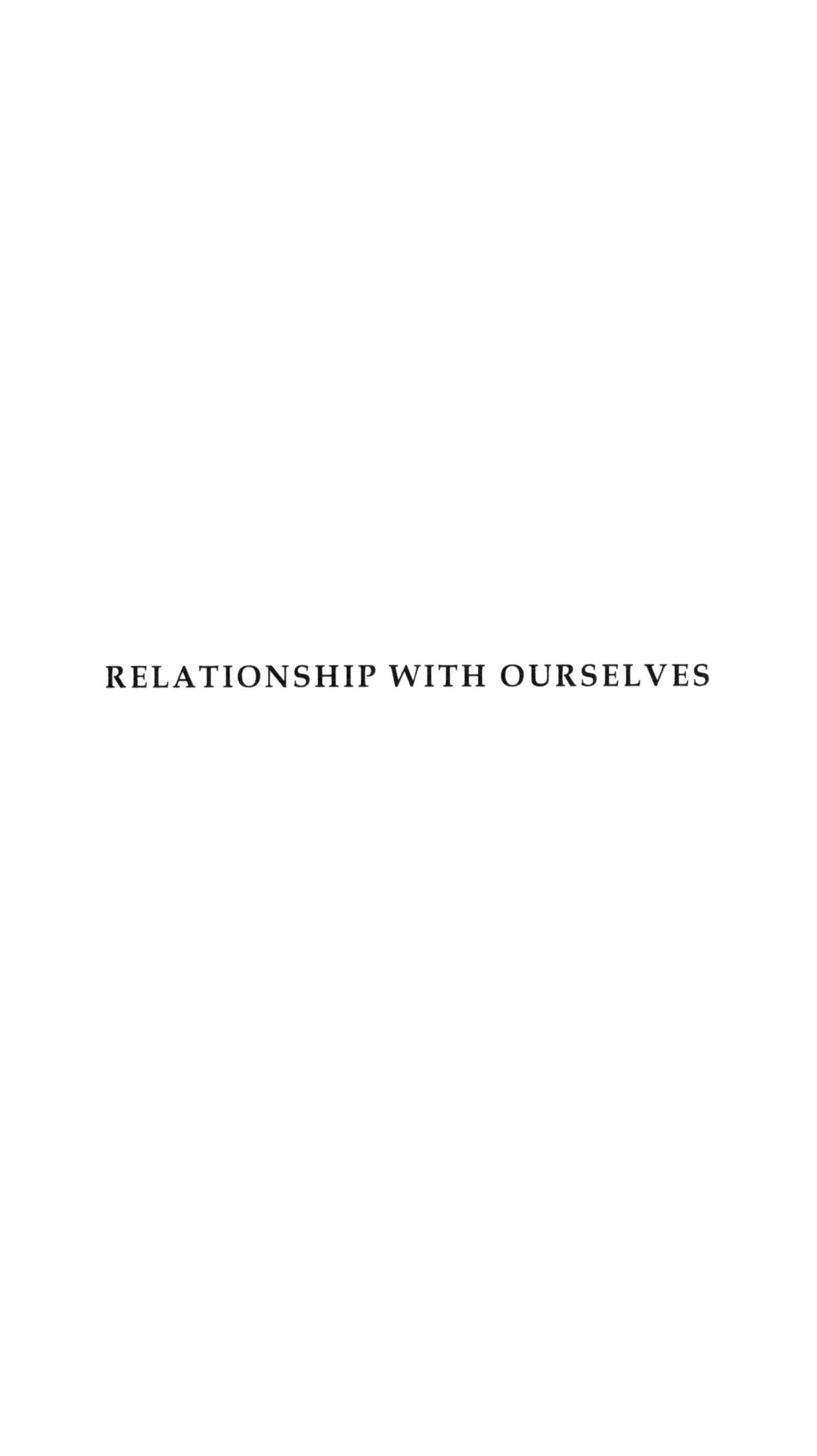

RELATIONSHIP WITH OURSELVES

10

Compass: Our Identity

In chapter one we talked about God's GPS and the fact that we need it to choose a destination and determine how we are going to get there. Sometimes in survival situations we find ourselves stuck in the woods of life with many roads and options to choose. It is times like these that we need navigational skills, specifically, the ability to read a compass to guide us out of thickly forested areas and foggy sage brushes. Few areas require the ability to read a compass more than determining who we are as pastors' wives. In this chapter we will look at some of the obstacles we face in trying to establish and maintain our identity.

Enter At Your Own Risk

Have you noticed that ministers' wives are eternally introduced as "the lovely wife of So and So?" We are always lovely and we never have any identity of our own.

—Pannell, 65

Sisters, our focus up to this point has been about relationships: with God, with our husband, and with other people. Building and maintaining strong relationships is essential if we are to survive as pastors' wives. In building relationships, there is a relationship that we are often prone to neglect: relationship with ourselves.

Men and sisters who are not pastors' wives: forewarned is forearmed. If I had a "No Trespassing" or "Enter at Your Own Risk" sign, I'd put it up right now. Some of what I write here will sound like a "dump" session, and it is. My rationale is, if I can't be candid and transparent with my sisters who are pastors' wives at a soul-bearing level, who can I be real with? Please bear with me—I promise you I won't pull a fast one and write another chapter like this.

Will The Real Me Please Stand Up?

Ninety percent of the world's woe comes from people not knowing themselves, their abilities, their frailties, and even their real virtues. Most of us go almost all the way through life as complete strangers to ourselves.

—Sydney J. Harris

Never be bullied into silence. Never allow yourself to be made a victim. Accept no one's definition of your life, but define yourself.

—Harvey S. Firestone

Don't paint stripes on your back if you are not a zebra. Focus on building upon your unique abilities.

—Lee J. Colan

I was once afraid of people saying, 'Who does she think she is?' Now I have the courage to stand and say, 'This is who I am.'

—Oprah Winfrey

When I was in college I took a course titled "Life and Career Options." The purpose of the course was to answer a two-fold question: "Who Am I, and Where Am I Going?" The course appealed to me because one of the greatest tragedies is to live an off-purpose, misdirected life. During the course we studied our personality traits, our ambitions, our likes and dislikes. We also talked about our goals and dreams—even those things housed in the closed room of our heart. In addition, we discussed what we had done thus far in life to make a difference in the world and our plans for leaving a legacy for others to follow.

The last few weeks of the course were devoted to writing our obituary from the standpoint of what others who knew us would say about us. There was one caveat: we couldn't write about any accomplishments that had an impact on us personally only; we had to write about those that made the world better for others.

I learned so much in that course that it has influenced my life thirty-five years later. I found out from the course that I really didn't know who I was as well as I thought I did. I also found out that the path my life had taken was one that really left little behind for others to follow. Since that time I've tried to live a life that would benefit others and leave a legacy beyond my own time that would cause others to say, "I'm glad she lived, and I'm glad she passed my way." Unavoidably, though, as a pastor's wife, I'm still asking the question, "Who am I, and where am I going, where am I in all of this, what about me?"

Have you ever asked yourself this question, sisters? It is common knowledge that pastors' wives live in a fishbowl world and are on display at all times. As is true of most fishbowls, all fish are not alike.

Lorna Dobson, author of *I'm More Than the Pastor's Wife: Authentic Living in a Fishbowl World*, surveyed 230 women representing every state in four foreign countries. She received a 59 percent response. Half of the women surveyed were comfortable with their identity being tied to their husband's occupation, the other half struggled in varying stages and at different times with being called the "pastor's wife," or "missionary's wife", etc. —Dobson, *35*

Which side of the coin are you on? Completely satisfied with being known as pastor's wife, or, depending on the situation, struggle with this issue? If you're struggling, check your job description—if you can find it.

Has Anyone Seen My Job Description?

All I can do is play the game the way the cards fall.

—James A. Michener

Things turn out best for the people who make the best of the way things turn out

—John Wooden

In September 2006, Greta Van Susteren of Fox News ran a special about Laura Bush, wife of 43rd President of the United States George W. Bush, when the heads of nations came to New York for the UN Conference. To take advantage of the moment, Laura hosted a World Literacy Conference. As she was accompanying Mrs. Bush, Greta made the comment, "The first lady has no job description, she has no manual. She has to determine the role she wants to take as first lady."

While not intentional, Greta's comments easily refer to a pastor's wife. Let me see if I can clarify what I mean. Pretend for a minute that you are an employment agency and had to hire someone as a pastor's wife for a month. What would be her job description? If one hundred of you are reading this book right now, and I took a poll, I'd probably find one hundred different answers.

Here's a joke I read about how confusing our role as pastors' wives can be:

> *A pastor was upset because his wife and children were running late for church. To show how upset he was, he honked the horn several times. Finally, he stormed into the house to find out what was wrong. His wife said, "Why don't we switch roles today? You get the children washed, dressed, and fed, and I'll sit in the car and blow the horn."*

Hopefully this joke doesn't describe your situation on Sunday morning, though there have been times when I've felt like switching roles with Earl. I don't want to be the pastor and sit in the car and blow the horn, but I would like to have a blueprint of what a congregation should expect of me. The majority of churchgoers have knowledge of what a pastor should do. Roles for pastors' wives vary with the congregation. Undeniably, one of the steepest hurdles we have as pastors' wives is trying to please other folk and fill their expectation of what our role should be.

Sisters, you don't have to spend another moment of your life focusing on people pleasing. Each of you can determine the role you want to take as a first lady. The keys to unlocking the mystery of our missing job description is: know who you are, appreciate who God made you to be, do not let insecurity dominate your life, and be comfortable in your own skin.

With these keys in hand you can resist the temptation to follow the lines others have written for you. You cannot wear another pastor's wife's shoes, nor be the wife to your husband that she is to her husband. That's why you must ignore how people perceive you, or how you think they perceive you. Your job is not to please other folk. Your only desire should be working with your husband to accomplish God's will for both of your lives.

Avoid the comparison trap by looking down the street to see how Mrs. First Lady Neighbor is handling her role. Every situation is unique, and you don't know what goes on behind closed doors. If you did, it's still not wise to compare yourself with others (2 Corinthians 10:12). The gaffe is you will never measure up to the standard; the grass always looks greener on the other side of the fence. I believe if you looked hard enough at the Proverbs 31 woman, you would even find something wrong with her.

Your identity also includes your temperament. That's another reason why you can't compare yourself to someone else. According to Tim LaHaye:

> *Temperament influences everything we do: eating habits, driving skills, the way we shop, yard care, study habits, handwriting, communication skill, bill paying, child discipline, exercise, sleep, decorating, selecting clothes, hobbies, and everything else.*
>
> —*LaHaye, 9–20*

You also do not have to envy one another. God gave us different gifts. For instance, all of you do not sing like a nightingale or play the piano. To my chagrin, I can't do either well, and I am jealous of those of you who can with a godly jealously—if this is possible. I believe at least two of you are in the same camp I'm in. We're not going to swallow cyanide flavored Kool-Aid about it because Ephesians 4 tells us that the Holy Spirit gave us each gifts. He didn't ask us what we wanted; He gave us exactly what He wanted us to have. They're not for ourselves, but for the equipping of the saints, so we don't have to envy one another.
I heard God say in Isaiah 45:9–10:

> *Woe to him who strives with his Maker!*
> *Let the potsherd strive with the potsherds of the earth!*
> *Shall the clay say to him who forms it, "What are you making?"*
> *Or shall your handiwork say, "He has no hands?"*
> *Woe to him who says to his father, "What are you begetting?"*
> *Or to the woman, "What have you brought forth?"*

Here's a story that about a man who was comfortable in his own skin:

> *A story is told of a man who hired an artist to paint his picture. The man was quite unattractive as warts covered many areas*

of his face. The artist wanted to paint him in the best light, so he decided that he would paint the portrait without the warts. When the portrait was completed the artist presented it to the man with pride in what he had done. The man was not pleased and told him to repaint the portrait, warts and all—for that's who he was, and that's what he wanted the portrait to reflect.

—*Anonymous*

I'm moving on, but I want you to know that I'm not quarreling with God. I still want to sing a Spirit-led "hair-raising, foot-stomping" solo before I transcend to glory. In the meantime, heres a lesson from Carly:

"Who Do You Think You Are?" is the title of Chapter 7 of Joel Osteen's book, *Your Best Life Now.* Joel writes about a woman named Carly who was overweight, unattractive, one leg was shorter than the other, and she worked in a male-dominated field. Despite these handicaps she was eventually promoted to CEO of her company and became a highly sought after expert in her field. Why? Because she had a positive self image. She believed she was made in the image of God and that she had value and worth not determined by man. —*Osteen, 35*

Where's the Ram?

The measure of love is what we are willing to give up for it.

—*Anonymous*

People are always blaming their circumstances for what they are. The people who get on in this world are they who get up and look for the circumstances they want and if they can't find them, make them.

—*George Bernard Shaw*

We must look for the opportunity in every difficulty instead of being paralyzed at the thought of the difficulty in every opportunity.

—Walter E. Cole

Give your complaints to God; give your compliments to others.

—Ruth Graham

I'm grateful to God that we can live our best life now as successful pastors' wives. Now that we're secure, let's talk about sacrifice for a moment.

Sacrifice is not a word I particularly like to have associated with me, but a pastor's wife can't avoid it. A large part of our calling is sacrifice; we can't get away from that, no matter how much our hair stands on end. Remember chapter one about God's design for marriage, and we talked about submission? Well, you can't have submission without sacrifice. The only problem is, where is the ram?

Most often we associate this question with Abraham and Isaac. You may know the story; it is legendary among Christians, and is told in Genesis 22. Abraham was Isaac's father. At God's command Abraham went to sacrifice Isaac. Abraham had the fire and the wood, but no lamb. Isaac observed this—the Bible doesn't say he was blind, right? So Isaac asked his father, where is the lamb? To which Abraham replied, "God will supply the lamb." Instead of finding a four-legged lamb, Abraham found a two-legged one—Isaac. He tied Isaac up and put him on the altar and prepared to kill him (how was he going to explain that to Sarah when he got home?). God provided a four-legged ram when He saw Abraham's obedience even to the point of being willing to sacrifice his son. What did God say? "Because you've obeyed Me, I'll multiply your blessings as numerous as the stars in heaven and as the grains of sand on the seashore." (Genesis 22:15-17).

I have a hot off the press newsflash, sisters. God still provides a ram. It's not in the thicket, it's you. You know it's you, too. Some of you could make a woodpile as high as Mount Moriah of the sacrifices you've had to make as a pastor's wife. For instance, in addition to the sacrifices we've talked about in previous chapters, many of you have had to shorten, postpone, or cancel a vacation because of church business. Many of you have had to relocate to parts unknown because of your husband's "calling: (If you want to read a good book about this, I recommend *After the Boxes are Unpacked* by Susan Miller). Yes, you are the ram. Hence, find a full length mirror, look at yourself, and say, "Here's the ram—board certified." You don't have to moan and groan about it, because it is what it is.

Ah, but being the ram isn't as bad as it sounds. God is faithful, and will rescue you from the fire. If He came through for Isaac, He'll come through for you too, for He is the same yesterday, today, and forever (Hebrews 13:8).

Besides being faithful, God provided the world with the greatest sacrifice that ever lived—our Lord and Savior and elder brother, Jesus Christ. Jesus wasn't a ram caught in a thicket; He was the precious Lamb of God. I heard John say in John 1:29 "Behold the Lamb of God Who takes away the sins of the world."

My Bible tells us in Hebrews 12:3 to consider Him when we are suffering. Jesus hung, bled, and died on Calvary's cross. He knew no sin, but took on our sins that we could become the righteousness of God (1 Corinthians 5:21). Isaiah 53:5 tells us that He was wounded, bruised, and chastised for us.

Ephesians 2:8–9 lets us know that it is by grace that we have been saved. I heard someone say, "What was God doing on the cross?" Someone else answered the question: "Being hung up for our hang-ups, looking beyond our faults and seeing our needs."

With this in mind, sisters, use some of those matches we talked about in chapter three to burn up your woodpile. While you're at it, please do me a favor—burn up those comments I made in chapter four about finding my place in Earl's ministry—and please hide the knife. If not, I might be charbroiled ram chops before you finish reading this book. Then plan your next vacation or time alone with your Honey. You may only be able to plan five minutes at a time, but enjoy every last one of those three hundred seconds. Perhaps he'll enjoy them so much that he'll learn to readjust his calendar. Well, there's nothing wrong with wishful thinking, is there?

Whew! I'm sure glad we got this chapter out of the way.

P.S. Did I mention "Anniversaryitis?" I know this isn't a word, but I'm referring to attending every kind of church-related anniversary at every church you can think of. I'm not batty enough to delve into this, especially since I really look forward to our pastor and wife's anniversary. You probably do too, but you know what I'm talking about!

Let's Pray...

Be a blessing!

11

Life Vests: Caring for Our Body & Soul

Life vests are essential to survival and should never be considered optional. They provide flotation and keep your head well above water when the boat flips and protect you from bruises should you strike a rock. Caring for your body and soul also helps you keep your head above water. We are tripartite beings. The Bible states emphatically that man was created in a trinity of spirit, soul, and body even as the eternal God is himself a trinity of Father, Son, and Holy Ghost. In fact, 1 Thessalonians 5:23 reads," Now may the God of peace Himself sanctify you completely; and may your whole spirit, soul, and body be preserved blameless at the coming of our Lord Jesus Christ. James 2:26 tells us, "For as the body without the spirit is dead, so faith without works is dead also." In this chapter we will talk about caring for our body and soul by keeping them physically, mentally, and emotionally fit.

Our Bodies

The greatest wealth is health.

—*Virgil*

Sisters, on a scale of one to ten, how's your health? Why do I ask? Caring for our bodies require self-discipline and self-denial. We have an obligation to keep them at peak performance by exercising regularly and eating properly. Increased health means increased work for God, and that means winning more souls for God. In addition, it gives you a better quality of life as a pastoral wife. Men are visual and like to look—including your pastor husband. If the truth were known, when someone looks good to him, he likes to take a second look. Thank God for a husband who resists the devil.

Still, knowing that your husband likes to look—give him something to feast his eyes on: you. Pause and take a good look in the mirror and then look in the album. Is there a big difference in size? If the answer is yes, perhaps it's time for a change.

It is my hope that the following discussion will motivate you, if needed, to pull away from the table and do a few push-ups or two, rather than take the path of least resistance and do nothing. Before I go further, I want to make it plain that no book can serve as a substitute for medical advice. This book is no different. I urge you to seek the counsel of your doctor for help with specific health issues.

Exercise & Fitness

Those who think they have not time for bodily exercise will sooner or later have to find time for illness.

—*Edward Stanley*

Along with a healthy diet, exercise is the cornerstone of good health.

Physical activity produces a multitude of benefits for your overall health and well-being. You don't need a doctor or me to tell you that exercise is essential. Paul said in First Timothy 4:7–8 that bodily exercise profits little compared with our spiritual well being, but it is still needful. That may be one of the reasons that Paul often used athletic illustrations in his letters.

For optimum results, exercise must be aerobic. Aerobic exercises involve sustained activity that stimulates the heart and lungs long enough to produce beneficial changes in the body. Brisk walking, jogging, swimming, cycling, and skipping rope are aerobic exercises. These exercises may make you sweat. I know you are probably not an eager beaver when it comes to sweating all over yourself, but it's a by-product of being fit.

To be effective, plan on spending at least twenty minutes each day, at least four to six days a week exercising. Less than this will keep you from performing at full capacity. On the one hand, this may be a lofty goal, especially for those of you like me who'd prefer spending those minutes being babied in a spa. On the other hand, time is out for being dumpy, grumpy, and frumpy. You don't have to be skin and bones, but you'll look better without saddlebags on your thighs and tires around your waist. My goal is to go to the gym at least three times a week. It doesn't always work out, but that's my goal—and you have to hold me accountable. I'll hold you accountable too.

Dr. Don Colbert tells us that exercise prevents cancer and heart disease:

> *Studies show that approximately one-third of cancer deaths can be linked to diet and sedentary lifestyles. Simple movement and exercise decrease the risk of certain cancers such as breast, colon, and possibly endometrial and prostate cancers.*
>
> —*Colbert, 119–20*

Some of you may have medical conditions that prohibit you from being able to endure strenuous exercise; low-impact aerobic programs may work for you. Sisters with arthritis, exercise can benefit you too. I know arthritis is painful because I have a small amount in my left hip, and the pain often prohibits me from exercising as much as I would like to, but I always feel better afterwards.

According to the Arthritis Foundation:

> *Exercise is an important component in staying healthy when you have arthritis. Moderate physical activity on a regular basis helps decrease fatigue, strengthen muscles and bones, increase flexibility and stamina, and improve your general sense of well-being.*
>
> —*ARTHRITIS.ORG, TOP THREE TYPES OF EXERCISES*

Diet & Nutrition

> *To lengthen thy life, lessen thy meals.*
>
> —*BENJAMIN FRANKLIN*

Good nutrition can help you achieve good health. If you are to stay in shape, exercise alone will not do it; you have to modify your eating habits. It's no surprise to any of us that we are what we eat.

I often find myself succumbing to food that I know isn't healthy, but it sure tastes good. I don't believe I'm by myself on this. A good rule of thumb about what we put in our mouths is, "Can I pray over it and not lie?" You see, when we say grace, we say, "Good Lord, make us truly thankful for this food I'm about to receive, nourishment for my body. In Christ Jesus' name we pray, amen."

Now ask your liver. How much nourishment is there in a sack of potato chips? Or in a giant Milky Way bar? Or ten Chips-a-Hoy cookies? Or five Oreos with the double filling? Or a couple of slices of sweet potato pie? While we're at it, let's throw in two scoops of ice cream…

You get my point—if it doesn't nourish your body, change your prayer or change your diet. Do any of you have an alternative prayer I can use? I've become addicted to multi-grain tortilla chips, but I can't continue to eat them without bulging out all over the place.

I'm going to come clean with you—again. I have fifteen stubborn pounds that are determined to stay on this already sufficiently overweight frame of mine. A couple of years ago I joined Weight Watchers to help me shed what I knew I didn't need.

I'm not promoting Weight Watchers, but I'm pleased to report that I did lose the fifteen pounds, received my lifetime membership and was on the maintenance program to help me keep the pounds off. To my detriment, I gained them back by not sticking to the plan. Since then I started the Daniel Plan with Earl and several members of our church. That plan is rather flexible and I'm not starving to death, so hopefully by the time this book is completed the fifteen pounds I needed to lose will be history. If you are interested in the Daniel Plan, the website is thedanielplan.com. If it doesn't work for you Google lists so many weight lost plans that it can make your eyes boggle, so I'm sure you can find something that suits you, if this is a path you want to take.

Beyond looking good for your husband, or even looking good for yourself, you have an obligation to God to keep your body as healthy as possible because He is concerned about your health. In 3 John 2, the Apostle John's opening comment to his friend Gaius was, "I would that you would be in health and prosper as your soul prospers." We also are reminded in 1 Corinthians 6:19–20 that our bodies are the temple of the Holy Ghost. Let's make His dwelling place as pleasant as possible. Now, put this book down for about thirty minutes and run around the block. Just a thought.

Our Souls

Unless the soul is fed and exercised daily, it becomes weak and shriveled. It remains discontented, confused, restless.

—*Billy Graham*

Run your fingers through my soul. For once, just once, feel exactly what I feel, believe what I believe, perceive as I perceive, look, experience, examine, and for once; just once, understand.

—ANONYMOUS

We must also care for our souls. Caring for our bodies alone is like riding in a four-wheel wagon that has two wheels missing. We can still ride, but the ride is going to be bumpy and not nearly as enjoyable as it would be with all four wheels.

Our soul comprises our mind, will, and emotions. It is different than our spirit. Here's an explanation that may help you to distinguish between your soul and your spirit:

Whenever the word "spirit" is used, it refers to the immaterial part of humanity that "connects" with God, who himself is spirit (John 4:24). The word "soul" can refer to both the immaterial and material aspects of humanity... In its most basic sense, the word "soul" means "life."

—GOTQUESTIONS.ORG, *WHAT IS THE DIFFERENCE BETWEEN THE SOUL AND SPIRIT OF MAN?*

Let's discuss our mind, will, and emotions:

Our Minds

Our limitations and success will be based, most often, on our own expectations for ourselves. What the mind dwells upon, the body acts upon.

—DENNIS WAITLEY

Doctors are not sure exactly how physical and mental healths influence each other, but the mind/body connection is real. There is a distinction between the brain and the mind.

The brain is a wonderful organ: it starts working the moment you get up in the morning and does not stop until you get into the office.

—Robert Frost

The brain has two functions: storing information in the memory and processing information. The right brain and the left brain are different. According to the right-brain, left brain dominance theory, the right brain is very expressive and creative. It is the right brain that allows you to have all of those wonderful daydreams. The left side of the brain is very logical and analytical. That's the side of your brain that likes to edit out what your creative right brain does. If you want to stimulate your brain try crossword puzzles, games, reading and studying. Vitamins can also be effective.

But what do we know about the mind? Our mind is our intellect. It is the control center of our body. It can shift our thoughts and actions and our whole perspective of life.

There are many books written about the mind. Psychologist Dr. Amanda Bowie told me of a book by Dr. Daniel Siegal, psychiatrist, titled *The Mindful Brain*. According to Dr. Bowie, in the book, Dr. Siegal tells us in every situation we have to be present in the "Now" by focusing on one thing at a time. In chapter six, he defines mindfulness as "a form of paying attention in the present moment on purpose." This means being receptive, self-observant, and reflective.

Dr. Bowie broke this down in layman's terms, as being aware of and paying full attention to whatever is going on now. For example, if you are standing in the church, you are aware of everything that's going on around you. Even with outside influences such as the choir singing, you are still aware of your immediate surroundings. If a child comes up to you and hugs you will still be able to engage that child and hug him back for you are focusing on the experience of the present moment.

I didn't read Dr. Siegal's book, but I read books by other psychologists and psychiatrists relating to the mind and mental stability. Two of these are Dr. Mark Hayman and Dr. Jeffrey C. Woods, Psy.D.

Dr. Hayman recommends developing an ultramind lifestyle to improve mood and brain functions. He describes this as dietary changes and supplements, exercise, relaxation, improved sleep patterns, brain exercises.—*Hayman,* 313

Dr. Jeffrey recommends administering self-assessment tests. He has written a book that is a good resource for mental health evaluations. It is a definitive guide to mental health care and provides a 264-item self-assessment inventory that can help you clarify and diagnose mental health problems. —*Woods, pub. 2007*

The Biblical View

> *Let this mind be in you, which was also in Christ Jesus.*
>
> —*Philippians 2:5*

> *Set your minds on things above, not on earthly things.*
>
> —*Colossians 2:3*

While it certainly can be a blessing to follow the prescripts of psychologists and psychiatrists in dealing with the mind, as pastors' wives, our primary source is and will always be the Bible. The Bible has much to say about the mind. In fact, there are more than 100 occurrences of the word "mind" in the King James Version of the Bible. Understanding the biblical view does not require psychological or psychiatric training.

The Bible uses the word "heart" to describe our thoughts, motives, and attitudes. God knows what's going on inside our minds, and the innermost aspects of our being matters most to Him. We are admonished in Proverbs 4:23 to keep our hearts with all diligence, for out of it are the issues of life. Keep means to protect or shield.

Joyce Meyer describes the mind as a battlefield. Our minds are constantly fighting against wrong mindsets that cause us to have negative visions for our lives. To overcome these negative conditions and mentalities we must have the mind of Christ—a mind that causes us to think like Christ thinks.—*Meyer,* Battlefield of the Mind, *15, 163, 186-187*

Renewing Our Minds

I would like to ask you two questions: (1) what do you think about when your mind is idle? and (2) what do you feed your mind when it is not idle? I ask the first question because as the old adage tells us, "An idle mind is the devil's workshop," and the second because, as the National Negro foundation slogan reminds us: "A mind is a terrible thing to waste." The bottom line is when our minds are idle we think about the things we've been feeding them. Are you feeding your mind junk food or nutritional food? Put another way: what TV shows do you watch? What Internet sites do you frequent? What books do you read?

Considering some of you are like me, you would do well to renew your mind.

> *I beseech you therefore, brethren, by the mercies of God, that you present your bodies a living sacrifice, holy, acceptable to God, which is your reasonable service. And do not be conformed to this world, but be transformed by the renewing of your mind, that you may prove what is that good and acceptable and perfect will of God.*
>
> —ROMANS 12:1–2

How Do You Renew Your Mind?

- *Keep your mind on God.* When you keep your mind open to the endless possibilities of our limitless God, you will not succumb to mind deprivation, but will triumphantly use your mind to focus on a better tomorrow.

> *You will keep him in perfect peace, whose mind is stayed on You, because he trusts in You.*
>
> —ISAIAH 26:3

Jesus said to him, 'You shall love the L*ORD your God with all your heart, with all your soul, and with all your mind.'*

—MATTHEW 22:37

- *Have the mind of Christ.* What kind of mind did Christ have? A spiritual, submissive, serving, sacrificial, secure mind. Someone said, "your attitude determines your altitude, and your altitude determines your attitude. Attitude also determines outcome. Have a bad attitude, everything else is going to be downhill."

Let this mind be in you which was also in Christ Jesus.

—PHILIPPIANS 2:5

- *Rededicate your mind to God daily.* You face so many things daily that enter into your mind that you need a daily cleansing. Yesterday's cleansing is not sufficient for today.

Who can understand his errors? Cleanse me from secret faults

—PSALM 19:12.

- *Meditate.* Meditation relaxes and refreshes the mind. When you meditate you use mental activities to focus your thoughts on things that heighten your spiritual awareness and bring inner peace.

And now, dear brothers and sisters, one final thing. Fix your thoughts on what is true, and honorable, and right, and pure, and lovely, and admirable. Think about things that are excellent and worthy of praise.

—PHILIPPIANS 4:8 (NLT)

Let the words of my mouth, and the meditation of my heart, be acceptable in thy sight, O Lord, my strength, and my redeemer.

—Psalm 19:14 (KJV)

- *Don't be double-minded.* Make up your mind what you want and go after it without being concerned about what other people say or think.

He is a double-minded man, unstable in all his ways (James 1:8)

- *Know God has you on His mind.*

For I know the thoughts that I think toward you, says the Lord, thoughts of peace and not of evil, to give you a future and a hope.

—Jeremiah 29:11

How precious also are Your thoughts to me, O God! How great is the sum of them! If I should count them, they would be more in number than the sand; When I awake, I am still with You.

—Psalm 139:17-18

See, I have inscribed you on the palms of My hands; Your walls are continually before me.

—Isaiah 49:16

Our Wills

Life is not a result of the dreams that you dream, but the choices that you make.

—*Otto Malone, quoted at Fontaine Baptist Church, Houston, Texas, February 27, 2011*

Our will is our instinct. It motivates, empowers, drives, and gives us energy to do what our mind confirms. It is housed in our soul, and requires much care. How many of you have heard the saying, "that's a strong-willed" child—a child who wants to do whatever he wants to do. He knows better but he does it anyway—because of his will. The will is often in conflict with the mind. For example, let's go to Romans 7 and read what Paul had to say about the struggle between his will and his mind:

For we know that the law is spiritual, but I am carnal, sold under sin. For what I am doing, I do not understand. For what I will to do, that I do not practice; but what I hate, that I do. If, then, I do what I will not to do, I agree with the law that it is good. But now, it is no longer I who do it, but sin that dwells in me. For I know that in me (that is, in my flesh) nothing good dwells; for to will is present with me, but how to perform what is good I do not find. For the good that I will to do, I do not do; but the evil I will not to do, that I practice. Now if I do what I will not to do, it is no longer I who do it, but sin that dwells in me.

I find then a law, that evil is present with me, the one who wills to do good. For I delight in the law of God according to the inward man. But I see another law in my members, warring against the law of my mind, and bringing me into captivity to the law of sin which is in my members. O wretched man that I am! Who will deliver me from this body of death? I thank God—through Jesus Christ our Lord! So then, with the mind I myself serve the law of God, but with the flesh the law of sin.

My sisters, Paul is not the only one with this struggle, we all have it. You may not have been a strong-willed child, but many of us are strong-willed adults. Our flesh is governed by our will, and there will be times when our mind and will are not in harmony. One of the messages God allowed me to preach was, "Help For My Messed-up Want-to." The term was taken from Beth Moore (*Get Out of That Pit*, p. 61). In that message, I reminded the congregation, as Beth did in her book, that we all have a "messed-up want-to"—our carnal or fleshy nature that makes us do what we don't want to do, but we do it anyway.

What can you do when your will is in conflict with your mind?

- *Recognize your limitations.*
- *Bring your will under subjection to the Holy Spirit (Galatians 5:16-22)*
- *Be truthful to yourself by being mindful of the issue you're battling and knowing the consequence of your behavior.*
- *Restate the following I WILL Scriptures:*

I WILL bless the Lord at all times, His praises shall continually be in my mouth!

—*Psalm 34:1*

I WILL remember the works of the Lord; surely I WILL remember Your wonders of old.

—*Psalm 77:11*

I WILL delight myself in your statutes; I WILL not forget Your word.

—Psalm 119:16

Emotional Health & Well Being

For God has not given us a spirit of fear, but of love, power, and a sound mind.

—1 Timothy 4:7

Emotions are temporary states of mind. Don't let them permanently destroy you!

—Unknown

Our emotional health correlates with our mental health. We've discussed emotions numerous times in this book, and I've devoted a section in chapter twelve to anger management. Many pastors' wives are taught not to display their emotions, thinking that any display of emotions is a sign of weakness and is not "spiritual." There is nothing wrong with displaying your emotions. God gave them to you, but you must restrain them if you are to be successful as a pastor's wife. If not, this can lead to emotional disorders.

Human Pendulums

You don't have to be bubbling all of the time, but you don't have to be in the tank all the time, either. Worst yet, you don't have to be a human pendulum, swinging from highs and lows all day long. The following quote is pertinent here:

You can't expect to prevent negative feelings altogether. And you can't expect to experience positive feelings all the time...The Law of Emotional Choice directs us to acknowledge our feelings but also to refuse to get stuck in the negative ones.

—Greg Anderson

The prophet Habakkuk stands out in my mind as one who properly applied the Law of Emotional Choice:

Habakkuk was in an emotional upheaval because of the injustice he was witnessing. The wicked were prospering and the godly were suffering, and God didn't seem to do anything about it. To make matters worse, God was going to send the wicked Chaldean army to punish Judah for their sin. Habakkuk was perplexed because he couldn't understand how God could use such wicked people to punish his own nation. He went to his watchtower to pray, meditate and wait on God. God answered him and told him that He was going to execute justice, but encouraged Habakkuk that He was still on the throne.

After hearing from God, Habakkuk's emotions changed from sorrow to joy. His expression of joy is one of the most memorable in the Bible:

> *Though the fig tree may not blossom, nor fruit be on the vines; though the labor of the olive may fail, and the fields yield no food; though the flock may be cut off from the fold, and there be no herd in the stalls—yet I will rejoice in the Lord, I will joy in the God of my salvation.*
>
> —*Habukkuk 3:17–18*

Emotional Stability

Sisters, I don't know your current situation. Whatever it may be, God is still on the throne, and your emotional health is more under your control than you think. You have access to more information about how to control your emotions than ever before and can learn how to live a healthier, longer life if you are interested. But how stable are your emotions?

I'm not referring to emotional upheavals like major stresses, loss of a job, or the death of a loved one. I'm not necessarily talking about the emotional impact of menopause, or other hormonally related conditions. I'm referring to your day-to-day affairs. Are you on an emotional roller coaster, up one day and down the next depending on our circumstances or people, or are your emotions stable and under control?

Again, I refer to Amanda Bowie, Psy.D. I asked Dr. Bowie to provide an explanation for emotional instability and recommendations for managing our emotions. According to Dr. Bowie:

> *Emotional instability is based a person's belief and values. When I get a referral of a person who is depressed or anxious, I attempt to determine how they manage their emotions based on their values and beliefs. The first question I may ask is how do they make decisions—are they based on facts or feeling (emotions)? If they make decisions based on feelings, I know there is a problem, because emotions change.*
>
> *There are negative or positive emotions. Negative emotions can come from negative experiences from different stages of life. For example, childhood: parents who are unavailable emotionally to their children, insecurities, self-doubt, coming from an abusive household; adolescence: peer pressure, relationships with parents; adulthood: self-concept, parenting, marriage, health. In the church it can be people's beliefs, opinions, and expectations.*

Dr. Bowie's recommendations for stabilizing your emotions are:

- *Take "me" time and learn to relax.*
- *Pursue what brings you joy.*
- *Regulate who you bring into your circle (friends, family, acquaintances).*
- *Protect what comes into your mind.*
- *Feed your spirit and replenish your soul with the word of God.*
- *Be true to yourself and know when to reach out for help.*

The Importance of Godly Character

I'd like to share with you a teaching that Pastor Ray A. Riley, former pastor of my home church, taught which I believe summarizes what we have been discussing in this chapter about caring for our body and soul. His subject was *The Importance of Godly Character.* Scripture reference, Genesis 2:7— "And the Lord God formed man *of* the dust of the ground, and breathed into his nostrils the breath of life; and man became a living being."

Here's an excerpt from Pastor Riley's teaching:

> *Many people have wondered: "Why didn't God in the beginning simply create humans as spirit beings without human nature? Why did He first make us physical—from the dust of the earth—then offer us eternal life only if we vigorously resist the weaknesses of our flesh? If God can do all things, why didn't He just create us with perfect character?"*
>
> *Of course, God could have done all that—if He had been willing to create us without the personal character we need for making personal choices. It all gets back to our free will, our freedom of choice. God Himself had a choice about how man would be created. He could have made us automatons, functioning like programmed robots whose only course of action is to carry out the instructions of their maker. But He chose to create us like Him, capable of making choices that are limited only by our knowledge and character. This requires that we learn right from wrong and that our character develop gradually by our decisions under God's guidance and assistance.*
>
> *God is not finished with us. We are still His workmanship (Ephesians 2:10). He is creating in us "righteousness and true holiness"—His character. As long as we are human, our character is not firm; it is not permanent. We can change our minds and behavior. We can make mistakes and learn from them. We can learn from the fruits of our right and wrong choices.*
>
> *Since we can change our minds—and repent of our errors—God can change us even more and create in us the will and the capacity to steadfastly choose what is right over what is wrong. For it is God who works in you both to will and to do for His good pleasure (Philippians 2:13).*
>
> *Of course, God requires that we first recognize and willingly reverse our wrong behavior by allowing his Spirit to empower*

us to make those changes. Then we can become a new person "created in righteousness and true holiness."

You know I can't add anything to that.

Let's Pray…

Be a blessing!

12

Rechargeable Flashlights: Stress, Anger, and Time Management

Though it is not common, you might find yourself in quicksand. Quicksand is a condition and not a soil type, and some of the things we see on TV are not accurate. Still, there are quicksand situations we have to deal with as pastors' wives that will take us under in a New York minute if we let them. I'm speaking of stress, anger, and overcommitted schedules. Wouldn't it be wonderful if our lives as pastors' wives included no stress, no anger, and no time constraints? That sounds nice, but it's not going to happen. That's why we have rechargeable flashlights in our success kit. We'll explore these three topics in this chapter.

Stress Management

I still find each day too short for all the thoughts I want to think, all the walks I want to take, all the books I want to read, and all the friends I want to see. The longer I live, the more my mind dwells upon the beauty and the wonder of the world.

—*John Burroughs*

When you get to the end of your rope, tie a knot and hang on.

—*Franklin Delano Roosevelt*

Too Stressed to Be Blessed?

I treasure Dr. Suzan Johnson-Cook's book, *Too Blessed To Be Stressed: Word of Wisdom for Women on the Move.* I met Dr. Cook several years ago at a conference in New York, and I have in my possession an autographed copy. In the book Dr. Cook tells us how we can take control in stressful situations so stress doesn't stress us out. Dr. Cook is more than qualified to tell us how, as she is a wife and mother, was the first female pastor of New York's oldest American Baptist church, and was appointed by President Clinton to serve on his Initiative on Race and Reconciliation.

Every head bowed and all eyes closed. Please raise your hands if you are stressed out right now. Yes, I see them. As pastors' wives we certainly are too blessed to be stressed. Let's clear the air, however. The truth of the matter is that some of you are running on fumes, your reserves have been depleted, and one more incident can blow you to smithereens. Why? You've pushed yourself to the limit. Many of your days are similar to the lady on my faded turquoise "She does it all" nightshirt. She's talking on the phone, stirring the pot of dinner on the stove, mopping the floor simultaneously—and she has a big grin on her face. Some of you have also plastered a grin on your face.

Externally you look like a tower of strength; internally you've become sticky wickets. I'm talking to Sena too.

Sisters, this is a crisis. According to Proverbs 24:10, "If you fall to pieces in a crisis, there wasn't much to you in the first place." I think there's something to us—we've just to stop the three-ring circus. We only have one life to live.

One Life to Live

Earl delivered a sermon titled, "One Life to Live." In the sermon he talked about Sylvester and Tweety Bird. You know, the "I tought I saw a putty-cat" bird?

Well, anyway...Earl spoke of how Sylvester tried over and over to eat Tweety Bird and in the process got killed himself. Each time he died he went to hell. Of course he was upset, but the devil told him there was no need to be flustered, for he was a cat and cats had nine lives. With that information in hand, Sylvester tried with all of his might to kill Tweety, but instead he kept getting killed himself. Finally, Sylvester gets down to his last life and comes to himself. He told himself that he had better be careful, because now he only had one life to live.

The main point of the sermon is that as humans we only have one life to live, and we have to live that life carefully. One day we will stand before the judgment seat of Christ and give an account of what we've done in this world, good and bad (2 Corinthians 5:10). I'm a firm believer that part of the account we'll have to give is how we handled stress, for Jesus gave us the cure for anxiety in Matthew 6:25–34 and told us not to stress. Stressing can't add one day to our life. Philippians 4:6–7 warns us not to be anxious for anything. We must heed the warning. Unmanaged stress can cause all types of medical problems.

Here's a portion of an article written by Jen Laskey and medically reviewed by Rosalyn Carter-DeWitt, MD about stress titled, *Six Ways to Reduce Stress and Protect Your Heart*:

> *The body's natural response to stress can increase your heart rate, raise your blood pressure and release stress hormones, according to experts at the Journal of American Medical Association.*

> *Stress also forces the heart muscle to work harder. The American Heart Association (AHA) suggests that acute and chronic stress may also affect other risk factors and behaviors, such as high cholesterol levels, a person's inclination toward smoking, the urge to overeat, and lack of interest in physical activity.*
>
> —*Jen Laskey,* Everydayhealth.com

The worst thing about stress is that it can kill you if it is not managed properly. How many of you will agree that if you kill yourself quickly, like shooting yourself in the head or slowly by stressing yourself to death, you have still committed suicide?

Good vs. Bad Stress

As you manage your stress you can be comforted by the fact that stress is not necessarily bad. Moderate amounts of "good" stress can enhance your performance and push you to successfully achieve your goals. However, if you continually place your body under stress you will create "bad" stress. Eventually your body will break down, leading to heart attacks and even death.

One tale-tell sign of bad stress is burnout. Ayala Pines and Elliott Aronson define burnout as:

> *A state of physical, emotional, and mental exhaustion caused by long-term involvement in situations that are emotionally demanding. Burnout candidates are idealists who choose a career in which they thought they could make a difference. Instead, they find themselves running into chronic situational stresses.*
>
> —*Soundview Executive Book Summaries, 36.*

Being a pastors' wife is not necessarily a career choice. However, our "push ourselves to the limit" mentality makes us fertile soil for burnout. Did you ever stop to think that we normally don't push things to the limit? For example, my car can go 160 mph, but I've never driven that fast. If I decided to drive at 160 everyday, how long do you think the engine would last? Why then do we put our pedal to the medal and fly down the road every day wearing our Superwoman capes and our super first-lady bulletproof vests and frayed nerves? Yes, I'm waiting for an answer. I didn't hear one, so I'll go on.

Short-term vs. Long-term Stress

Then there is short term positive and long term negative stress. I realize what's stressful to one person may be relaxing to another, but no one can function well with sustained periods of long-term negative stress. Short-term positive stress is rejuvenating. Long-term negative stress is depleting.

Stress Relief Tips

Sisters, you can re-acclimate your stress level by adapting a lifestyle that minimizes long-term negative stress in your life. If you had altitude sickness, the way to re-acclimate is to go to a lower elevation or to live with it until the body adjusts. You don't have to do this with long term negative stress. You can significantly reduce your stress by incorporating stress relieving tips into your daily life. Here's a few you may wish to try:

Aromatherapy

The right fragrance can relieve stress. The article, *Use Aromatherapy Stress Relief to Gently Remove Tension* stated "Aromatherapy stress relief uses the sense of smell to gently move our bodies and emotions to a feeling of greater balance, safety and well being."—*gentle-stress-relief.com*.

Now, don't stress yourself out by running out to your favorite store and charging ten bottles of your favorite scent to the credit card we'll discuss in chapter seventeen.

Drink Tea

According to *Women's Health* magazine, drinking tea prior to stressful tasks helps reduce stress. Cocoa has stress-reducing properties also.—womenshealthmag.com, *Stress Relief Tips*

Frequent Breaks

This suggestion is from Pastor T. D. Jakes:

> *Take a break and restore yourself. Walk down an unfamiliar street during your lunch hour. Instead of going straight home from work, stop at a bookstore and browse around. Or, best yet, find a quiet place to pray. The world can wait for an hour. It can wait because, believe it or not, it will go on without you. This realization can cause some folks to panic, to scurry even faster. In order to sustain ourselves, though, we must realize that since the world will race along without us, we must find our own pace and make our journey our own and not the world's.*
>
> —*T. D. Jakes*, Maximize the Moment, *76*

Rest

The best solution for relieving long-term negative stress is rest. God initiated rest, and His directive is that we should take a day of rest every week of the year. He illustrated rest by resting on the seventh day after He created the world. God wasn't tired, for He created the world just by saying, "Let there be." God continues to work; if not we wouldn't be here today. Jesus told us in John 5:17 that God is always working. So God didn't rest for Himself; He rested so we could enter into rest. The following Scriptures confirm God's desire that we rest:

Come to me, all you who labor and are heavy laden, and I will give you rest.

—MATTHEW 11:28

For in repentance and rest is your salvation in quietness and trust is your strength.

—ISAIAH 30:15

When you lie down, you will not be afraid; yes, you will lie down and your sleep will be sweet.

—PROVERBS 3:24

I will both lie down in peace, and sleep; for you alone, O Lord, make me dwell in safety.

—PSALM 4:8

I lay down and slept; I awoke, for the Lord sustained me.

—PSALM 3:5

However, one of the most prominent sins pastors' wives commit is failure to rest. Let's make every effort to eliminate this sin in our lives. And don't miss church going to the church building—even on Sunday. God may want you to stay home and rest in Him. As my friend Evangelist Ruby Lewis said during a women's conference:

We have to start listening to God, and stop thinking about what people think. Sometimes the Lord may tell you not to go to church today and to spend time with Him. Sometimes we are at every

> *service but our hearts are not right. God has told you to stay home and pray, but you are at church. We have to listen to God.*
>
> —Evangelist Ruby Lewis

And she was right.

Let me tell on myself again. Though I know rest is essential to well-being, I had a problem with resting—even in Jesus. Since Earl shepherds so far from home it is not practical that he drive home from church every night. On the days he was not at home, I spent countless hours complaining and tossing and turning and giving myself pity parties because he wasn't there with me. There were times when it really felt as though I was single, and I had a hard time with this. It didn't help the situation when I went to my home church, and folk would ask me if Earl and I were still together.

When it was time for me to go to bed at night, it wasn't easy because I was lonely. Then I read in Jill and Stuart Briscoe's book, *In a Quiet Place*, about Elijah and the difference between loneliness and solitude. This knowledge revolutionized my life. I found that loneliness is involuntary isolation from others; solitude is deliberate and voluntary seclusion. Jesus enjoyed solitude. Mark 1:35 tells us that Jesus rose up early in the morning before day to depart to a solitary place and pray. I haven't gotten to the point of rising up very early in the morning before day, but I am able to handle being alone much better knowing that God has given me these times of solitude to withdraw to a quiet place and rest in Him.

Something else that helped me: I went to the Christian bookstore and found a beautifully inspirational painting of a young lady falling asleep on a large Bible in the shape of a mattress. The caption under the picture reads, "My Comfort." I hung the painting right above my bed, and that is the last thing I look at before going to sleep for the night.

God's Sabbath Rest

Your taste in books and paintings may differ from mine, sisters, but as you live a life that brings glory to God, you have the assurance that no matter how stressful this world may be, there is rest for the saints of God. It's called God's Sabbath Rest, and He has prepared it for you. This is the ultimate rest for those who have faith in God and are obedient to His Word. Hebrews 4:9–11 tells us to make every effort to enter into that rest.

Warren Wiersbe provides an exposition of this text:

> *God's Sabbath rest is a type of our present rest of salvation, following the finished work of Christ on the cross. It is also a picture of the "eternal Sabbath" of glory. Israel's Canaan rest is similar to the life of victory and blessing we gain as we walk by faith and claim our inheritance in Christ.*
>
> —*Wiersbe, 684*

In the Valley of Decision

> *Standing in the middle of the road is very dangerous; you get knocked down by traffic from both sides.*
>
> —*Margaret Thatcher*

> *Life's rewards go to those who let their actions rise above their excuses.*
>
> —*Lee J. Colan*

My sisters, I've written about stress management as candidly as I know how. As we prepare to discuss anger management, may I remind you again that you are too blessed to be stressed? You must decide for yourself if you are going to stop stressing and get the rest you need or keep running on empty. Just remember, there is no crown in heaven for stress-out, burnout, rust-out, or give-out!

As you spend time in the valley of decision, my prayer is that you will make up in your mind you are not going to let long-term negative stress lead you to an early grave. If you don't decide, your body will decide for you. Unlike Sylvester, you only have one life to live. Kick out this killer!

Anger Management

One commonly overlooked danger in traveling through the wilderness is high temperatures. If not addressed, they can bring on heat stroke or even death. The slippery slope of unresolved anger can also lead to stroke and death. Your heart is not designed to pump effectively while you are boiling on the back burner.

Boiling on the Back Burner

> *Cease from anger and forsake wrath; Do not fret; it leads only to evildoing.*
>
> —*Psalm 37:8, NASB95*

> *For every minute you are angry you lose sixty seconds of happiness.*
>
> —*Ralph Waldo Emerson*

> *Keeping score of old scores and scars, getting even and one-upping, always make you less than you are*
>
> —*Malcolm Forbes*

The Anguished Repose website posted an article about stress: *It's Not The Stress That Gets You, but How You Respond To It,* in which they included excerpts of research published February 2011 in the *journal Brain, Behavior, and Immunity.* The researchers suggested that there is a correlation between anger and heart disease, and noted that people who react to challenging situations with anger instead of calm may have higher risk of heart disease risk.

Dr. Judith Carroll who conducted the study at the University of Pittsburgh was quoted:

> *People who reported high levels of anger and anxiety after performing a laboratory-based stress task showed greater increases in a marker of inflammation, than those who remained relatively calm. This could help explain why some people with high levels of stress experience chronic health problems.*
>
> —*ANGUISHREPOSE.COM, FEBRUARY 18, 2011*

My sisters, you don't want to experience chronic health problems because you can't handle your anger properly. Still, an albatross around many pastors' wives' necks is an inability to manage anger. This is so persistent among some of us that it has wrecked our lives. One of the reasons we stagger as pastors' wives is because we think anger is sin, so we deny it rather than deal with it. As a result, we keep our anger inside and manufacture ulcers.

We must break the chains that attempt to enslave us to a life of hypocrisy. Many of you know what it's like to come apart at the seams because you've bottled your feelings. I do. Although I'm a communicator, I've been borderline ballistic many times about things that just weren't right. I couldn't talk to anyone about it—Earl, a church member, or even another pastor's wife, because it would seem like complaining. So I privately boiled. Silly me, instead of being bent out of shape I should have unveiled my anger and moved on. Do I have a witness?

What's Broke?

Before you can deal with your anger you have to find out what's broke. As we've discussed in previous chapters, the pastor's wife has many opportunities to get angry. Since I'm not pulling punches, one group of persons that can anger you the most is church members. You may care for them dearly, yet there are going to be times when you will not see eye to eye on the matter under discussion. You must seek to reconcile quickly and biblically (Matthew 18) and refuse to let anger consume you and taint your relationships with the members of the church. Michelle Obleton, a pastor's wife, tells us that many of us even harbor resentment toward our husband's ministry:

> *Many pastors' wives resent the ministry because of the all-consuming hold it has over their husbands. They are aware of the many people who look to their husbands for daily guidance. It appears that their husbands eat, sleep, live, and breathe for the church.*
>
> —Carter, 95–96

I totally agree. How many times have I boiled because I felt like the fifth wheel, second fiddle, or odd woman out? Some of you may be, or have been, in the same pot.

An Alternative to Boiling

Sisters, if we want to crockpot all of the things that potentially cause us to be angry we could simmer until the cows come home. Worse, we will be boiling when the sun goes down, and find ourselves walking in sin and disobedience to God's commands. We must have an alternative to our boiling.

Let me offer a few solutions:

- *Get to know yourself.* This helps you to predict how you will act in an anger-provoking situation. James tells us that much of our anger and fighting comes from unresolved lusts within us (James 4:1–2), so we have to be honest with ourselves.

- *Don't rehearse it.* I can't tell you the number of times that I've done this: rehearsed how I'm going to tell Earl about what he did and how angry it made me. That got me nowhere.
- *Don't allow it to become the subject of every conversation you have.* Did you ever meet someone angry? Everything they talk about is this particular instance. After a while you do an about face when you see them coming.
- *Resolve it before the night is over* (Ephesians 4:26-27). Don't go to bed angry, get up angry, and stay angry all day. The person you are angry at may be surfing in the Bahamas while you are huffing and puffing and blowing your house down.
- *Develop ministries for yourself without sitting around moping about your husband's ministry.* Nothing ventured, nothing gained. A great ministry is blazing a trail for young women. You can serve as an invaluable resource. They need to know about the pitfalls to avoid. Don't be reluctant to tell them about the minefields, and the mines that you've stepped on, but by the grace of God, you've survived. Thanks be to God, in 2005 I founded Ministers of the Heart, Inc., a national interdenominational fellowship of female ministers and other women of God. Please write to me at earsen@att.net if you would like additional information about our sisterhood. We'd love to have you join us.
- *Use discretion.* The proper way to handle anger towards your husband is not to wait until he's in bed and getting ready to fall off to sleep, and you decide that you want to talk about it Now! Trust me, I tried that, and that's not the way. Wait until morning when both of your heads are clearer.

Time Management

Experts in survival tell us time management is important. Their advice is that whenever you go camping or hiking in the wilderness, you should determine in advance how long you are going to stay there and tell someone what time you will return. If you don't get back in time, start searching.

Redeeming the Time

> *I think the world today is upside-down. It is suffering so much because there is so little love in the home and in family life. We have no time for our children. We have no time for each other. There is no time to enjoy each other, and the lack of love causes so much suffering and unhappiness in the world.*
>
> —*Mother Theresa.—quoted in Benenate and Durepos, 129.*

You can turn your world right side up by redeeming the time, sisters. Time is a gift from God, and Ephesians 5:16 instructs us to redeem the time for the days are evil. Redeeming the time means managing your time well by taking full advantage of the time God has given you on this earth to fulfill your purpose. You each have an individual purpose, but we all have one purpose in common—kingdom advancement, and it takes time to do it.

Barbara Hughes writes:

> *What will history record about your pilgrimage as a ministry wife? Think about what you want your legacy to look like. Pray about how you can take steps toward achieving what the Lord wants you to do—and then redeem the time and do it.*
>
> —*Hughes, 73*

Whether or not you redeem your time is contingent on your response to the question: do you make time or find time? Making time requires forfeiting necessary tasks to squeeze unplanned activities into your already busy schedule. Finding time requires centering your schedule on your priorities and eliminating non-essential unplanned activities.

Where Do You Find Time?

May I see a show of hands—How many of you are addicted your Smartphones, Ipads, Daytimers, or anything else to help you make the best use of our time? It looks as if a few of us are (yeah, right!).

Problem is, these gadgets don't give you more time; they just allow you to crowd more things into an already crowded day. That's why we put a frozen entrée in the microwave and stand by waiting impatiently for those five to seven minutes to hurry and pass. Let's not even think about the ordeal of waiting for the two minutes we are supposed to let our food remain in the microwave after the cooking time is up. Can anyone tell me why we are supposed to do this anyway?

What about drive-thrus and drive-bys? You seldom have to get out of your car these days. Did you know there are drive-by funeral homes? Instead of going inside and signing the register to let the family know you took time to pay your respects, all you have to do is go to the window, ring the buzzer, speak a name into the speaker, and they wheel your favorite aunt or uncle to the window for your final parting glance. I'm not kidding here; I saw one. I'm not telling you where I saw it because I can't remember, but trust me, they do exist.

You may not be at the point yet where you want to frequent a drive-by funeral home, but since this is a success kit, not one to unload and walk away empty handed, let me share a few tips for managing your time:

Tips for Managing Your Time

- *Know your biological clock.* Are you a morning or afternoon person? You should know and schedule your work accordingly.
- *Just Say No!* Interruptions are often one of the biggest challenges in managing time. If you don't want to find yourself frustrated at the end of the day with little or nothing accomplished, you have to say no. Saying no doesn't come easy to all of us, so let's say it all together, "no!" And make sure your Sunday "no" is nice and sweet. After all, you are the pastor's wife. An acquaintance of mine has a creative way of saying "no." She says, "You just missed me." That means she is not going to do it. Who could get mad at that approach? Now, I'm not recommending that you be lazy and trifling when someone

asks you to help them do something. Pastors' wives have to pitch in where needed. However, if your plate is full, it's okay to tell someone, "I'd love to do it, but my plate is full right now. Can you ask me again next week, or next month, or next year, or next decade?" Honestly, a decade may be too long.

- *Monitor calls.* Telephone calls are a real time stealer so you must learn to monitor the number and length of your calls. Set aside time everyday to check your calls; you don't have to jump every time the phone rings. Set your phone to a different ring-tone for your husband and for family members to distinguish the calls from bill collectors. Try not to talk on the phone while driving—and certainly don't text. Debra Jones, the saint at our church who was responsible for our church marquee, placed a sign on the marquee that read, "Honk if you love Jesus. If you're texting while you're driving you'll meet Him soon." I know we all want to meet Jesus, but I don't want to have to explain how I got to heaven before my mansion is ready, and neither do you.
- *Delegate.* You can't, and don't have to do it all. When you delegate, hold others accountable, but don't micro-manage. You wouldn't want someone breathing down your neck would you? I wouldn't.
- *Limit unexpected visitors.* Something that worked for me when I was employed by ExxonMobil was a "red" and "green" time indicator on my office door. Red meant "please do not disturb"; green meant "come in." When I was in the office with the door closed most visitors respected my need for privacy. I learned to be kind to those who didn't as I eased them out of my office. Conferring standing up also helped to limit unwanted visitors. Taking a restroom break may work. I say "may" because there were times when I tried this and it didn't work. On more than one occasion the same male visitor walked with me to the restroom and waited until I came out. I'm sure he was glad I'm a Christian.

Well, sisters, that's enough about management. I'm stressed, angry, and running out of time. Just kidding.

Let's Pray…

Be a blessing!

13

Gas Mask: To Prevent Haughtiness

The primary function of a gas mask is to prevent toxic gases or poisonous material from entering the lungs and attacking the person. It does not provide its own oxygen supply, but filters out the particles. The mask can also protect the face from contact poisons or gases. Our success kit must include a gas mask to protect us from being contaminated by haughtiness. Let's take a moment to discuss this toxin and how we can filter it out of our hearts.

Haughty Women

> *What does the Lord require of you, but to love mercy, do justly, and walk humbly with thy God?*
>
> —*Micah 6:8*

Of all the marvelous works of God, perhaps the one angels view with the most supreme astonishment is a proud man.
—CHARLES CALEB COLTON

A young boy went to a restaurant and asked the owner if he could use the phone to call the grocery store. The owner thought this was strange, but allowed him to do so and hung around to listen to why he was calling the grocery store. When he called the store, the boy asked to speak to the manager. When the boss came on the line he told the manager that he was looking for a job and asked if he had any openings, to which the manager responded "No, I already have somebody." The boy told him that he would work hard if he would hire him. The manager said, "No thank you, I'm very pleased with the boy that I have now." The boy then told the manager that he was willing to work for almost nothing, to which the manager said, "No thank you; I want to keep the boy I have; he's a great worker." When the boy hung up the phone, the restaurant owner said, "I'm so sorry that you weren't able to get the job, it seemed like you really needed one." The boy said, "No sir, I work at the store; I was just calling to check up on myself."—*Source unknown*

Sisters, when was the last time you called to check up on yourself to see if your heart was contaminated with haughtiness? *Merriam Webster* dictionary describes haughtiness as being "blatantly and disdainfully proud." Haughtiness says, "The best way to lift myself up is to put someone else down."

A haughty heart cannot please God because it is an abomination to Him. In fact, "haughty eyes" is listed in Proverbs among the seven things that God hates (Proverbs 6:17). Richard Exley et al. list pride and hypocrisy as two of the greatest spiritual sins. They write that pride often looks and feels like commitment, devotion, and sacrifice for the kingdom; and like hypocrisy, self-righteousness takes on many wily forms, such as "holier than them" and "better than them" attitudes.—*Exley and Galli, 19–23*

Dr. Henry Blackaby summarizes it this way:

Pride is the great enemy of the Christian. It is an overly high opinion of yourself. It motivates you to do things that are not

> *Christ-like...if you succumb to its influence, there will be consequences: Pride holds you back from asking forgiveness, discourages you from admitting your sins, convinces you that you deserve better treatment, impedes your serving others, will have you striving for places of prominence, have you listen to flattery and ignore honest counseling. Pride will lead you to isolate yourself so that you are not accountable to others.*
>
> —*Blackaby, 179*

Sadly, haughtiness is the Achilles heel for many pastors' wives. Ego tripping and the tendency to be "puffed up" with pride hang as a millstone around their neck and tarnish their testimony for Christ. They may try to cover it up, but God sees, and He knows. I heard God say in Jeremiah 23: 24, "Can anyone hide himself in secret places so I shall not see him?" and "Do I not fill heaven and earth?" God also tells us in Proverbs 16:18 that pride goes before destruction and a haughty spirit before a fall.

To cap it off, many persons put all pastors' wives in the same bag whether or not the label fits. I have never felt better than anyone, and most likely you haven't; but let's cut through the chase. The dichotomy is that while many of us don't want everything that goes along with being the pastor's wife, we like the prominence that comes with being a first lady. There's no sin in that, until we start acting like proud peacocks, or like we are the cat's meow, the rat, the trap, and the cheese. Yes, I said it.

Sometimes we are haughty because of our own insecurity. We feel that people are against us, so we have to put on airs and act like we're God's gift to the world. Let's stop that nonsense, and repeat together: "Everyone is not against me. In fact, I know that there are more for me than against me."

The gangrene of haughtiness can also lead to a judgmental spirit. Romans 14:4 admonishes us against judging another man's servant. We all belong to God, the righteous judge. Seeing that, there's no need to play games with each other by saying, "I'm not being critical, I'm just inspecting their fruit." When was the last time we inspected the fruit in our own lives? Or, when was the last time we noticed that people don't want to be around us when we are critical and judgmental?

Sisters, we can't afford to be detached from people. We need each other. What we sing on Sunday morning, "I need you, you need me; we're all a part of God's body" is true. The Bible tells us in Ephesians 4:16 that we are one body joined and knitted together. I don't know about you, but I need every piece of me. I sure need you.

Humility: The Antidote for Haughtiness

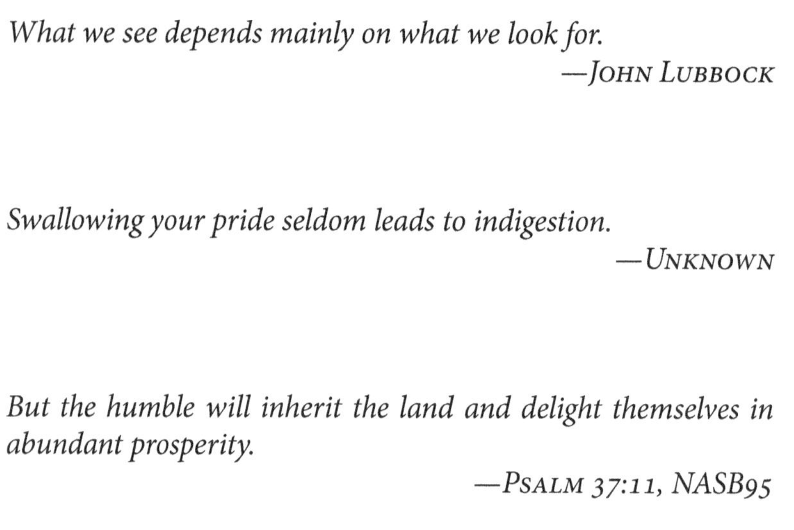

What we see depends mainly on what we look for.

—*John Lubbock*

Swallowing your pride seldom leads to indigestion.

—*Unknown*

But the humble will inherit the land and delight themselves in abundant prosperity.

—*Psalm 37:11, NASB95*

What is the antidote for haughtiness? Humility. Humility is the quality or state of being humble. When we are humble, we are unpretentious, and offer ourselves in a spirit of deference or servility. God tells us in Luke 14:11 "For whoever exalts himself will be humbled, and he who humbles himself will be exalted."

Romans 12:3 addresses the topic of humility by telling us we are not to think of ourselves more highly than we ought to. That doesn't mean we should be shrinking violets. Still we can't lose sight of the fact that God called us, not because of who we are, but in spite of who we are. No matter how much we have going for us, we are only dusty participants in this thing called life. Tall dust, short dust, slim dust, fluffy dust, but still dust. One hundred years from now when someone digs up our body, all they will find is dust and dentures.

There is nothing more humbling to me than looking at the board in my own eye. When I concentrate on my own rafter it's real hard to see the riffraff in my sister's eye (Matthew 7:3–4). Instead of being critical, judgmental, and suspicious, I can't help but extend more grace—realizing that there is good in the worst of us and bad in the best of us—and knowing that my train hasn't arrived at the station yet.

I'm also humbled when I look at the list in Galatians 5:22-23 and read about the fruit of the Spirit. I'm a minister but I find my spiritual development appalling. I'm not even proficient in the first fruit on the list: "love." Let's re-read 1 Corinthians 13. We talked about love earlier, so we aren't going to spend a lot of time talking about it here. If you've mastered love, God bless you. How is your long-suffering? All I'm trying to say is that we don't have time for haughtiness; we have enough to do by asking God to make us, shape us, and remold us. Then we can show others the right way.

All things considered, sisters, I realize the haughtiness label may not fit you today, but it might tomorrow; so please take heed lest you fall into this sin (1 Corinthians 10:12). In the event some of you are still not motivated to walk in humility, read what God said in Isaiah chapter three to the haughty women of Zion:

> *The Lord says, "The women of Zion are haughty, walking along with outstretched necks, flirting with their eyes, tripping along with mincing steps, with ornaments jingling on their ankles. Therefore the Lord will bring sores on the heads of the women of Zion; the Lord will make their scalps bald. In that day the Lord will snatch away their finery: the bangles and headbands and crescent necklaces, the earrings and bracelets and veils, the headdresses and ankle chains and sashes, the perfume bottles and charms, the signet rings and nose rings, the fine robes and the capes and cloaks, the purses and mirrors, and the linen garments and tiaras and shawls. Instead of fragrance there will be a stench; instead of a sash, a rope; instead of well-dressed hair, baldness: instead of fine clothing, sackcloth; instead of beauty, branding."*
>
> —*Isaiah 3:16–24, NIV*

Now, you know you don't want to be walking around smelling bad with bald heads, no jewelry, and wearing sackcloth. I know I don't. So, please be humble, not haughty.

Let's pray…

Be a blessing!

PS- What I said about the cat's meow, the rat, the trap, and the cheese was an observation, not a criticism. Smile, please.

14

Duct Tape: Guarding Our Tongues

Duct tape (sometimes called duck tape) is always good to have in an emergency. It is a vinyl, fabric-reinforced, multi-purpose pressure-sensitive tape with a soft and tacky pressure sensitive adhesive. Duct tape helps prevents glass from shattering and water from leaking. We can also duct tape ourselves in place. We can duct tape ourselves to a large tree or duct tape our family leg to leg so we don't lose one another. It's even been suggested using duct tape to make a glider to fly above the hurricane or duct tape yourself to the side of a bus to get out of town.

Pastors' wives need duct tape in our success kit. I'm not suggesting we go through drastic measures to tape ourselves to the side of a bus. But duct tape can be useful in helping to guard our tongues. After all, if duct tape can give us a free bus ride, why can't it help our tongues? Let's talk about that in this chapter. Not free rides, our tongues.

You Can't Unscramble An Egg

Remember: if you speak in haste, apologize in haste, too.

—Old Codger Wisdom

Lord, I have been so good today. I haven't raised my voice to anyone. I haven't called anyone rude names. I haven't yelled and screamed, ranted and raved at anyone. I haven't even broken anything or hurt anybody. But Lord, I'm getting out of bed in about five minutes, and I will probably need your help then. Amen.

—*Quoted by Dorothy Patterson in* A Handbook for Ministers' Wives, *18.*

Sisters, would your sugar be a little sweeter if you could say a few choice words to a few choice people, and you were able to take back what you said? I asked because pastors' wives have a plethora of reasons for verbally tanning a few hides. This book barely scratches the surface in disclosing some of the supersized atrocities that make us battle-weary. One big problem: "loose lips sink ships." Words are powerful and they either hurt or heal. Once you've said something you can't take it back. Unscrambling words is like trying to unscramble eggs. You can't un-ring a bell either.

I know you can't unscramble eggs or un-ring bells because I'm a repeat offender at trying. God has given me the gift of gab, and I tend not to mince words. As sure as eggs are eggs, I've gibberishly said things I shouldn't have. Then I have to turn flips trying to take my words back. I think this is called "hoof and mouth disease." But once it's said, it's said. Trying to "unsay" it is futile.

For some reason I don't think I'm the only one who has ended up with eggs on my face because I disengaged my brain before I engaged my tongue. Yes, I see you. Thanks for being honest. May we talk about our tongues for a few moments?

Deadly Poison

James describes our tongues as deadly poison. He tells us they must be tamed if they are to be God honoring:

> *For every kind of beast and bird, of reptile and creature of the sea, is tamed and has been tamed by mankind. But no one can tame the tongue. It is restless and evil, full of deadly poison. Sometimes it praises our Lord and Father, and sometimes it curses those who have been made in the image of God. And so blessing and cursing come pouring out of the same mouth. Surely, my brothers and sisters, this is not right! Does a spring of water bubble out with both fresh water and bitter water? Does a fig tree produce olives, or a grapevine produce figs? No, and you can't draw fresh water from a salty spring.*
>
> —*James 3:7, NLT*

God is so good. He prompted Deborah Smith Pegues to write a book about taming our tongues titled, *30 Days to Taming Your Tongue: What You Say (and Don't Say) Will Improve Your Relationships.*

In the book Ms. Pegues refers to thirty kinds of tongues—one to be tamed each day. I recently found out that Ms. Pegues also wrote a workbook, so those of us who suffer from "disengaged" tongues can purchase the entire package.

As always, our best source is the Word of God. The Bible gives us much advice about our speech habits. Here are a few Scriptures to meditate on that I find helpful in controlling my runaway tongue:

> *There is an appointed time for everything. And there is a time for every event under heaven—a time to be silent and a time to speak.*
>
> —*Ecclesiastes 3:1, 7b (NASB95)*

Pleasant words are a honeycomb, sweet to the soul and healing to the bones.

—PROVERBS 16:24 (NASB95)

The mouth of the righteous is a fountain of life. But the mouth of the wicked conceals violence.

—PROVERBS 10:11 (NASB95)

A soothing tongue is a tree of life, but perversion in it crushes the spirit.

— PROVERBS 15:4 (NASB95)

Death and life are in the power of the tongue, and those who love it will eat its fruit.

—PROVERBS 18:21 (NASB95)

Like apples of gold in settings of silver is a word spoken in right circumstances.

— PROVERBS 25:11 (NASB95)

For the mouth speaks out of that which fills the heart. The good man brings out of his good treasure what is good; and the evil man brings out of his evil treasure what is evil. But I tell you that every careless word that people speak, they shall give an accounting for it in the day of judgment. For by your words you will be justified, and by your words you will be condemned.

—MATTHEW 12:34B–35 (NASB95)

A servant of the Lord must not quarrel but must be kind to everyone, be able to teach, and be patient with difficult people. Gently instruct those who oppose the truth. Perhaps God will change those people's hearts, and they will learn the truth. Then they will come to their senses and escape from the devil's trap. For they have been held captive by him to do whatever he wants.

—*2 Timothy 2:24–26 (NLT)*

Speaking the Truth in Love

The truth is incontrovertible. Malice may attack it and ignorance may deride it, but in the end, there it is.

—*Winston Churchill*

Truth is not beautiful, neither is it ugly. Why should it be either? Truth is truth.

—*Owen C. Middleton*

The great enemy of the truth is very often not the lie—deliberate, contrived and dishonest; but the myth—persistent, persuasive and unrealistic.

—*John F. Kennedy*

Tact is the art of making a point without making an enemy.

—*Isaac Newton*

Pastors' wives have to be truthful, but tactful. It's not what we say; it's how we say it. When we use tact we can speak the truth in love. I believe when Earl preached a message, "Hung By The Tongue," he had me in mind. I don't know how many times I've been hung because of my lack of tact. I said the right thing but it came out the wrong way. Some of my barb wires may be cultural earmarks as I'm from Philadelphia, Pennsylvania living in Texas. In Philly we just come out and say it without beating around the bush. The majority of Southerners I know, including Earl, use a gentler approach than some of my Northeastern counterparts. My parents were both from the South, and I've lived in Texas longer than I've lived in Philly. Still, like Ragu, it's in me. That's no excuse.

You may not be from the Northeast, but I may not be myself. Therefore, let me take another moment and tell you no matter how good you look on the outside, being tackless damages your witness to the world: "Like a gold ring in a pig's snout is a beautiful woman who shows no discretion." (Proverbs 11:22. NIV) If this is your testimony, sister, ask God to set a trap over your mouth. He'll do it.

If you can't remember any of the aforementioned Scriptures, before you speak **THINK**, using this acronym:

Is it **T**rue?

Is it **He**lpful?

Is it **I**nspiring?

Is it **N**ecessary?

Is it **K**ind?

If not, keep it to yourself!

A word of caution: If your husband bombed during the sermon, don't tactfully criticize him on the way home from church, even if he told too much of your business in the message. Believe me, he's beating himself up all ready. We ministers personally know the feeling. It is none too pleasant. I'm just being real.

Can I Get a Bow Wow?

There is no evidence that the tongue is connected to the brain.

— *Frank Tyger*

I don't at all like knowing what people say of me behind my back; it makes me far too conceited.

—Oscar Wilde

Who gossips with you will gossip of you.

—*Irish Saying*

Another way we have to guard our tongue is to refrain from gossiping. I titled this section, "Can I Get A Bow Wow?" because gossiping is like living a dog's life. What does that have to do with being a pastor's wife? Plenty. The Bible tells us in Philippians 3:2 to beware of dogs. It may startle you to find out that the Bible may be talking about us. 1 Corinthians 15:33 says, "Do not be deceived. Bad company corrupts good morals." This is definitely true when it comes to gossip.

Bob Gass explains what living a dog's life looks like in his devotional about Mandy, his next-door neighbor's dog who loved Friday's because it was the day Mr. Gass put the garbage out. Mandy would rip open the garbage that held all of the "family secrets" and spread it all over the street, so Gass had to go up and down the street to pick up the garbage. He warned us to beware of dogs that spread garbage and admonished us not to be those that did. —*Gass, 255*

Sisters, if we are to ensure we are not classified as dogs, we, too, must not mess with other folks' garbage and stop it if we are now doing so. We have more than enough of our own garbage to worry about.

In my neighborhood, trash day is on Tuesday and Friday. Earl and I have lived in our home a long time, and do you know what I found? It doesn't matter how much trash we put out on Tuesday, we still have some more to put out on Friday. We may not see each other's trash, but we all have it. Just because someone is close to us, and the Mandy's of the world bring that mess to us, we can reject it in the name of Jesus.

And please don't fall into the devil's snare of being contaminated by "religious gossip." There is a big difference between honest concern and religious gossip. Religious gossip is pretending to be concerned, but your real motivation has malicious intent. Proverbs 17:9 tells us

"He who covers a transgression seeks love, he who repeats a matter separates friends."

A story is told of three pastors who went on a retreat to confess their sins to one another and pray for deliverance. The first pastor admitted to being an alcoholic. The second pastor confessed to being a gambler. The third pastor confided that he was a gossiper, and couldn't wait to get home to tell all of the other two pastors' business.

Don't let this be said of you, sisters...be an example in word and deed. The law of witnesses is established in Deuteronomy 19:15: "One witness shall not rise against a man concerning any iniquity or any sin that he commits; by the mouth of two or three witnesses the matter shall be established." Ephesians 4:29 instructs us to let no corrupt communication proceed from our mouths. So don't get caught in the rumor mill—gossiping and listening to dirt about others. When the balloon goes up, those who talk about others will talk about you, too.

While we're at it, let's also stay out of the hen's house.

Stay Out of the Hen's House

> *Learn from the mistakes of others. You can't live long enough to make all of the mistakes yourself.*
>
> —*Anonymous*

Sometime ago I bought a figurine of three monkeys. Under each monkey was a short saying: "See no evil, hear no evil, say no evil." That's good advice. Let's look at a culprit that can keep us in the henhouse if we don't guard out tongues: lying.

Lying

> *A half truth is a whole lie.*
>
> —*Yiddish Proverb*

Much of what we don't call a lie is a lie. The May 2011 issue of *Christianity Today* featured an article by Sarah Sumner titled *Seven Levels of Lying*. According to Ms. Sumner, "we lie more than we think. And that's just the problem. Every person on the planet is at times an Oscar-winning liar."

In the article, Ms. Sumners refers to a book by J. Budziszewski, author of *What We Can't Not Know* in which she mentions "the seven degrees of descent." Ms. Sumners calls them the seven levels of lying. They range from lying to self-protect to developing your lying technique, and seeing it as your duty to lie.—*christianitytoday.org*.

Acts 5: 1–11 gives an example of a woman who had a well-developed lying technique. Her name is Sapphira, and she was married to a man named Ananias. The Bible doesn't say that Ananias was a pastor, but he was her husband. Even so, Sapphira knew that she had no right to lie just because her husband lied.

Ananias and Sapphira sold some property and brought part of the money to the apostles. With mutual consent they kept the rest, but claimed it was the full amount. Ananias and Sapphira didn't have to lie because it was their property, and they could have given any amount they wanted to, but they chose to lie.

The Holy Spirit conveyed to Peter that Ananias and Sapphira had lied. Peter told Ananias what he had done and that he had not lied to men but to God. As soon as Ananias heard these words he fell to the floor and died. About three hours later Sapphira came in (probably switching), and Peter confronted her by asking her if she and her husband sold their land for the price they told the apostles. Sapphira answered yes. Peter asked her how could she conspire with Ananias to lie to God, and, instantly, she fell to the floor and died.

You may be a liar and not know it—even though your technique is not as developed as Sapphira's. Ms. Sumners says in her article, if you tell your husband you are going to meet him at a certain time and show up late, you've lied. I've done that more times than I can count. If you are like me and know you have to improve in this area and other areas, repent and ask for God's forgiveness. Jesus told us that Satan is the father of lies, and you certainly don't want to give others the false notion that you're his daughter (John 8:44). You are a child of the Most High God. God told us in 1 John 1:9 if we confess our sin He'll forgive us. We will talk more about repentance and forgiveness later.

Integrity

The integrity of the upright will guide them, But the perversity of the unfaithful will destroy them.

—*Proverbs 11:3*

In matters of style, swim with the current; in matters of principle, stand like a rock.

—*Thomas Jefferson*

There can be no happiness if the things we believe in are different than the things we do.

—*Freya Stark*

It is incumbent upon pastors' wives to be women of integrity. Our character must match our reputation. God has honored us with the privilege of living lives that demonstrate His moral character to a watching world. Lest we get twisted, integrity is not just for pastors' wives, it is for everyone reading this book. Linda Dillow comments:

We don't often hear the word integrity. It seems like something from George Washington and John Adam's era. But integrity is a word of deep meaning: a biblical word. Integrity is defined as the quality of being honest and upright in character."

—*Dillow, 69*

Integrity is built through consistency, transparency, and a controlled tongue. When you are a person of integrity you don't have to say "I swear" every time you say something. Your word should be your bond. In the distant past contracts were sealed with a handshake. Now we need a lawyer, notary, and ten to twenty witnesses. That's because integrity is a dying art. Don't let this be said about you.

Avoid using God's name to make an oath, and don't make commitments lightly. Let your yea by yea, and your nay be nay. Listen to what Jesus said in Matthew 5:33–37:

> *Again you have heard that it was said to those of old, "You shall not swear falsely, but shall perform your oaths to the Lord. But I say to you, do not swear at all: neither by heaven, for it is God's throne; nor by the earth, for it is His footstool; nor by Jerusalem, for it is the city of the great king. Nor shall you swear by your head, because you cannot make one hair white or black, but let your 'Yes' be 'Yes,' and your 'No,' 'No.' for whatever is more than these is from the evil one.*

Start Declaring

Sisters, on the whole, in this chapter we've talked about several ways our unruly tongues can bring forth bitter water that dishonors God. I suppose we all are guilty in one form or another, though I didn't want you to leave this chapter ruminating about Sapphira's lying lips. You can leave this chapter using your tamed tongue to bring forth sweet water that honors God. Specifically, declaring is sweet water, so you can start declaring right now. Job 22:28 tells us: "You will also declare a thing, and it will be established for you; so light will shine on your ways."

I want light to shine on your ways, sisters. Thus, I declare what God has ordained for you:

> I declare that you will know the height, depth, and breath of the love that God has for you.
>
> I declare that showers of blessings will rain upon you, overtake you, and chase you down the street.
>
> I declare that you will have joy in proportion to your sorrow.

I declare that you are the head and not the tail.

I declare that you will go over and not go under.

I declare that you walk in abundance, prosperity, peace, and joy.

I declare that you have love, power, and a sound mind.

I declare that you are healed, delivered, and set free.

Not tomorrow, but today!

Let's Pray…

Be a blessing!

15

Cold Weather Gear: Dress Codes

Hypothermia is a killer. It is a condition in which core temperature drops below the required temperature for normal metabolism and body functions, which is defined as 35.0 °C (95.0 °F). If exposed to cold and the internal mechanisms are unable to replenish the heat that is being lost, a drop in core temperature occurs. As body temperature decreases, characteristic symptoms occur such as shivering and mental confusion. We can't do anything about the weather, except be prepared with the appropriate clothing and appropriate gear. In this chapter we will talk about appropriate attire for first ladies—for any kind of weather.

Shopping is a woman thing. It's a contact sport like football. Women enjoy the scrimmage, the noisy crowds, the danger of being trampled to death, and the ecstasy of the purchase.

—Erma Bombeck

Buying something on sale is a very special feeling. In fact, the less I pay for something, the more it is worth to me. I have a dress that I paid so little for that I am afraid to wear it. I could spill something on it, and then how would I replace it for that amount of money?

—RITA RUDNER

Fashion can be bought. Style one must possess.

—EDNA WOOLMAN CHASE

Pastor Valetta Shaw preached a message titled, "It's Personal." In her message, Pastor Shaw talked about the passion of Christ and told us that our response to His passion was personal. We each had to make a decision about what Christ's agony, crucifixion, and resurrection meant to us—nobody else could do it for us.

Sisters, it is almost sacrilege to discuss the way we dress in the same chapter as making a decision for Christ. The only reason I dare to do so is because the way we dress is so personal. If three of us decide to go camping in the wilderness together, it's unlikely we will dress the same way; if we did, two of us would want to go home and change, for we are not a choir—right?

Still, just as we need to dress appropriately to survive in the wilderness, we need to wear the proper attire if we are to be successful as first ladies. I'm aware that you may not agree with 10 percent of what I write. Please do with this chapter as Earl always reminds us when we hear someone preach: shovel out that which you want to throw away and rake in that which you want to keep. I don't want to hear any shovels—okay?

Modest Dress

Don't be concerned about the outward beauty of fancy hairstyles, expensive jewelry, or beautiful clothes. You should clothe

> *yourselves instead with the beauty that comes from within, the unfading beauty of a gentle and quiet spirit, which is so precious to God. This is how the holy women of old made themselves beautiful. They trusted God and accepted the authority of their husbands.*
>
> —1 PETER 3:3–5 (NLT)

For starters, can someone tell me where the modest dress department is?

I love shopping, but haven't found it yet. I'm also finding out day by day that modest dress is apparently relative. Just as what grandma wore may not work today, what appeals to a senior or middle-aged pastor's wife does not necessarily work for a young pastor's wife. Some churches have contemporary and traditional services. So, what's appropriate?

You and I may not come to a consensus on taste and style, but can we agree that a pastor's wife should dress as a holy example to all women of the church, young and old? Proverbs 31:25 tells us that we are clothed in strength and honor.

The Short, Low, and Tight of It

Now how short is too short? It depends on what you want folk to see, sisters. If you don't want them to see your posterity, don't show it. Enough said.

And how low is too low? Some of you who are my age remember the limbo dance. The aim was to go under the limbo stick. They kept lowering it each time you were successful, until you were unable to go under the stick. But the cry was, "How low can you go?" This seems to be the cry in the church nowadays. You see all kinds of low, particularly low-cut tops. Folk want to show everything God gave them, it seems. Regardless of how well endowed you are, you do not need to show all of your cleavage when you come to the church house. If you wear a nice top, all will still know that you are well endowed or not so well endowed.

How Tight Is Too Tight?

Some folk wear their clothes so tight they have to walk like penguins. Oh, I hope that's not you, sisters. I think as a pastor's wife, your rule of thumb should be simple:

Wear clothes that fit you well, unless you are trying out for a part as the Jimmy Dean sausage lady. You know what I mean. If you put it on, and it doesn't fall down naturally, it's too tight. Don't try to pull on it, it's just too tight. Put it back in the closet until you lose weight. If you know you aren't going to lose weight, give it away.

By the way, I wear size ten. Does anyone have a size ten that you know you'll never wear again? I'll make you a bargain. I have some size eights that have seen their better days on me. Don't think I'm not trying to squeeze myself into them, either. However, I need to let bygones be bygones.

Arms in or arms out? Oh, I know this is personal, and you have to decide. Some pastors' wives believe they shouldn't wear dresses to church with their arms out. I used to think this way, but it's hot here in Texas. I don't wear sleeveless dresses on Sunday morning because it would send some of our members into a tailspin. You may not have any objections to wearing dresses with your arms out on Sunday. Whatever the case, I think we can at least set some standards. What do your arms look like? Are they trim or flabby and wrinkled? Did you shave under your arms, or is that a beard I see? What does your husband say about the matter? If the negatives outweigh the positives you may opt to settle for a nice short-sleeve top.

What about pants? Should a pastor's wife wear pants to church? That too is a personal decision. If you are comfy, and your husband is not opposed to you wearing them to church, wear them. I've seen some sisters come to church in appropriate pantsuits and some that were inappropriate. We don't want to be in the inappropriate group. If you are going to wear pants, please, loosen up. No one wants to see the cellulite in the pastor's wife's thighs. Or worst yet, dimples in her backside.

Before I leave this section, it's befitting to discuss congregational preferences. Some members don't think a pastor's wife should wear makeup or jewelry, color her hair, or do anything to beautify her appearance. While I feel we need to consider the congregation, I don't think it's sinful to ignore legalistic folk who attempt to put us in bondage because they are not free.

I ran into this situation when I was a recurring guest speaker at a church whose denomination was different than mine. I started out wearing makeup and jewelry, but it was obvious they had a problem with it. Well, I had a problem with them, and I was determined to wear both. Then I read in 1 Corinthians 8:13, "Therefore, if food makes my brother stumble, I will never again eat meat, lest I make my brother stumble," so I stopped wearing jewelry and makeup when I ministered there. I would fix myself up as soon as I left the church because I personally agree with Robert W. Schambach—"even an old barn needs a little paint sometime." No, I'm not calling myself old!

You may also want to consider praying for wisdom before wearing expensive, extravagant clothes if God has called your husband to pastor a poor struggling congregation. No need to hide them in your closet, just use wisdom. You may find the article by Linda Ozirney, *Fashions for the Pastor's Wife* helpful.—*torchleader.com.*

Hats

Another personal choice. Many pastors' wives are known for their hats. Visit any national convention and see the hat parade. Do you have to wear a hat just because it's popular to wear one? Absolutely not.

I like hats, have lots of them, and wear one when I feel like having a hat day. If you know of a store that sells nice, inexpensive hats please let me know. Don't stop at hats; tell me where I can find some nice inexpensive shoes and clothes, too. This is one secret you don't have to keep to yourself. In case you are interested, I found a great website: firstladyexchange.com. You can shop and sell "sanctified seconds"—hats, clothing, and accessories.

His Clothes

I know the way your husband dresses is personal. This doesn't have to stop you from shopping for him periodically to enhance his wardrobe. Help him whether or not he asks for it. If he doesn't seem to appreciate it, don't get an attitude. You don't want him to go out there with uncoordinated clothes, do you? If your answer is yes, shame on you.

Earl dresses nice and has good taste in clothes, but I've had to help him upgrade his wardrobe by adding colors. His favorite color is brown, and most of his clothes are in the brown family. While he looks good in them, I love colors, my favorite being blue. Therefore, I convinced him to add soft shades of blue to his wardrobe, then purple, and other light colors. I haven't convinced him that he'll look good in a red suit yet, and other than a shirt, yellow is still out of the range for him.

Incidentally, sisters, a whole lot of men are color blind. Just ask them to look at something purple or burgundy and tell you what color it is. Some can't even distinguish black from brown from navy blue, so let's help them out. Earl's not too bad, but I've helped him ward off disaster by matching the wrong colors. I'm glad I did; folk wouldn't talk about him, they'd talk about me. How could she? And there's something in it for us, too when our husbands match—it'll make us look better when we are walking with them. No one wants to be walking beside a big red and green Coke can! You may also want to color code your outfit with your husband occasionally if he doesn't object too much. It lets everyone know who he came with and who he's going home with.

As we bring this chapter to a close, lest you take what I said as condemnation for the way you desire to dress, let me clear the air to say this: when it gets down to the meat of it, what you wear is between God and you. If God tells you it is okay for you, then it is okay for you. You don't need anyone to validate what God said is right for you.

Our outer woman is not really something we should focus all of our attention on anyway. We are more than our outer woman. In fact, the real we are inside looking out of our eyes. God just gave us our body so we could be legal on Earth. I heard Paul say in 2 Corinthians 4:16, although the outer man perishes, the inner man is being renewed day by day.

There are two sets of clothing we all must have in our wardrobe regardless of personal preference: the armor of God referenced in Ephesians 6 and the garment of praise described in Isaiah 61:3. Keep your armor on at all times; as first ladies we have to always be dressed and ready for service. If you are going through trials and tests, wrap yourself securely in your garment of praise. It will hold you better than ten girdles.

For ministers: Preach to women as though they are already where they need to be. In other words, preach the love of God. Let them know who they are and how much God loves them, and how they can be new creatures in Christ Jesus (2 Corinthians 5:17). Too many preachers "preach the clothesline," and spend entirely too much time talking about hemlines (the way folk dress), necklines (how low cut the blouses are), and curvelines (how short and tight the skirts are). Their hope, of course, is that people would get their lives in order so God could use them and bless them.

We can't deny that this type of preaching and teaching is needed, but it should not be our focus. I wore inappropriate revealing garments, but God cleaned me up and changed my clothesline; He can do the same for other sisters. If there is a need to take someone aside and talk to them about modest attire, do it in love. Make sure you are not asking someone to do what you are not doing yourselves.

Let's pray…

Be a blessing!

16

Medication: Cheerfulness

It is always good to have medicine in your survival kit. There are all kinds of medicine: pain relief, topical applications, allergic reaction drugs, antibiotics, cough suppressants, decongestants, skin care. In this chapter we will discuss God's drug for pain relief: a cheerful heart. No pastor's wife can afford to leave home without it in her success kit.

Take Three Times a Day Before Meals

> *Too often believers give the impression that the Christian experience is a cheerless journey of harsh self-discipline that must be painfully endured until the heavenly rewards are finally realized.*
>
> —*Osbeck, July 2*

Wake up with a smile and go after life...Live it, enjoy it, taste it, smell it, feel it.

—JOE SNAPP

Life is too short not be happy and too long not to do well.

—BRYAN DODGE

A happy person is not a person in a certain set of circumstances, but rather a person with a certain set of attitudes.

—HUGH DOWNS

Okay, sisters, are you truly a happy person? Put another way, how cheerful is your heart? Solomon, the wisest man who ever lived, said, "A cheerful heart is good medicine, but a crushed spirit dries up the bones" (Proverbs 17:22, NIV). Doctors have known for ages that a cheerful person is a healthier person. This is definitely good news when we think of the amount of money many of us pay for prescriptions.

According to the Kaiser Foundation, "In 2007, 90 percent of seniors and 58 percent of non-elderly adults rely on a prescription medicine on a regular basis.... Furthermore, the drug industry's profit margins have raised considerable attention. Pharmaceutical manufacturing was the most profitable industry in the U.S. from 1995 to 2002, and in 2008 it ranked third with profits after taxes of about 19 percent." —Kaiser EDU.org, *Prescription Drug Costs, Calculations Using National Health Expenditures Data from Centers for Medicare and Medicaid Services*

How would you like to make 19 percent profit on your investment? Add this figure to the amount of money we pay to pharmacies, and the statistic becomes even more staggering. By the way, did you ever check out the list of side effects? Everything from ingrown toenails to death. Many of our doctors don't have any problem reaching behind their desk and loading us up with a handful of "free" samples, even before we have an opportunity to fully explain what our problem is. It's easy to get our prescriptions filled since there's a Walgreens and CVS on almost every corner. In the meantime, we remain as sick as ever, and our hearts are anything but cheerful. It's hard to be cheerful when you are sick and broke.

Cheerful Heart Gauge

By perseverance the snail reached the Ark.
—Charles H. Spurgeon

One gauge of a cheerful heart is having a good sense of humor and being generous with your laughter and smiles. Let me ask it this way: has anyone ever told you to smile? I've been told that many times. I guess when I have a non-smiling face on I look like a mule or something, because frequently someone will ask, "Are you having a good day?" That tells me that I have to increase my medication.

There is some debate about how many muscles it takes to smile versus frown. I don't know and frankly, it isn't something that I will spend a lot of time researching. I do know that a smile looks better than a frown. Let me see the hands of those of us who are in the teaching and preaching ministry who teach or preach to folk who look like they have gas or are sucking on a lemon. I know we can't be that bad.

A No Fail Prescription

My sisters, here is a no fail cheerful heart prescription you can take three times a day that is guaranteed to give you cheer 365 days of the year. It won't cost you a dime and you can't overdose on it, so take it more often than that if you need to. I'm not asking you to throw your doctor-prescribed medicine down the drain; I'm not qualified to do that nor would I suggest you stop taking it without your doctor's consent. The cheerful heart prescription is not intended to diagnose, prevent, or cure any disease. I'm just asking you to take it at least three times a day for a merrier you:

- *Start each day off with joy no matter how you feel.* Affirm Psalm 118:24, "This is the day that the Lord has made, I shall rejoice and be glad in it" over yourself before you get out of bed. Determine that you will not let anyone or anything defraud you of your joy. Joyce Meyer reminds us that joy is not a giddy high feeling; it is calm assurance knowing that God is with us and that He will take care of us.

  Bishop Dr. Victor Couzens, preached to our congregation from this text and told us that rejoice means to regain the joy that you once had. He reminded us that God made the day just for us. It may have ups and it may have downs but it is custom ordered. God is sovereign and could have done things a lot differently than He did for us today, but He didn't. We can rejoice because whatever God made, He can handle. The Apostle Paul was in prison but he still rejoiced. He was so joyful that shared his joy with the church at Philippi. Paul told them: "Rejoice in the Lord always, and again I say rejoice" (Philippians 4:4).
- *Read and sing psalms of praise.* Ephesians 5:19 tells us to speak to one another in psalms and hymns and spiritual songs, singing and making melody in our hearts to the Lord. Psalm 150:6 sums it up: "Let everything that has breath praise the Lord."
- *Don't take yourself too seriously.* Learn to laugh at yourself. We've all done things we would consider numskulled, so there's no need to try to cover it up with an attitude. Just call it what it is, laugh about it, and have fun with yourself. I have lots to laugh about. Every time I remember Earl's and my first trip to Hawaii as husband and wife it makes me laugh. I wanted to enjoy the beauty of the ocean and take photos, but I had to go down slippery rocks first. Earl was already on the beach, and I sure wasn't going to be outdone. Well, as I was going down the rocks it started to rain. I knew the rocks were slippery, but I didn't want my hair to get wet, so I tried to put my umbrella up. Needless to say, it didn't work. Earl said that all he saw was me slipping down the rocks; he knew I had hurt myself—but God takes care of babies and me. It was still humiliating. Those who witnessed my downfall probably memorialized me as the silly lady who had an umbrella on a cliff.

Since I survived, I can also laugh at what I did on our trip to Mexico. I'm adventuresome and have a tendency to get myself into trouble. Earl has to bail me out. Against his better judgment, he and I went into a cave with water. We were told the water had a strong current. At first, Earl didn't want to go in, but I did because a few folk went into the water. So Earl went in, and I went in after him. They gave us a tube, and as soon as I went in, I started drifting toward the deep end. I thought I was going to drown, but, thank God, Earl came to the rescue again.

I have a long list of other blockheaded things I've done that God has brought me out of, and I could laugh until Jesus comes. You have "nuttier than a fruitcake" things that God has brought you out of too. So laugh at yourself.

- *Don't ridicule others.* It's okay to laugh at yourself, but it isn't okay to ridicule others. And it's not okay to make others the brunt of your jokes. Don't say something like, "She can take it." Can you take it if someone made ceaseless wisecracks about you? Most likely, no—so do unto others as you have them do unto you.
- *Memorize some good clean jokes.* Hordes of them are out there. You don't know any? Let me share a couple with you. They both involve males so we can laugh at their expense.

At Sunday school they were teaching how God created everything, including human beings. Little Johnny seemed especially intent when they told him how Eve was created out of one of Adam's ribs. Later in the week his mother noticed him lying down as though he were ill, and said, "Johnny what is the matter?" Little Johnny responded, "I have a pain in my side. I think I'm going to have a wife."

—Author Unknown, Christian-Jokes.org

The Sunday school teacher told the class about Lot being told to take his wife and flee out of the city. "Lot got away, but his wife disobeyed divine orders by looking back and was turned into a pillar of salt," the teacher explained. One little boy asked, "What happened to the flea?"

—Author Unknown, Christian Jokes.net

If these didn't make you laugh, here are some references that can help jump-start your funny bone:

A hilarious book that will have you rolling on the floor is, *Gettin' Old Ain't for Wimps* (although I still don't know what my sister-in-love Beverly had in mind when she gave it to me). It is a compilation of humorous stories and words of inspiration. In the book, author Karen O'Connor discusses aches and pains, and on page sixty to sixty-one, she gives a prescription for them: laughter. I believe the prayer she ended her prescription with is one that would do us all well to pray.

Another book I think you'll enjoy is *Mama Get the Hammer! There's a Fly on Papa's head!* Barbara Johnson writes a chapter, "Life Is a Great Big Canvas" in which she lists six realities we cannot change. You may also enjoy, Lindsey O'Connor's *If Mama Ain't Happy, Ain't Nobody Happy!*

- *Think yourself happy.* If you don't want to buy books, do like Paul, think yourself happy. The joy of the Lord is your strength (Nehemiah 8:10). The way to do this is to make merry in your heart (Psalm 104:33–34). I don't know how many of you have experienced uncontrollable laughter during worship service, but I did once, and it was wonderful. I was so caught up in enjoying the Lord that I started laughing and couldn't stop. Prior to this I had heard about folk who did it, but I didn't believe it. It's true.

If you are not comfortable laughing until you hurt in church, you can still tickle yourself pink. All you have to do is to start thinking about the goodness of Jesus. I don't know about you, but when I think of the goodness of Jesus I want to throw myself a merry heart party. In fact, when I think of the goodness of Jesus and all He's done for me, I could dance, dance, dance, dance, dance all night.

I know I'm not by myself; at least four of you feel like dancing too. So let's do a sister thing. On the count of three, think about one thing Jesus has done for you today that nobody else could do; smile about it; then kick up those heels, and dance, dance, dance, dance, dance… Nobody's mad but the devil, and we don't need his seal of approval!

Let's Pray…

Be a blessing!

17

Backpacks: Financial Management

Backpacks are a good way to carry your gear. When you backpack, it is like carrying your home on your back. Normally, a backpack will carry food, water, first-aid kit, poncho, flashlight, and many other items. So you have to ensure that your backpack is sturdy and can withstand the test of time. Our finances must be sturdy also if we are to be successful pastors' wives.

Whether a man winds up with a nest egg, or a goose egg, depends a lot on the kind of chick he marries.

—Old Codger Wisdom

A chicken doesn't stop scratching just because worms are scarce.

—Grandma Axiom

A Solid Financial Foundation

Tell me what you think about money, and I will tell you what you think about God, for these two are closely related. A man's heart is closer to his wallet than anything else.

—*Billy Graham*

Sisters, financial indiscretion can sabotage your life. Did you know, with the exception of love, Jesus talked about money more than any other subject? For instance, He warned us in Matthew 6:24 that we cannot serve God and money. Jesus asked in Matthew 16:26, "What profit is to a man if he gains the whole world and loses his own soul?" Why did Jesus emphasize money so much? He knew how easy it was for us to be tempted to become slaves to our money and the things it can buy.

If financial indiscretion can sabotage our lives, it stands to reason that it can also sabotage our marriages. In fact, the number one cause of conflict in marriage is finances. It's improbable that most of us reading this book were born with silver spoons in our mouths, have a tree that grows money, or find pennies from heaven every time it rains. We must have a solid financial foundation. Incorporating fundamental principles of financial management into our marriage is imperative if we are to survive in today's economy and manage our money in a way that pleases God.

T. D. Jakes discusses the importance of financial management in his book, *Reposition Yourself*. Bishop Jakes tells us that we each have three voices within our head that speak to us. One voice is concerned about our addiction to apathy regarding our finances. This apathetic attitude has ruined us financially, resulting in lost business opportunities, poor credit, and other financial maladies—p 25.

In my experience, a solid financial foundation must be built on the following fundamental principles to be effective:

Budgeting

Cast but a glance at riches, and they are gone, for they will surely sprout wings and fly off to the sky like an eagle.

—PROVERBS 23:5

"My doctor gave me six months to live, but when I couldn't pay the bill, he gave me six months more."

—WALTER MATTHAU

You have to budget, sisters.

I know this from personal experience. My financial situation got out of control, and I found myself living beyond my means: buying what I wanted, not what I could afford. Before long, I had a problem with creditors, my wages were levied, and my home was almost foreclosed. I'm so thankful that God stepped in and rescued me and taught me how to be a better steward of His resources by learning to budget. Don't' panic Culverhouse, Inc. family; this was long before Earl and I met!

Webster's defines a budget as "a plan or schedule adjusting expenses during a certain period to the estimated or fixed income for that period." I learned when it comes to budgeting and spending, one simple rule will do: if you don't have it, don't spend it. You want your husband to minister as freely as possible. Debt ties him down. I know you like to look good, but Neiman Marcus may not be the place for you to shop at this season of your life. It might be Wal-Mart, and there's nothing wrong with that; a few accessories will go a long way. Remarkably, the eighty-inch-screen TV may not be the right purchase now.

Keep in mind that you are not a white knight; you can stop saying, "Charge," and put yourself on auto-pilot as you reach into your handbag and bring out the plastic. It's unreal how quickly you can find yourself surrounded by creditors. In case you don't know these folk, they are the ones who can own you if you are undisciplined and prone to making financial mistakes. Be real—it's embarrassing to have a 350 credit score out of a possible 850.

Not only that, it's embarrassing to get in the check-out line and be told that the bank didn't approve your credit-related purchase because you've gone over your limit. I've been there and I know what I'm talking about. If you are over your limit and desperately want to charge another outfit, let me shoot straight as an arrow with you and save you the embarrassment. Name it and claim it, and call it and haul it, and grab it and sack it won't reverse the bank's decision. Binding your credit card bill doesn't work either. Until you make a payment you still owe the piper. After all, you did dance to the music, didn't you? Instead of sulking, look in your closet and find one of the outfits you still haven't worn. You know the ones I'm talking about: those you purchased a month ago because the price was right, and the store now has them on sale for 70 percent less than you paid for them. Don't feel bad, I have some too.

Another question: Outside of applying for more credit, when is the last time you checked your credit report? You don't need surprises in this area—especially like finding out you've become a victim of identity theft. If you aren't already doing so, get into the habit of checking your credit report at least annually. By law you are entitled to receive a free copy of your personal credit report every twelve months. The biggest three credit reporting companies—Experian, Equifax, and TransUnion—have created a website where you can request your report.—*www.annualcreditreport.com, Official Site to Help Consumers Obtain Their Free Credit Report*

Financial Weight Management

In addition to budgeting, it is helpful to know if you are financially overweight. Ellie Kay, author of *The Debt Diet*, gives advice on how you can know if you are financially overweight. This is a must read if you really want to lose unwanted debt pounds. Two tale-tell signs are using credit card cash advances to pay for living expenses and using and depending on overtime to meet the month's expenses.

Debt vs. Investment

There is a difference between debt and investment. Investments build financial security; debts take it away.

If you are in debt, Crown Financial Ministries gives you five basic steps you can follow to become debt free and stay that way: 1) transfer ownership of all of your possessions to God; willingly surrendering your will to His will, 2) give God His part by tithing off of your gross income, 3) allow no more debt until everything has been paid off; this includes using credit cards to pay for purchases, 4) develop a realistic budget, 5) retire the debt by paying extra on those with the highest interest rate. If interest rates are the same pay on those with the smallest balance.—*crown.org, Crown Financial Ministries, Getting Out of Debt*

Hi Ho Hi Ho Off To Work I Go

Hard work never killed anybody, but why take the chance?

—Edgar Bergen

The only place where success comes before work is in the dictionary.

—Donald Kendall

Some of you may have drained your savings through no fault of your own. The weakened economy and smaller incomes have forced you to make significant lifestyle changes. Others of you may be experiencing unemployment, illness, and other expenses that have left you financially crippled. If you are not working currently outside your home, but are considering it to make ends meet, talk to God and your husband first, for they both are interested in your finances.

Once you get the go ahead abide by God's principles. Everything you do is a mission field. Work unto the Lord vertically (2 Corinthians 5:20), and God will do the work horizontally.

Here are a few tips:

- *Treat your boss with respect; see your job as a ministry or place of sharing.* Ask yourself the question: If I were the owner of this company, would I hire me, knowing my work ethic? If you are slothful you lose your influence. Remember, you are working unto the Lord, not unto your boss. When you get tired of working, having a "take this job and shove it" is not a good witness for the pastor's wife. We don't even want to think about going there.
- *If you didn't buy it, it's not yours.* Leave the paper and pens in the office. You can buy these items at the office supply. They really aren't that expensive. You can save even more money by shopping at the 99 Cents store for these items.
- *Be on time; punctuality is a virtue.* Don't let flextime be an excuse for being late. Just because you are the boss doesn't mean you can stroll in any time you want to. I have to fess up: the virtue of punctuality is still unfolding in me. When I was employed outside the home I used flex-time many times to justify my tardiness. No comments, please.
- *Unpleasant assignments? Don't have heart failure over them.* I've tried that, and that gets you nowhere. Until you drop dead after your heart failure, you are still faced with the project.
- *Go for excellence, not perfection.* You will never be perfect, only Jesus is perfect. Just do the best job you can do.
- *Don't always do something looking for the next promotion.* God knows what you are doing, and He'll reward you. You may be working for company X, but it's all in God's hands. Psalm 75:6 reads: "For exaltation *comes* neither from the east, nor from the west nor from the south. But God is the Judge: He puts down one, and exalts another."

To those of you who are doing your best, but still cannot make ends meet: God knows what you need before you ask (Matthew 6:8). His economy is not like our economy and His mathematics are different than ours. We seem to specialize in division and subtraction, while God majors in multiplication and addition. There's nothing too hard for Him, nothing impossible for Him. Remember how Jesus took five barley loaves and two fish—a small boy's fish sandwich—and fed 5,000 people? On another occasion He fed 4,000. He'll take care of you, too. That's why He told us not to worry (Matthew 6:24–34).

Another passage of Scripture that I find encouraging in times of financial blowout is 2 Chronicles 25:1-9. Earl preached an uplifting message from this text titled, "When Loss is Gain." In the text, Amaziah, King of Judah, paid one hundred talents of silver to hire 100,000 men of valor from Israel to help him fight against Edom. God sent a prophet to tell him not to use these men. Needless to say, the king was disturbed because of the money he spent. But the prophet encouraged him not to be troubled by reminding him that God was able to do much more than this. King Amaziah obeyed God and he came through victorious.

Sisters, God is still able to do much more than this, whatever your this is. Therefore, stay the course if you are in a financial mess. Express quiet hope that things will return to a better normal soon. If you do your part, God will get you out of your financial spaghetti bowl. He specializes in turning ashes into beauty. If He did it for me, He'll do it for you, too!

Miscellaneous Money Matters

Here is an assortment of money matters to build into your solid financial foundation:

- *Tithe.* To tithe is to give God 10 percent of your gross income. I know some people don't believe in tithing, but I do. Therefore, since I have the pen, regardless of how little or how much you make, how little or how much debt you have, please give God His money cheerfully (2 Corinthians 9:7). Don't participate in a Sunday morning holdup (Malachi 3:8-9). That's not becoming for a first lady. After all, everything belongs to God. Job 1:21 tells us we came into this world naked and we are going to leave this world naked. The clothes we're buried with will remain in our caskets, unless grave robbers steal them. Further, you won't need any money in heaven; the streets are even paved with gold.
- *Grace Give.* This is giving in addition to your tithes. Grace giving has no ceiling. When you grace give you become a channel for receiving more of God's blessings. Jesus said in Luke 6:38:

Give, and it will be given to you: good measure, pressed down, shaken together, and running over will be put into your bosom. For with the same measure that you use, it will be measured back to you.

When you don't grace give you are like the Dead Sea. The Dead Sea is a lake in Israel the Jordan River empties into. God blessed Earl and me to travel to Israel and see it. It's lovely to look at, but it's still dead. That's because it is a giver and not a taker. The salt and mineral content is over 30 percent compared with 6 percent for oceans. Why? Water only leaves the sea by evaporation (about one inch a day), and there is no life in it except for simple organisms. (Source: Travel Jordan Agency, *What is the Dead Sea?*)

- *Put your trust in God not money.* Paul advised Timothy to "Command those who are rich in this present age not to…trust in uncertain riches but in the Living God" (1 Timothy 6:17), and this advice is still good. We cannot trust in money as our ultimate source of security and happiness. We must trust in God.

Listen to what Beth Moore has to say about trusting God:

> *No bank account under heaven can promise complete immunity from economic disaster. Even if, God forbid, we withdrew every dime from our accounts and buried them in airtight chests in the family graveyard, the question would still remain: what will the dollar be worth when we dig it up? People who have placed their trust in money are shaking in their boots on slippery sand right now.*
>
> —*Moore, So Long Insecurity, 203*

None of us have to be the person Beth described. Regardless of our financial situation, we have a sure foundation, our faith in God. Habakkuk 2:4 tells us, "The just shall live by (his) faith." When we live by faith, we put our confidence in God, not man.

Dr. David Jeremiah puts it this way:

> *Don't get caught up in the cultural clamor for wealth and security; trust your future to God and take care to live out the gospel, reaching your loved ones, your neighbors, and your friends with the only message of real hope to a world at risk of entering eternity without Christ.*
>
> —*Jeremiah, 36*

- *Take inventory of your stuff.* No matter what your financial situation, it is probable that you have too much stuff. Pastor Ray A. Riley preached a message, "What Do I Do With All This Stuff?" It ministered so much to me that I hope to attempt to preach it one day, God willing. I don't have time to go into detail with the message, but Pastor Riley reminded us that stuff generates more stuff. If you find yourself asking questions about your stuff, you don't need more.
- *Become financially wise.* For example, don't fall for Ponzi schemes—a swindle in which a quick return, made up of money from new investors on an initial investment, lures the victim into much bigger risks.—Ask.com.
- *Stand in your truth.* This helpful advice came from financial czar Suze Orman:

> *In order to create lasting security you must learn to stand in your truth. You must recognize, embrace, and be honest about what is real for you today and allow that understanding to inform the choices you make. Only then will you be able to build the future of your dreams.*
>
> —*Orman, 22*

One Final Word

My sisters, God has given us everything pertaining to life and godliness (2 Peter 1:3). You may not have all of the latest blings and things, but regardless of your financial situation, be godly; godliness with contentment is great gain (1 Timothy 6:6). As Philippians 4:19 reminds us, our God shall supply all our need according to His riches in glory by Christ Jesus. Have any of you been to God's "Shall" station lately? My nephew, Elder Chester Whitaker, told me about it. It's open 24/7 and has everything we could ask or think.

Let's pray…

Be a blessing!

18

Bandages and Dressing: Infidelity

A bandage is a strip of woven material used to hold a wound dressing or splint in place. A dressing (also called a compress) is an immediate protective cover placed over a wound to assist in the control of hemorrhage, to absorb blood and wound secretions, to prevent additional contamination and ease pain.

Our success kit must also contain bandages and dressings, for at any time we can find ourselves cut and bruised and in pain. That's what this chapter is about.

Torn Asunder

There were three of us in this marriage, so it was a bit crowded.
—*Diana Princess of Wales*

No adultery is bloodless.

—Nina Ginzberg

The only reason I don't want to commit adultery is because I love my wife and I love my Lord.

—Joseph Prince

Yes, this chapter is about committing adultery, infidelity, or extramarital affairs, if that sounds better. Few experiences are more painful than adultery. I shouldn't dare address that subject with you holy women of God, for it is the premier forbidden folly. You already know what the Bible says about adultery, and it's settled in your heart that you are going to be faithful to your husband until death do you part. When you are parted by death, if he goes first, you are going to remain pure and chaste, unless you choose to remarry. No discussion should be needed, and I shouldn't insult you by talking about it further.

However, although it is a difficult and painful subject, and you've already read this far, there's no need to paper it over: Pastors' wives can be involved in adulterous affairs (I promised you I would keep it real). We even get the seven year itch and yearn for a change. Willard F. Harley Jr. and Dr. Jennifer Harley Chalmers advise us not to be under the false illusion that an extramarital affair could not happen to us. *—Harley and Chalmers, 13–27*

Furthermore, I believe the Holy Spirit would tell me to omit this chapter if there was 100 percent certainty that each of us would never find ourselves involved in the clutches of an adulterous relationship. We can't be certain of this. While adultery is something I earnestly pray that none of us ever have to face, we have to have something in our success kit to help us in the unfathomable event that it does happen. I ask that you keep an open mind as we journey through this chapter.

His Cheating Heart

Before I focus on us, I want to take a few moments to discuss our husbands. Many books have been written about a husband's infidelity.

It is no wonder. Men are vulnerable, and that includes our husbands. Even though they are pastors, they can fall into the traps and snares of the devil and become victims of adultery, so we must do everything we can to keep them away from this evil.

Two books that come to mind are *His Cheating Heart*, a book written by Jenny Sanford, wife of South Carolina Governor Mark Sanford, after his affair with his "soul mate." Another book is *When His Secret Sin Breaks Your Heart: Letters to Hurting Wives*. In the book author Kathy Gallagher presents answers to letters from wives whose husbands have committed adultery and other sexual sins. She writes:

> *Many women lack compassion for their husband's struggles because they have never been controlled by sexual desires themselves. The problem is that they don't understand how powerful the sexual drive is in a man and how susceptible he is to temptation in a culture that is full of sexual images.*
>
> —Gallagher, 28

Sisters, this susceptibility is not isolated to low-down, down-low brothers in the pastorate. Things often happen when our husbands are not low-down. I'm not excusing their behavior in any way, but we have to be aware of the temptations our husbands face. Outside the church they are bombarded daily with breath-taking Halle Berry's and Beyonce Knowles' look-a-likes who would gladly pay them to be their mistress. Additionally, any day of the week they may be called to counsel attractive married women inside the church with problems, including husbands and relationships. Then there are single cute as a kitten women sitting on the pews with problems for which they need a man's opinion. Look who's available—our husbands, misters jack of all trades. Moreover, we can't dismiss the Delilah's that may be in the congregation who want to replace us if they have a chance (I told you she would come up again).

Before long, things can get way above our husbands' heads. They may be prayed up and fasted up, but they can be pulled by the flesh into improper relationships. We can't fool ourselves or walk around naïve. I don't care how many times the choir sings "I Surrender All" we have to stay on our post and guard our husbands to make sure they stay on theirs.

Given these temptations, sisters, we must be tough with our love. We can't do much about the women on the outside except tie a hidden camera around our husbands' neck so we can monitor their every move. I don't think any of us want to do that; it would be costly, exhausting, and aggravating. We can do something about their involvement with women inside the church though, like requiring our husbands to counsel women only in our presence, or with a deacon, or other male member. That shouldn't bother them one bit. It's common to have a nurse in the room when the male doctor is examining a female patient. It never hurts to play nurse once in a while, amen?

When we issue mandates such as these, we must refuse to waffle. There is no sloppy agape or greasy grace. Our husbands can't have their cake and eat it, too. That doesn't sound very Christian—but it is. Furthermore, this concept is not novel; we've just been loosey-goosey about it. And it has nothing to do with being jealous. If it did, so what? We wash the handkerchiefs we packed in chapter four.

Our Cheating Hearts

> *Ministerial infidelity is indeed becoming more frequent. We are products of our culture; there are no moral fences anymore. This has certainly affected the church and its leaders. And they have to struggle to keep our thought life clean and holy. All other battles pale in significance to this one.*
>
> —*Merrill, 182.*

What happens when we are the one with the cheating heart, and are breaking our husbands' heart? What happens when we are the one who's been unfaithful?

We must guard against two types of adultery: emotional and physical. Dr. Gary and Barbara Rosberg tell us we are susceptible to an affair if we are experiencing boredom or lack in our marriage in areas such as sexual activity, compliments and validation, attention and intimate time in prayer and God's Word.—*Rosberg, 71*

Let's talk about emotional adultery first, then physical adultery.

Emotional Adultery

> *Our notion of faithfulness in marriage is too often shallow. We generally think of it only in the physical realm. Yet, in many marriages spouses are physically faithful but not emotionally faithful. They are faithful with their bodies but not with their hearts.*
>
> —*Cloud and Townsend, 131*

Sisters, because we are pastors' wives doesn't mean we are immune to emotional adultery. Similar to other women, we can be swept away by another man if our heads are not on straight. There are some Denzel Washington's and George Clooney's out there who can turn our heads straightway, suddenly, and at once. There may also be attractive men inside the church who give us the attention we crave from our husband. We are most vulnerable when we're lonely; and let's face the facts, as a pastor's wife, we can have a lot of lonely times. We may not stoop so low as to have a physical relationship with another man, but we can be emotionally bonded to him.

So, what do you do to stay pure emotionally? Do you walk away when you feel more than you want to when your eyes meet those of a man not your husband's? Or do you feel that your marriage has become humdrum and you need something more exciting? Do you get caught up in sexual fantasies—especially when you focus on the time your husband is apart from you? Do you look around and see other "normal" marriages and ask why isn't mine like that? Do you turn on the TV and see wonderful relationships between husbands and wives, and ask, "What's wrong with my marriage?" If so, you are a prime candidate for emotional adultery, as we all can be. There is no way to continue a healthy relationship with your husband while your mind is taken up with thoughts of another man. Jesus said in Matthew

5:18, "If you lust after a woman you have committed adultery already." That verse also applies to your lusting after a man—real or fantasy.

Physical Adultery

Being a pastor's wife also doesn't not keep us from physical adultery, so resist it at all costs. You may know some pastors' wives who are already statistics and I've known some too, but we can't be too quick to throw stones. Instead let us try to minister to those who have gone astray, and tighten our resolve to keep our marriage bed undefiled. In one moment we could sell our marriage down the drain. All of the tea in China cannot compensate for the damage. We are most vulnerable when we don't realize how vulnerable we are. Paul said in First Corinthians 10:12, "If you think you are standing, be careful less you fall."

Awareness of what the Bible says doesn't stop the battle within; we have to be doers of the Word (James 1:22). In *Every Young Woman's Battle Workbook*, authors Shannon Ethridge and Stephen Arteburn address the sexual battle women face and give advice about how to pursue purity in a sex-saturated world. The authors remind young women that the sexual battle begins in the heart and mind and the way to overcome it is by developing a deep-seated level of intimacy with God.

Regardless of our age, Ethridge and Arteburn's advice is applicable for each of us. The only way we can win the battle of adultery is to keep ourselves pure, unlike the adulteress in Proverbs 7:6–24 (NLT) who enticed a young man. Let's read this passage together:

> *While I was at the window of my house, looking through the curtain, I saw some naive young men, and one in particular who lacked common sense. He was crossing the street near the house of an immoral woman, strolling down the path by her house. It was at twilight, in the evening, as deep darkness fell. The woman approached him, seductively dressed and sly of heart. She was the brash, rebellious type, never content to stay at home. She is often in the streets and markets, soliciting at every corner. She threw her arms around him and kissed him, and with a brazen look she said, "I've just made my peace offerings and fulfilled my vows. You're the one I was looking*

for! I came out to find you, and here you are! My bed is spread with beautiful blankets, with colored sheets of Egyptian linen. I've perfumed my bed with myrrh, aloes, and cinnamon. Come, let's drink our fill of love until morning. Let's enjoy each other's caresses, for my husband is not home. He's away on a long trip. He has taken a wallet full of money with him and won't return until later this month."

So she seduced him with her pretty speech and enticed him with her flattery. He followed her at once, like an ox going to the slaughter. He was like a stag caught in a trap, awaiting the arrow that would pierce its heart. He was like a bird flying into a snare, little knowing it would cost him his life.

If You Are Involved in an Affair

> *Regardless of the immediate source, anytime we receive input that is not consistent with the word of God, we can be sure Satan is trying to deceive and destroy us. What we read or hear may sound right, may feel right, may seem right—but if it is contrary to the word of God, it isn't right. If we could only see that the forbidden fruit, fruit that looks so ripe and tastes so sweet in the first moment, always leads ultimately to death and destruction.*
>
> —*DeMoss, 32.*

While I still pray that none of you reading this book will ever be unfaithful to your husband, if you are involved in an affair, what can you do?

- *End the affair immediately.* Sing your swan song and make haste—even if you have to quit your job or move. And don't rant and rave with the lame excuse, "I'm just praying for him." That's just a cop-out. If he needs prayer ask your husband to pray for him. Better yet, ask your husband to pray for the both of you as you seek your husband's forgiveness.

- *Take responsibility for your actions.* Admit it! You can't fool God, your husband, or yourself by pointing the finger at anyone but you. I've had opportunity to counsel persons whose marriages have been torn asunder by infidelity. Often the first response to the question, "why?" is because of something their spouse didn't do. The cheating spouse usually admits to being responsible for their actions after a few electrical shocks, but this is a waste of time and prolongs the recovery process.
- *Repent.* We'll talk more about repentance in chapter twenty two. For now, know that God is a God of another chance.
- *Ask God to fill you with the Holy Spirit.* When you are Spirit-filled you won't have to fight the battle of the flesh by yourself. You can make it with supernatural help.
- *Get an accountability partner to report to and pray with.* Give her full access to everything that has a powerful ungodly grip on you, or the devil uses to tempt you. And don't lie and connive when she confronts you. Be honest and open.

To sum it up, sisters, we must be extremely careful and bend over backward to preserve purity in our marriages. That's why Jesus taught us to pray against being led into temptation. Take that to mean, "Give me the good sense, Lord, to keep out of alluring situations, because if I get into them, I know exactly what I'm capable of doing and what I *will* do."—*Source Unknown*

Let's pray…

Be a blessing!

19

Storm Shelter: Contrary Winds

Climatic conditions can be contrary. Storms can arise with no warning. As a storm progresses, circulating winds may shift in the east and the northeast, culminating in heaving rain or snow and increased velocities. This is the "nor'easter" and is rarely a gentle storm. One thing is certain, the weather will not change until there is a shift in the wind. Don't look for a nor'easter to abate so long as the wind howls out of the northeast, not even if it drops somewhat. Only when the wind shifts toward the west will the storm end.

—RIVIERE, 4–6.

Pastors' wives are routinely buffeted by contrary winds. If we are to be successful, we need a storm shelter when the wind shifts and great storms arise in our lives.

Storms

> *Wouldn't it be great if every morning when we woke up, all the issues that existed the previous day were gone? Life rarely works that way. Adversity is a part of life, and all of us will face challenges that test our ability to endure, continue, and survive. There is nothing like adversity to reveal how strong we really are.*
>
> —COTTRELL, 72

> *To realize the worth of the anchor, we need to feel the stress of the storm.*
>
> —RBC MINISTRIES, JULY 4

> *If you want to see the sun shine you have to weather the storm.*
>
> —FRANK LANE

Pastors' wives have not been promised an exemption from any of life's storms. The Scriptures teach that "man is born to trouble as surely as sparks fly upward" (Job 5:7). As someone has said, "We are in a storm, coming out of a storm, or going into a storm." Sometimes you can protect yourself because you predict storms by the clouds, and you can find shelter in your tube tent. Many storms happen before you can make it to the tent.

I would venture to say that some of you reading this book today are like me—in an unpredictable Euroclydon (Acts 27:14). Bishop Cedric Kenebrew said it this way: "We can be up today and down tomorrow, in the penthouse today and poverty tomorrow, on Easy Street today and Destitute Boulevard tomorrow, on the Mount of Transfiguration today, and on Calvary tomorrow."

When you are in your Euroclydons, you can find yourself musing like David:

> *Fearfullness and trembling have come upon me, and horror has overwhelmed me. So I said, "Oh, that I had wings like a dove! I would fly away and be at rest. Indeed, I would wander far off, and remain in the wilderness. I would hasten my escape from the windy storm and tempest.*
>
> —*Psalm 55:5-8*

Sisters, God knew what He was doing by not giving you wings, so you don't have to fly away or wander off. You have something to hold on to as God strengthens, guards, and protects you. Nahum 1:3 tells us that clouds are the dust of his feet. You don't have to let the winds and clouds of this life put you in a state of helplessness and hopelessness. As with everything else, God has a purpose for our storms.

Purpose for Our Storms

I'd like to share with you some words of encouragement that help me better understand the purpose for our storms:

> *Everything God permits in a Christian's life is for His glory and for our good.*
>
> —*Bishop Jerry Maiden*

> *Difficulties can deepen your faith, teach patience, develop maturity, build wisdom, force you to pray, remind you of what is truly important.*
>
> —*Gray, et al., 182*

> *Suffering is a necessary part of life, growth, and any meaningful relationship. No truly mature person or marriage has ever escaped suffering.*
>
> —*Cloud and Townsend, 237*

Getting Through the Storm

Life is not about waiting for the storm to pass...it is about learning to dance in the rain.

—ANONYMOUS

Behold, God is my salvation, I will trust and not be afraid.

—ISAIAH 12:2

No matter what the storm, you also have the assurance that God can outlast the storms in your life, so when you can't trace His hand, trust His heart. I'm not trying to give you platitudes or attempting to be politically correct because I'm in a storm even as I write. While I minister to you, I'm ministering to myself.

Mother Wilhelmenia Hardy, our church mother, told me this story: Two sisters were driving home when they encountered bad weather. One was a Christian, the other was not. As the storm got worse, the Christian sister prayed softly to herself, "Lord, you promised to protect me, give me peace, and keep me safe no matter where I am." The other sister heard her and said loudly, "And you had better make Him keep His promise!"

My sisters, you can't make God do anything He doesn't want to do; He's sovereign. However, you can rejoice because God promised us peace and He keeps His promise.

Listen to Jesus' words in John 14:27:

Peace I leave with you, My peace I give to you; not as the world gives do I give to you. Let not your heart be troubled, neither let it be afraid.

You must also keep in mind that peace is not the absence of trouble, but knowing that God is there in the midst of your trouble. Here's an illustration of peace:

> *Two artists were commissioned to paint a portrait of peace. The portraits were to be judged by a panel of persons who were going through troublesome times in their lives. The first artist painted a picture of a beautiful day with a beautiful sunset, blue ocean, palm trees swinging in the breeze, not a ripple anywhere. The second artist painted a picture of a hurricane. The sky was covered with dark ominous clouds, the ocean was foreboding, and the trees were bending, almost to the point of breaking. But on one of the limbs was a robin singing praise to God.*
>
> —*Source Unknown*

Who do you think won the contest? The artist who painted peace with no trouble or the one who painted peace in the midst of trouble? You guessed it, the second artist. Because peace is not the absence of trouble, it is assurance in the midst of trouble that God will see you through.

Mark 4:35–39

I went to a funeral a few years ago and I heard Pastor Robert Owens preach a sermon titled, "Does Jesus Care When I'm in a Storm?" The text was taken from Mark 4:35–39 of a storm that the disciples encountered:

> *As evening came, Jesus said to his disciples, "Let's cross to the other side of the lake." So they took Jesus in the boat and started out, leaving the crowds behind (although other boats followed). But soon a fierce storm came up. High waves were breaking into the boat, and it began to fill with water. Jesus was sleeping at the back of the boat with his head on a cushion. The disciples woke Him up, shouting, "Teacher, don't You care that we're going to drown?" When Jesus woke up, He rebuked the wind and said to*

> *the waves, "Silence! Be still!" Suddenly the wind stopped, and there was a great calm. Then He asked them, "Why are you afraid? Do you still have no faith?" The disciples were absolutely terrified. "Who is this man?" they asked each other. "Even the wind and waves obey Him!"*
>
> *—NLT*

In his closing Pastor Owens talked about storms in our lives and reminded us that even though we are in relationship with Jesus or have faith, that doesn't keep us from storms. Eventually we are going to encounter some turbulence, lighting, and rain. During a storm Jesus is not like human pilots. When we are flying and hit turbulent weather, often human pilots go around the storm; Jesus flies through the storm with us. There is no storm in life that is not under His authority.

Sisters, with this in mind, trust Jesus PERIOD—even in a storm. If Jesus has brought you through a storm, will you please join with me in lifting Him up and praising His holy name? He's worthy! I'm not asking you to praise all day, just praise Him for two minutes as you think about the storms that He has brought you through. When you finish praising, please pray for those who are still in a storm. May each of you be assured that Jesus is still in control, and His peace is available to you.

Words from Hannah Whitall Smith end this chapter:

> *I am not called upon to glorify him (God) by any especially fervent or delightful emotions as some of you are. My mission is to glorify the Lord by the steadfastness of my faith in the midst of a storm of doubts and reasonings and by my unquestioning acquiescence in his will in circumstances of peculiar trial.*
>
> *—Smith and Dieter, July 3*

Let's pray…

Be a blessing!

20

Tissue Packs: Grief Protection

Tissue packs are essential to our success as pastors' wives.

Biologically, a tissue is an outer organ that protects the muscles from exposure and harm. To distinguish a minor burn from a serious burn, the first step is to determine the degree and the extent of damage to body tissues. The three burn classifications: first-degree, second-degree, and third-degree will help you determine emergency care. First-degree burns are the least serious. Only the outer layer of skin is burned, but not all the way through. When the first layer of skin has been burned through and the second layer of skin (dermis) also is burned, the injury is called a second-degree burn. Third-degree burns are the most serious. They involve all layers of the skin and cause permanent tissue damage. Fat, muscle and even bone may be affected. So, tissues are important.—mayoclinic.com.

—Burns: First Aid

Sisters, there is a burn that goes beyond biological proportions. I'm referring to the burn of grief associated with widowhood. Just as tissues protect our vital organs, tissue packs offer grief protection and are indispensable to pastors' wives as we pour out our heart to God in the midst of sorrow.

Widowhood

Though he brings grief, he also shows compassion because of the greatness of his unfailing love. For he does not enjoy hurting people or causing them sorrow.

—*Lamentations 3:32–33, NLT*

Every minister's wife will experiences agony and ecstasy, the best and the worst, the good and the bad. Only when the Lord allows you to go through the experiences of pain and suffering do you reach for his strength and providence. He must be found faithful in meeting your needs in order for you to have a worthy testimony for someone else. Accompanying your tears must be a determination to trust the Lord and believe that he is able to deliver from any fiery furnace.

—*Patterson, 198.*

I'm aware that I've mentioned hurt and pain numerous times in this book, my sisters. Widowhood warrants its own chapter. Each pastor's wife has to have the proper outlook on widowhood. It is three-dimensional:

First, your outlook must recognize God's love and great heart for widows. Here are a few Scriptures that confirm God's special love for widows:

You shall not afflict any widow or fatherless child.

—*Exodus 22:22*

> *He administers justice for the fatherless and the widow, and loves the stranger, giving him food and clothing.*
>
> —*Deuteronomy 10:18*

> *A father of the fatherless, a defender of widows, is God in his holy habitation.*
>
> —*Psalm 68:5*

> *For your maker is your husband, the Lord of hosts is his name; and your redeemer is the holy one of Israel; he is called the God of the whole earth.*
>
> —*Isaiah 54:5*

> *Do not oppress the widow or the fatherless, the alien or the poor. Let none of you plan evil in his heart against his brother.*
>
> —*Zechariah 7:10*

> *Honor widows who are really widows.*
>
> —*1 Timothy 5:3*

Second, your outlook cannot be a pipe dream. It is possible that many of you reading this book will find yourselves facing the reality and pain of widowhood before the day ends. That's another justification for cultivating communion with God during peaceful times. Without this you cannot be victorious when the difficult times come.

Here is a horrific account of the murder of a young pastor on March 6, 2011, inside the church he shepherded:

> *Hours after the Reverend Clint Dobson was suffocated with a plastic bag and his assistant severely beaten inside NorthPointe Baptist Church, the suspects in his slaying laughed while watching a television news report about the case, according to court documents.—Scott Goldstein, Men arrested in Arlington pastor's death laughed and bragged, court papers say.*
>
> —*Dallas Morning News, March 7, 2011, dallasnews.com*

This is no laughing matter. Pastor Dobson had no idea when he went to work that morning he would never see his wife again. Of course, Mrs. Dobson didn't know, either. With one cruel act she went from being the pastor's wife to the pastor's widow.

I can't imagine Mrs. Dobson's pain, but I know firsthand the heartbreak of being a pastor's widow. There are those of you who have felt the twinge, too. In addition to being apart from your husband, there is the agitation of going to church and not hearing him minister again, the ache of the congregation's tears, and the discomforting pang of not knowing where you fit in since you are no longer the first lady of the church. Yes, there is much pain with being a pastor's widow.

Third, your outlook must include an uplook. There is light at the end of the tunnel, and hope for widows in the midst of the shudder and vale of tears. If you are widowed, you do not have to crumble up and die. God still has great things in store for you. If God wanted your life to end, He would have removed your name from today's "Wake-Up" list.

The Grief Process

> *God gave us our memories so that we might have roses in December.*
>
> —*J. M. Barrie*

If you have the proper outlook on widowhood you do not sorrow as those who have no hope (1 Thessalonians 4). It is important to realize, however, that we will all go through the grief process.

Hospice Foundations of America tells us that grief is not a stage but a series of roller coasters:

> *It is best not to think of grief as a series of stages. Rather, we might think of the grieving process as a roller coaster, full of ups and downs, highs and lows. Like many roller coasters, the ride tends to be rougher in the beginning, the lows may be deeper and longer. The difficult periods should become less intense and shorter as time goes by, but it takes time to work through a loss. Even years after a loss, especially at special events such as a family wedding or the birth of a child, we may still experience a strong sense of grief.*
>
> —HOSPICEFOUNDATION.ORG., GRIEF, WHAT IS GRIEF?

Here's what helpguide.org has to say:

> *There is no right or wrong way to grieve—but there are healthy ways to cope with the pain. You can get through it! Grief that is expressed and experienced has a potential for healing that eventually can strengthen and enrich life.*
>
> —HELPGUIDE.ORG, COPING WITH GRIEF AND LOSS

Thomas Attig tells us even though we grieve we don't have to let our loved ones go completely when they die:

> *Grieving persons who want their loved ones back need to look for some other way to love them while they are apart. Desperate longing prevents their finding that different way of loving. Letting go of having them with us in the flesh is painful and necessary. But it is not the same as completely letting go. We still hold the*

gifts they gave us, the values and meanings we found in their lives. We can love them as we cherish their memories we found in their lives. We can love them as we treasure their legacies in our practical lives, and spirits. But there is nothing in all of this that implies that we must let go completely. There is no reason to let go of the good with the bad.

—*Attig, 50*

My story…

We must learn to weep before we can dry another's tears.

—*Our Daily Bread,155*

Out of difficulties grow miracles.

—*Jean de la Bruyere*

"I want him resuscitated, and I want him resuscitated now!" No, these weren't words from a sitcom; they were the words that came out of my mouth when Pastor Joel Jerome Thompson, my spouse of nineteen years, passed away from lung cancer on June 28, 2001. He went from one life to the next, and joined the citizens of heaven. I didn't relish God's timing. Joel and I had many fruitful years of marriage and ministry together.

Joel had been hospitalized after falling in the driveway and breaking his hip. The doctor said it was unusual for someone his age to break a hip without something else going on. Needless to say, he and I were both devastated by the doctor's diagnoses of stage four lung cancer on May 18, 2001, his fifty-ninth birthday. Joel had not smoked in thirty years. How could he have lung cancer?

Joel was full of life and wanted to live to be at least 500 years old. He told me several times over that he wanted to be resuscitated if he died. In jest, he also told me that if he died he wanted his cremated ashes painted on our bedroom ceiling. I was totally against resuscitation, so when I was presented with DNR (Do Not Resuscitate) papers a week or so before his death, I quickly signed them. It was a different Sena when I stood in his room at Diagnostic Hospital in Houston, and the doctor announced that he was gone. Gone? Gone where? Then it dawned on me that the doctor meant he had passed away.

With tears cascading down my face I told the medical staff that I wanted to have him resuscitated. They reminded me of the papers I had signed, and I hastily signed new papers.

My head pounded furiously as I asked if the hospital had a place where I could pray. I found a small room and cried out to God to bring Joel back to life. I was certain God was going to do just that. When I returned to Joel's room a few minutes later a team of doctors was working hard on him trying to resuscitate him for about what seemed to be ten minutes. Finally, Joel's primary doctor turned with tears in his eyes and shook his head. I knew then that God's answer was No! How could God call Him home only six weeks after his diagnosis?

I was numb. I didn't know what to do. Even though Joel never came back home after he was hospitalized I still looked to him for comfort and support. But now what?

I finally garnered enough strength to call my brother and former Overseer, Bishop Jerry Burley, who met me at the hospital, prayed with me, and waited until the mortician came to remove Joel's body. I left the hospital still stunned. I don't remember much of what happened that night, other than someone had broken my car's right side-view mirror while it was parked in the hospital parking garage. In some ways I guess the mirror represented my broken heart.

Fast-forwarding, I got through the funerals, graveside service, and burial. We had two funerals—one in Houston and one in Chicago, Joel's hometown. I delivered the eulogy at both. Since he wanted to be buried in Philadelphia, we had graveside services there for family members who couldn't travel to Houston or Chicago.

Leaving Joel's body at the gravesite was one of the most onerous times in my life. He and I had done just about everything together. We were both called into the ministry the same time. In fact, we were both surprised when we'd broken the news to one another and wrote Pastor Price, our pastor, to tell him what God had done. We both preached our first messages on March 15, 1987: I preached during the 8:00

a.m. service; Joel preached at 11:00 a.m. He and I ministered together for eleven years at the Church of the Living God in Cleveland, Texas where he served as pastor. We celebrated many good times together, and cried together when my mother and Omar died. Now I was alone, and that burned.

Thank God, my sisters Elyse, Martha, and Bert were with me the first time I went to the church Joel was called to pastor. The congregation was exceptional. They were hurting as much as I was and did everything they could to wrap their arms around me. Our associate minister, Elder Danny Rone, preached that morning from the subject, "I Still Have Joy," reminding us that no matter what goes on around us, we can still have joy on the inside.

Elder Rone spoke the truth; but my heart was unbearably heavy for months—especially when I went to a restaurant to eat. It was horrible eating by myself, and I didn't like this new experience.

But God...

Sisters, I didn't tell you all of the gory details to have you take out your tissue packs and snot all over your Jones New York new suit. I told you the whys and the wherefores to bring you to this point. The whole nine yards is, with all my fast-forwarding, I did a lot of rewinding, too. I went through every stage of grief and know what it is like to be on the roller coaster. I would be up one moment and down the next. I also had many sleepless, tearful nights. I even bargained with God to let Joel return. I promised God I would be a better wife to Joel if He would allow him to come back (I did admit in chapter one that I had a problem with submitting to his authority). I even told God that Joel would want to come back if he could. The Holy Spirit quickly told me that was not the case, and, of course, Joel was not coming back.

But God...

I can earnestly say, through my experience as a widow, I've learned to trust in God and to lean more on Him than ever before. He's faithful and His grace is sufficient. Widowhood is difficult because death is a physical separation; but God the Father saw me through every trial, the Holy Spirit comforted me, and Jesus was my valley Friend. I also came to grips with the reality that death is the doorway to heaven, although it was bittersweet—I missed Joel so.

Yet, there was never a time when God didn't walk with me and talk with me. There was never a time when I did not feel His consoling power and presence. He was there when I looked out the window and saw leaves all over the front yard and sidewalk from the trees in front of the house. What made it worse is that we live on a corner lot and leaves were all around the side of the house.

I looked out of the window and cried out to God, "Who is going to rake all of those leaves?" We had a gardener, but he went AWOL on me, and since I live in a deed-restricted sub-division, I knew I had to take action. I waited for God to give me the name of someone to rake the leaves. Instead, I heard Him say, "You are!" Me, I don't think so! About thirty minutes later, God and I were out raking leaves. I must have filled about two-hundred bags (just an exaggeration), but He was with me all of the time. When I finally finished, I was exhausted, but I made it.

God carried me through every one of my trying days. He reminded me through a plaque hanging on my bathroom wall that He was with me. The plaque has Isaiah 41:10:

> *Fear not, for I am with You; be not dismayed, for I am your God. I will strengthen you, yes, I will help you, I will uphold you with My righteous right hand.*

But God...

God let Earl find me. The Bible says Proverbs 18:22, "He who finds a wife finds a good thing, and obtains favor from the Lord." I'm so grateful to be Earl's good thing and that he has obtained favor from God. I have been favored too. Earl is one of the greatest blessings that God has given to me, and I love him from the very depths of my heart. If it wasn't for Earl, this book would have not been written, so I really owe him one—but let's keep that a secret.

Moving Ahead to Brighter Days

I'd like to take a few moments to talk to those of you who are widows before I close this chapter.

Though I don't know your story, my prayer is that you will find the same comfort that God provided for me. You'll have "tear times," and there will be times you feel like you can't go on, but don't give up. You'll understand it better by and by when you meet God face to face. Until then, may you look forward to the day when you can move beyond your sadness and into a bright new sunshine.

Here are some recommendations that helped me:

- *Find others with whom to discuss your pain and sorrow.* Each person grieves uniquely, yet we all need to share our hearts, our burdens, our questions, and our sadness with someone else.
- *Don't forsake your church's fellowship,* though it will be difficult not seeing your husband in the pulpit.
- *Embrace the congregation fully*—remember, you lost a husband, but they lost a pastor. They are grieving, too.
- *Continue to serve God.* You are still living and have work to do. Glorify Him every season of your life.
- *Invest in the lives of others.* It takes your mind off of your pain.
- *Draw comfort from joining a grief support group and by reading books written on grief*—especially by women who have experienced widowhood.

Let's Pray…

Be a blessing!

21

Signaling Mirror: Attracting Help

No success kit is complete without tools for searching and rescuing trapped victims. Among these tools is the signaling mirror. Of all signaling devices known in our air-rescue age, possibly the most useful one is the smallest, simplest, the one least used, and carried by the average outdoorsman. Everyone, as it is said, talks about it, or knows about it, but nobody happens to have one. This is the signaling mirror. You should have one in your pack!

—*Dalrymple*, 265

Pastors' wives need a signaling mirror to summon the help God has made available to each of us to rescue us when we are trapped. We will discuss sources of help in this chapter.

911

He who dwells in the secret place of the most high shall abide under the shadow of the Almighty. I will say of the Lord, "He is my refuge and my fortress; my God, in him I will trust."

—*Psalms 91:1–2*

No rose without a thorn.

—*French proverb*

Every winner has scars.

—*Herbert Casson*

There was a hurricane coming towards a small town, and they served an announcement for everyone to evacuate. A young man of high faith in God refused to leave. The water began rising and a truck came by packed with people evacuating, and the driver asked the man if he was leaving, and he replied, "No, I have faith in my Father. I'm covered in the blood and I'm not leaving." So the water began rising, at this point, over his porch and a boat arrived. The driver asked the man if he wanted to evacuate and the man replied, "I am highly favored, covered in the blood of my Father, and He will not forsake me—I'm staying!" So the water, at this point, gets to the man's roof, and a helicopter comes with a ladder. The pilot asked the man if he wanted to evacuate, and the man replied, "I am highly favored by the Lord, and covered with the blood, and I will not leave." So the man drowns and goes to heaven, and he patiently waits in line for judgment. When it was his time to face the Lord, he asked God, "Why did you forsake me? I am highly favored, and served you all of my life, why did you allow me to drown?" And the Lord replied, "I sent you a truck, a boat, and a helicopter, what more could I do?"—Told to me by Corey Aldridge, Original source unknown

Sisters, my intention in writing this chapter is not to keep harping on our hurts, beat a dead horse, or milk the subject dry. I've written it to harmonize healing with hurt. As pastors' wives our lives are layered with joys and blessings, but they are also marbled with cuts and lacerations. Sometimes the bleeding does not stop—there is a severe deep puncture wound, and there is sign of infection. We find ourselves in a 911 situation, even in our tube tents and storm shelters, and we need to be healed.

Undoubtedly some of you have felt like the man in the story—in dire straits, calling for the Lord to help you, waiting for Him to respond, and drowning as you wait. Your life doesn't have to end with your going to heaven asking God why He forsook you and allowed you to drown. You can signal for and accept the help God sends. He is a very present help in the time of trouble, and He wants to heal you everywhere you hurt.

A Time for Healing

A time to kill, and a time to heal; a time to break down, and a time to build up.

—*Ecclesiastes 3:3*

Is there no balm in Gilead, is there no physician there? Why then is there no recovery for the health of the daughter of my people?

—*Jeremiah 8:22*

To be healed it is vital to know your limitations, weaknesses, and strengths. If you allow the silver-tongued orator who domiciles in your head to convince you that you are invincible, you are living in a fool's paradise. This is a sad state of affairs. It is also tragic that too often pastors' wives cave in to the perils of life by despairing or denying the problem exists, rather than seeking the help we need. This should not be. Ecclesiastes 3:3 tells us there is a time for everything, including a time for healing. Our time is now; there is a balm in Gilead.

Let me get on my soapbox for a moment: Guilt trips and self-condemnation are out when you are hurting. You don't have to have it together all the time. I know this may be a hard nut to crack because pastors' wives are often the "go to" and "be strong person." However if you become a basket case, or go berserk and lose your way, how can you guide anyone else? In any event, if you need to be on life support you are not by yourself. We've all been hurt, and we all need help. The story is told of a private that was in a war. His sergeant called out for him to come to someone else's aid. The private said, "Sir, I've been shot." The sergeant told him, "We've all been shot."

You also can't let church "politics" enslave you. Within the church there is often a stigma associated with needing help. When we seek counseling from the pastor we wait until no one is around, and then make a beeline to the office. We fear that folk think we are going ape, but we're just looking out for our own well-being and for the well-being of others.

Seeking Help

He that won't be counseled can't be helped.

—Benjamin Franklin

I believe the Christian community today needs to accept the reality of family dysfunction and become part of the healing process. For too long, we have shot our wounded with shame rather than offering the healing arms of Christ's grace and understanding. The time to pretend that Christians are perfect is over. It needs to be okay for Christians to struggle through problems and deep hurts in order to heal.

—Henslin, xi

Greg Groeschel, offers six questions to ask yourself to determine if you need help:

Do your family and friends say you have a problem?
Do you continue even though you are hurting?
Do you arrange your schedule, priorities, or spending around it?
Can you go one week without it?
Is it driving others away?
Are you denying it is a problem, or trying to keep it a secret? —*Groeschel, 85*

Resources

> *The Christian life is not a constant high. I have my moments of deep discouragement. I have to go to God in prayer with tears in my eyes, and say, 'O God, forgive me,' or 'Help me.'*
>
> —*Billy Graham*

> *When you pass through the waters, I will be with you; and through the rivers, they shall not overflow you. When you walk through the fire, you shall not be burned, nor shall the flame scorch you.*
>
> —*Isaiah 43:2*

Sisters, if you need healing you do not have to despair. God has provided many sources of help.

In addition to your true friends, a great source of help is an older, mature Christian woman. Or you may feel comfortable approaching another pastor's wife or someone similar who can identify with your situation and diffuse your frustrations.

It is also all right to share your hurts with the members of your congregation. They love you and are concerned about you.

Professional Care

Sometimes professional care is needed—there is no shame in this. One of the best ways to receive help is to turn to pastors and Christian counselors. When you go to a counselor, you can't oversimplify or over-spiritualize your problems. Be willing to risk being vulnerable, unmask your inner struggles, and talk openly about yourself. Don't get discomposed if your counselor refers you to someone else. Earl and I are Certified Christian Counselors, and when we were in school, we were coached over and over again to remember three words, "refer, refer, refer" when things got over our heads.

According to Dr. Amanda Bowie, you should seek professional help beyond your pastor and Certified Christian Counselor when you experience emotional, physical, or mental symptoms. How do you know something is wrong? Intuition.

Here are some symptoms Dr. Bowie advises us to look for:

Physical Symptoms

- *Sleep disturbance—problem getting to sleep or staying asleep*
- *Uneasiness*
- *Anger*
- *Tension headaches*
- *Panic attacks (chest pains, irregular heartbeats, such as feeling "the walls are closing in on me")*
- *Stomachaches (a lot of digestive problems, nervous stomach, nausea, queasiness, diarrhea)*
- *Muscle tension and tightness*
- *Weakness—feel weak all the time, have a hard time getting out of bed (things you do routinely are hard to execute)*
- *Changes in appetite or weight (anxiety)*

Emotional Symptoms

- *Unable to complete your daily activities, can't stay focused*
- *Crying all the time, constantly sad, depression*

- *Feeling hopeless*
- *Feeling helpless*
- *Agitated more than normally (like a ticking bomb on the inside, problem dealing with pressure)*
- *Self-mutilating behavior (cutting)*
- *Irritability (get upset at the smallest whim. This means you have a lot of issues to deal with—e.g., if you're telling me today that it's a good day, I get angry)*
- *No motivation or ambition*
- *Isolate yourself from others*

Psychologists, Psychiatrists, Licensed Counselors

Many times people seek psychological help as the last resort. We should change the way we go about seeking help. If needed, here is some information from Dr. Bowie that may help you make a better decision:

Therapist

A therapist is someone you can talk to to help you through situations and help you gain or improve coping skills. One of the main questions a therapist will ask is "What has to change to make you feel better about this situation?" If you are looking for a therapist, ask about her clinical perspectives and skill sets.

Types of Therapists

Licensed Clinical Social Worker (LCSW). They practice independently and provide counseling. They have a master's degree in social work and are licensed to practice as a therapist.

Licensed Professional Counselor (LPC). They have a master's degree in counseling and are able to practice as a therapist.

Licensed Marriage Family Therapist (LMFT). They focus on the family and marriage counseling.

Licensed Chemical Dependency Counselor (LCDC). Chemical dependent issues.

Psychologists (Ph.D, or Psy.D); Doctor in Psychology. They have a license and are able to perform therapy and make psychological assessments and diagnosis. In some states they are able to give medication.

Psychiatrists. They have a medical degree and are able to give medication and treat disorders. Psychiatric treatment will include medication intervention and a psychologist to follow-up and provide psychotherapy.

Dr. Bowie recommends if you are having physical symptoms to go to your doctor first to ensure nothing is going on medically. If the symptoms are not relieving themselves, and you are aware that other things are going on, you may desire to seek counseling. You may want to start with a LPC or LCSW. Ask what is her theoretical orientation, e.g., what she specializes in. If your problem is above her scope, she will refer you to a psychologist.

Costs

Many insurance plans have mental health benefits that pay for some of these services, or co-pays that will reimburse you. Check your mental health benefits. Samaritan Counseling Centers typically provide therapy free or on a sliding scale.

When you can't afford to pay, some colleges and universities have psychological services, so check with schools in your area.

Self-Care

Seeking another's help is essential for success. Since other people can't be with you at all times, and your budget may be limited, here's a few self-care items:

- *Admit you have a problem (Mark 10:27).* Be true to yourself by being mindful of the issues you're battling and knowing the consequence of your behavior. Then you can address your problem head-on and stop making excuses. As Billy Sunday said, "An excuse is the skin of a reason stuffed with a lie."—*quotegarden.com, Billy Sunday quotes.*
- *Know yourself.* How you respond to hurt often depends on how you view yourself. Check to see if your response to criticism, etc. is grounded in low self-esteem or if there is another problem. The bottom line is not how people view you, but how does God view you.
- *Own your own problems.* People may give you advice, but it is up to you to come up with workable solutions. If you come up with it, you own it, and you have buy-in. Then you can make the necessary changes without resorting to chemical abuse such as drinking and taking pills.
- *Encourage yourself.* God is still holding up the universe, so tell yourself, "This is just a temporary inconvenience." Weeping may endure for a night, but joy comes in the morning (Psalm 30:5). If you look out of your window, you'll find that morning is already here.
- *Minister to someone else.* Sometimes we spend so much time focusing on our problems that we forget there is always someone worse off than we. We've probably heard the saying, "I complained that I had no shoes, but then I saw a man with no shoes to use." You can go to the hospital, visit senior saints, fix meals for someone who is shut-in, even babysit for a single mother to get your mind off of your problems. Hint: if you are over fifty you may want to think twice before volunteering to babysit for a two-year-old.

You Will Rise Again

May your trails be crooked, winding, lonesome, dangerous, leading to the most amazing view. May your mountains rise into and above the clouds.

—Edward Abbey

Sisters, be assured that no matter what you've been through you will rise again. May I encourage you with a story author J. K. Gressett shared that was told by Samuel S. Scull, Pentecostal pioneer of Arizona:

> *Mr. Scull and his wife and children settled on a farm in the Arizona desert. One night a fierce storm struck and severely damaged the farm. As Mr. Scull was viewing the horrific damage he heard a stirring in the henhouse and saw an old wet and battered rooster climbing through the debris. He didn't stop climbing until he had reached the highest board in the pile. As the sun came up he still crowed even though he had gone through a storm.*
>
> —*Gressett in Pentecostal Evangel, 6*

We can learn a lesson from that old rooster: even when the storms of life assail, don't stop climbing. We still have a reason to praise!

Let's let Arthur Russell close this chapter:

> *It is not passionate appeal that gains the divine ear so much as the quiet placing of the difficulty and worry, in the divine hands. So trust and be no more afraid than a child would be, who places its tangled skein of wool in the hands of a loving mother, and runs out to play, pleasing the mother more by its unquestioning confidence than if it went down on its knees and implored her help, which would pain her the rather, as it would imply she was not eager to help when help was needed.*
>
> —*Russell, 37*

Let's pray.

Be a blessing!

22

The Recovery Room: Altar Call

The recovery room is sometimes referred to as the post-anesthetic room (PR) or anesthetic room (AR). It is a special nursing unit that accommodates a group of patients who have just undergone major or minor surgery. The purpose of a recovery room is to provide direct and continuous patient observation during emergence from general or regional anesthesia.

— ARMYMEDICAL.TPUB.COM, *FACTS ABOUT THE RECOVERY ROOM*

It is essential that pastors' wives spend time in God's recovery room after we've undergone major and minor surgery associated with our divine calling. Our recovery takes place at God's altar, where we find confession, repentance, forgiveness, and restoration. That's what this chapter is about.

The Altar

> *Man tells us in these days that sin is what you think it is. Well, it is not. Sin is what God thinks it is. You may think according to your own conscience. God thinks according to His.*
>
> —John G. Lake

> *What a Friend we have in Jesus, all our sins and griefs to bear! What a privilege to carry everything to God in prayer! O what peace we often forfeit, O what needless pain we bear, all because we do not carry everything to God in prayer. —Joseph Scriven, What a Friend We Have In Jesus*
>
> —*PDMUSIC.ORG, PUBLIC DOMAIN MUSIC*

My sisters, this is the last segment of my tour with you. I want you to know from the depths of my heart that I've enjoyed our journey. I leave this writing with mixed feelings—as one would feel heading home after spending time with a close friend. To women who are not pastors' wives, our pastor husbands, and other men of faith: Thank you again for your interest in this book. I earnestly hope you have benefited from traveling with the other pastors' wives and me, and that what I've written has broadened your understanding of our matchless life.

It is only befitting that we end this book at the altar. As Heather Hempley sings, "We're not perfect, we're simply redeemed." Therefore, the only way we will succeed as pastors' wives is to stay at the altar. The altar is God's recovery room. It is a place of peace and rest and the only place we can go for real solutions to our problems. It is also a place of renewing and refreshing before God. Everything we need is at the altar. We do our part, and God is faithful to do His part.

Bishop Cedric Kenebrew wrote a song titled "Altered at the Altar" in which Earl narrates on the CD. The song conveys that no matter what you are going through, God can alter you. He may not change your situation, but He can change you. God is not only a help in trouble; He's a great help in keeping out of trouble.

What Will We Find at the Altar?

Let's look at four things we will find at the altar: Confession, Repentance, Forgiveness, and Restoration.

Confession

> *Confession of errors is like a broom which sweeps away the dirt and leaves the surface brighter and clearer. I feel stronger for confession.*
>
> —*Mohandas Gandhi*

Confession is to admit your guilt. Romans 3:23 tells us that all have sinned and come short of the glory of God. We are all included in the *all*. Yes, we are pastors' wives and saints, but we still sin. In fact, God said if we say we have not sinned we call him a liar (1 John 1:10). Some of our sins were held under the microscope as we journeyed through this book; others were more elusive, but we still sin. You see, our spirit is saved, but our flesh isn't. Someone said all the flesh does when we are baptized is get wet; it is still drawn to and prone to sin. We must confess our sins at the altar.

If you are like me, it is painful to confess your sins at the altar. Confession brings pain as you react to your sin with shame, disgrace, and embarrassment. But we should expect pain at the altar. Pain is God's greatest teacher, and He disciplines those He loves *(Proverbs 3:11–12; Hebrews 12:5–11)*. As Charles Spurgeon has said, "The Lord does not permit his children to sin successfully."

So put your shame, embarrassment, and disgrace aside and humbly confess all of your sins to God. Don't hold back from telling Him about every area you know is displeasing to Him and that causes you to walk contrary to His will and way. He knows it anyway, so you might as well fess up. If you still can't remember the areas you need to confess, the Holy Spirit does. Ask Him to bring your sins to your remembrance, and He will. He is the Spirit of Truth, and He will lead you and guide you into all truth (John 16:13).

Repentance

Confession without repentance is just bragging.

—Rev. Eugene Bolton

It is not enough to confess our sins; we must repent when we walk unworthy of our calling as pastors' wives. Repentance is not simply a bad feeling or remorse. It is a "a change of mind" that leads to a change of heart (affections) and a change of life…it is therefore a decision to quit sinning" (*Nickelson*, 30).

How to Repent

- *Keep short accounts with God.* Keeping long accounts with God really doesn't make good sense. Lack of repentance brings on the chastening of God and has devastating consequences. Read what David wrote in Psalm 38, and you'll know what I'm talking about.
- *Call sin sin*—not problems, accidents, incidents, mistakes, or anything else that may sound better than sin. Jesus didn't die for problems and all of those other things. He died for sin—high treason against God.
- *Acknowledge your sins.* A good role model of repentance is found in Psalm 51. We know this psalm well. It is the psalm that David wrote after sinning with Bathsheba.
- *Go and sin no more.* This needs no explanation.

Forgiveness

Forgiveness—when God buries our sins and does not mark the grave.

—Louis Paul Lehman

To be wronged is nothing unless you continue to remember it.
—Confucius

Forgiveness is to grant relief for payment of a debt. Let's read two Scriptures about God's forgiveness:

The Lord is compassionate and merciful, slow to get angry and filled with unfailing love. He will not constantly accuse us, nor remain angry forever. He does not punish us for all our sins; He does not deal harshly with us, as we deserve. For his unfailing love toward those who fear him is as great as the height of the heavens above the earth. He has removed our sins as far from us as the east is from the west. The Lord is like a father to his children, tender and compassionate to those who fear him. For he knows how weak we are; he remembers we are only dust.
—*Psalm 103:8–14, NLT*

I, even I, am he who blots out your transgressions for my own sake; and I will not remember your sins.
—*Isaiah 43:25*

Sisters, I thank God for His tender mercy and compassion, for cleaning us up, and not remembering our sins after we ask for forgiveness. That's better than forgetting, for if God said He would forget, He could remember our sins and bring them up again. But since He won't remember, we don't have to remember them either and suffer the detrimental effects of guilt. As Dr. Mike Murdock said, "guilt is the thief of faith." (Dr. Mike Murdock, *Morning Motivation with Mike Murdock*, March 3, 2011).

But you have to remember, though revenge is sweet, God will forgive us only as we forgive others. Matthew 18:23–35 records the story Jesus told of a king and two debtors so we could understand how our sins against God compare to our sins against others. In this story, the king represents God, and we represent the unforgiving servant.

When we think of how much we've hurt God, and how God forgives, it should be unthinkable not to want to forgive others:

> *Therefore the kingdom of heaven is like a certain king who wanted to settle accounts with his servants. And when he had begun to settle accounts, one was brought to him who owed him ten thousand talents. But as he was not able to pay, his master commanded that he be sold, with his wife and children and all that he had, and that payment be made. The servant therefore fell down before him, saying, 'Master, have patience with me, and I will pay you all.' Then the master of that servant was moved with compassion, released him, and forgave him the debt.*
>
> *But that servant went out and found one of his fellow servants who owed him a hundred denarii; and he laid hands on him and took him by the throat, saying, 'Pay me what you owe!' So his fellow servant fell down at his feet and begged him, saying, 'Have patience with me, and I will pay you all.' And he would not, but went and threw him into prison till he should pay the debt. So when his fellow servants saw what had been done, they were very grieved, and came and told their master all that had been done. Then his master, after he had called him, said to him, 'You wicked servant! I forgave you all that debt because you begged me. Should you not also have had compassion on your fellow servant, just as I had pity on you?' And his master was angry, and delivered him to the torturers until he should pay all that was due to him.*
>
> *So My heavenly Father also will do to you if each of you, from his heart, does not forgive his brother his trespasses.*

Don Clowers tells us how we know we've forgiven someone:

> *One way to know whether or not we've forgiven someone is to examine ourselves for the presence of resentment or pain. When we no longer experience those feelings when thinking about the person who wronged us, we know we've been healed. When we remember the good times more than we remember the bad, we know that a healing has occurred. That doesn't mean we need to*

keep the person who hurt us close by, but we do need to move on to a place where that person no longer negatively dominates our thoughts.

—*Clowers, 21*

Building a New Relationship

Here are a few tips for building a new relationship with the forgiven person:

- *Understand what forgiveness is.* Forgiveness is a gift you give to yourself and to others. When you forgive, you are not condoning the wrong behavior, you are releasing the person who wronged you from being captive to your emotions.
- *Distinguish between forgiveness and forgetting.* Only God is capable of forgetting. He never told you to forget. But when you forgive you are turning the outcome over to the Lord. When you turn it over to the Lord you can move forward, because you know God is going to take care of things (Hebrews 10:30). You don't hide the ax and leave the handle sticking out—waiting for the next time.
- *Don't count offenses.* Matthew 18:21–22 records Jesus' conversation with Peter about forgiveness:

Then came Peter to him, and said, Lord, how oft shall my brother sin against me, and I forgive him? Till seven times? Jesus saith unto him, I say not unto thee, until seven times: but until seventy times seven.

Seventy times seven means forgive as often as your brother asks for forgiveness. Some people will hurt you time and time again, but you still have to forgive them. And even if they don't come to you, forgive them. That doesn't mean you have to be a doormat. If possible, remove yourself from the situation. Love them, but don't let them get so close to you that they can hurt you. If you cannot remove yourself, resolve in your mind that you are not going to let them affect you.

- *Learn to forgive yourself.* You made mistakes and didn't do the best job; but yesterday ended at midnight. Today is a new day. So don't be too tough on yourself. Move beyond your history into the larger terrain of your destiny (*Jakes, Let It Go, 33*). If you've offended someone, do as the Bible tells us to do: leave your gift at the altar, be reconciled to your brother or sister, and then offer your gift (Matthew 5:24).

Husband Specific Tips

- *Be first.* Be the first to extend forgiveness to make things right. Learn to say, "I'm sorry," "I'm wrong," "You're right," "Please forgive me," and "I forgive you."
- *Give your husband space to hurt you, and make room for mistakes.* There are really six people in your marriage: who you are, what you think you are, and who your spouse thinks you are, (and vice-versa), so at any given time one of you may mess up.
- *Delete the "D" word from your vocabulary.* Let forgiveness and reconciliation be first. Divorce is so easy now that people can get it in a couple of days. Make divorce the last resort, even if your husband has been unfaithful (murder, yes, that's an option if you want a prison ministry—no, I'm not serious). Seriously though, rebuilding the bridge between your husband and you may take several years, but by God's grace you can.
- *Never forget how much God has forgiven you.* We talked about this earlier, but I want to repeat it here. How good is your memory? Can anyone, including me, recall the number of times God has forgiven us? No. I didn't think so. Keep this in mind before you bring out the calculator and remind your husband of how many times you've forgiven him.

Restoration

He restores my soul.

—*Psalm 23:3*

> *So we praise God for the glorious grace he has poured out on us who belong to his dear Son. He is so rich in kindness and grace that he purchased our freedom with the blood of his Son and forgave our sins.*
>
> —*Ephesians 1:6–7, NLT*

Restoration is a bringing back to an unimpaired or improved condition. That's what God does when we confess, repent, ask him for forgiveness, and forgive others. He accepts us just as we are, and we don't have to perform to receive His acceptance. He accepted us in the past, He is accepting us in the present, and He will always accept us in the future (Ephesians 1:4–5). In spite of all you and I have done, God extends the same grace toward us that He did when He saved us (Ephesians 2:8–10). Some say that Grace is an acronym for God's Riches at Christ's Expense; some say it is God Rejects All Carnal Efforts.

I heard a story that illustrates what restoration looks like:

> *A young man quarreled with his father and left home. He kept in contact with his mother although he did not communicate with his father. As Father's Day approached he wrote his mother telling her he wanted to come home but couldn't until he knew his father still loved him and had forgiven him. His mother wrote back that she would talk to his father and if the father had forgiven him she would tie a white cloth on the tree close to the railroad tracks near their home. Since he was going to be traveling by train he would see the white cloth. If there was no cloth he was not forgiven.*
>
> *The young man took the train towards home accompanied by a friend. When the train approached the spot where the tree was he was afraid to look so he asked his friend to check to see if there was a white cloth hanging on it. His friend replied that there wasn't just one white cloth, white cloths were tied to every limb on the tree.*
>
> —*Source unknown*

God's love is greater than the father's love in this story. I don't know about you, sisters, but I thank God for the white cloth our Heavenly Father tied to the cross of Calvary—Jesus Christ. Jesus hung, bled, and died, and looked beyond our faults.

Furthermore, God writes our sins in pencil, not in ink. Our story is not over. The best of our story has never been told; Jesus is still writing the chapters. It doesn't matter what we've done. Our future is not determined by our past.

David was on the other side of Calvary, but he knew God and the joy of forgiveness. Look at his contemplation of the joy in Psalm 32:1–2, NLT:

> *Oh, what joy for those whose disobedience is forgiven, whose sin is put out of sight! Yes, what joy for those whose record the Lord has cleared of guilt, whose lives are lived in complete honesty!*

From Scabs to Scars

Sisters, when God alters and restores you at the altar you have the assurance that you can move from scabs to scars. The transition entails resisting the temptation to play the "what if" and "would've, could've, should've" game. There's no future in that. Instead, press on to higher heights and deeper depths.

Paul talks about pressing on in Philippians 3:12–14:

> *Not that I have already attained, or am already perfected; but I press on, that I may lay hold of that for which Christ Jesus has also laid hold of me. Brethren, I do not count myself to have apprehended; but one thing I do, forgetting those things which are behind and reaching forward to those things which are ahead, I press toward the goal for the prize of the upward call of God in Christ Jesus.*

The greater blessing is that you can have this assurance without groveling and begging. Our High Priest, Jesus Christ, invites you to come boldly to the throne of grace:

> *Seeing then that we have a Great High Priest who has passed through the heavens, Jesus the Son of God, let us hold fast*

our confession. For we do not have a High Priest who cannot sympathize with our weaknesses, but was in all points tempted as we are, yet without sin. Let us therefore come boldly to the throne of grace, that we may obtain mercy and find grace to help in time of need.

—*Hebrews 4:14–16*

That's real good news, my sisters. How I thank God for Jesus; He's a wonderful Savior. When we can't, He can.

I'm going to my seat now, as you may be bursting in anticipation of touring with Earl in the next segment of our journey—especially since he's writing to your husbands. However, as I sit down I have to tell you this: I feel like praising God! I don't need a drum roll, a chord from the organ, or a choir. I just think of God's grace and mercy toward me. Romans 5:8 tells us, "But God demonstrates His own love toward us, in that while we were still sinners, Christ died for us." Like the Clark Sisters say, "It should've been me, it could've been me, it would've been me—but the blood!"

Is there a shout in the house? Yes, I see you. Praise Him!

Let's Pray…

Be blessed!

P.S- I'll be back with a few closing comments after your tour with Earl.

Tour 2

From Pastor to Pastors

23

Letter From Earl To Pastors

Dear Brothers,

The great trust that our Lord has entrusted us with, as husbands, is to love our wives as Christ loves the church. Woman was made from man for his glory. She was made in the image and likeness of God, (spirit) from the rib of man, physical. This composite being loves and cares like her Maker and reproduces physically what she was made from. Adam was observably overwhelmed by this marvelous mate God made from him. Therefore, we should hold as precious and dear this great treasure we are trusted with, our soul mate. With great and holy reverence I relate, with God's divine enabling, we can sleep with our mates and their sleep will be sweet.

This thought of *"I'm Sleeping With The Pastor"* conveys the idea of a woman choosing to spend her life being a blessing to and being blessed by the man of God. Her sleeping with him is indicative of the fact he has found her, realizing he has found a good thing. He then makes a blood covenant to live with her in a life-long union called marriage. Marriage is not easy in the base case. Being married to a man of God has inherently even greater demands. Sleeping with the pastor suggests a man has found and chosen his life- long mate, and the woman has accepted the proposal.

The woman being taken from man is a significantly divine concept. It would have been easy for God to make woman from the dust of the ground, as he did Adam. However, God establishes over and over his divine principles. He makes the woman from man to bond them inextricably together, physically and spiritually. God is a God of order. He also has established that he desires fixed accountability and responsibility. The woman was given by God to man for him to love and to reflect his glory.

For a woman to sleep comfortably and securely with a man there must be three attitudes of heart passionately in place; he must love her sacrificially, sanctifiedly, and servantly. These three attitudes of heart and soul will make the marriage bed a place of blissful and serene repose.

Our Lord and Master Jesus Christ of Nazareth, loves his Bride the Church unconditionally. We are commanded by God, through the Apostle Paul, in Ephesians 5:25; to love our wives. This love by our Lord is experienced daily as we feel his presence, peace, provisions, and protection. Thankfully, this love is a divine choice. We are made in his image and after his likeness for his glory. When a man chooses to love is wife, he lives out, in a visual way for the world to see, what our Lord does for his church.

In Ephesians 5:25, the apostle Paul tells us; "Husbands, love your wives, just as Christ also loved the church *and gave himself up for her;*" this is sacrificial love. The husband must intentionally put the needs of his mate first. This attitude of sacrificial giving of one's self cannot be done without loving God with all your heart and walking in the power of the Holy Spirit.

Husband love your wife as Christ loves the church is best describe by the term *empathetic selflessness. "Submitting to one another out of reverence for Christ,"* Ephesians 5:21, is looking, as best we can, through the eyes of our mate and responding appropriately to what we see. Having made that empathetic observation we then proceed by placing the needs of our mate before our own. Real love is sacrificial in its nature. The most notable word for this attitude of heart is *agape*; the Greek word for the God kind of love.

The woman, taken from the man, suggests a birth, if you will. Therefore, one might say she becomes his baby. Godly humans are careful to care for their off spring. The scripture says: *Ephesians 5:1–2, Therefore be imitators of God, as beloved children; and walk in love, just as Christ also loved you, and gave himself up for us, an offering and a sacrifice to God as a fragrant aroma. Ephesians 5:28, So husbands ought also to love their own wives as their own bodies. He who loves his own wife loves himself; for no one ever hated his own flesh, but nourishes and cherishes it, just as Christ also does the church, because we are members of his body.* (NASB)

These passages reveal we imitate our Heavenly Father and our Lord when we "walk in love." The two becoming one cannot be demonstrated any clearer than the husband loving his wife as he loves himself. The phrase "but nourishing and cherishing" reveals demonstrative actions and attitudes of sacrificial love. The great bountiful product of God's masterful divine design is the more we give the more we receive. Hidden treasures are locked up in our mates that will only be released by their receiving sacrificial love. When she is loved sacrificially she feels sanctified by her husband.

When something or someone is sanctified, it has been set apart as special, it's to be consecrated, to hallow, purify, and it's designated, dedicated, or sacred. When a man sanctifies his wife, he extends to her supernatural grace. This atmosphere allows his wife to grow and mature into what God has purposed for her life. Flowers grow well in the right conditions. The flower requires rich soil, water, and sunshine to flourish and grow. The woman needs a stable and secure home environment to live out her God-ordained purpose. This stability has been characterized by the husband allowing his wife to experience *velvet steel*. Velvet is one of the softest and smoothest pieces of fabric.

Women must be treated with tenderness, care, and respect, while at the same time experiencing the solid strength and stability of their husband's masculinity. Statistics reveal, the number one need, out of the top five needs of a wife is security. In Ephesians 5:26, the Lord washes his bride, the church, with the word. The husband must take words and wash his wife's heart, soul, and mind from any improper thinking about herself. The powerful rays of the sun cause the flower to grow and flourish. As the man stands strong in the power of God's strength, velvet steel, his wife is nourished and nurtured by his Godly presence. This atmosphere of a man truly setting his wife apart for her graceful development is best defined as sanctification.

A husband's greatest challenge is to make his wife know that she is truly loved and has first place, after God, in his life. This challenge is greatly diminished by the husband knowing his wife's love language. Love languages are simply manners in which our mate desires to be related to. Gifts, touch, time, and words of endearment are love languages. If we are going to practice empathetic selflessness and create an environment where our mates will flourish and grow, their love language must be known and spoken on a consistent basis. Our wives desire and deserve to be treated special and cared for as God's divine design demands.

As we continue to love our wives sacrificially and sanctifyingly, our attitude of heart, more than anything else, must be a servant's heart. Jesus our lord and master on the night preceding his crucifixion took a towel and girded himself and began to wash his disciple's feet.

His climatic statement to this great expression of humility and care was John 13:14–15: *"If I then, the Lord and the teacher, washed your feet, you also ought to wash one another's feet. For I gave you an example that you also should do as I did to you."*

This posture our Savior and Lord takes is one of a dulos slave. In Christ's day, this position was one of the lowest, most menial jobs that one could have. However, our Lord uses it to give us an audio-visual of what true servanthood is all about. If we are going to love our wives as Christ loves the church, humility and love in the Holy Spirit are requisites. We serve our wives by *loving, listening, language, and lifting them.* Women have issues, so stated a late dear female minister friend of mind. When we know something is heavy for us, men, it's really a heavier load for our mate. By lifting heavy objects for our mates we show them their well-being is our concern. We should always be looking ahead to foresee the possibility of a struggle for our mate and then move to eliminate the problem. This lifting is not only anticipating and eliminating the physical, it's being observant of their countenance and responding appropriately. We may need to share something humorous, tell a non-threatening joke; offer a non-sexual hug, "just hold me," just listen to me, I don't need you to fix it, just listen to me. All of these are subtle, simple ways of serving, washing our mate's feet, while lifting our mate's countenance.

Our mates have to talk. Most often they will talk more than we do. If we don't make time to talk with them they often will find others to express themselves with. Women, I'm told get about 50,000 words per day to share with. On the other hand, men get about 30,000 words (this represent a very talkative man). This 20,000 word difference is potentially problematic. When the man gets home from work, or the wife gets home from her job, she may be working at home, the man has used up most of his words. However, his wife still has 20,000 to use. Men we must allow for a daily loving wrap-down. This wrap-down is where we listen to hear our mate's heart as she thankfully shares it with us. Remember she still has 20,000 words to share. These words will be best shared with her friend, lover, and soul mate, her husband.

A proactive way of listening is to use the term, *did I hear you say* (DIHYS) after your mate has shared something with you. Repeating back to your mate what you thought you heard helps her and you participate in affective listening and sharing. When she finds you are concerned enough to listen, she might share at a feelings level. This level of communication is where truth gets told and real bonding of souls takes place. Most often a twenty-five or thirty minute period is all that is required for this loving wrap down. Remember, the truth will make you free. This investment can often pay more dividends by creating a loving home environment than a mutual fund. It may lead to real mutual fun.

Intimacy begins in the kitchen. When our wives have served us all day a wonderful expression of thanks is to get up from the table, with real heart-felt thanks for a great meal, take all the dinner preparations and wash them. The wife's heart is warmed as she observes this care and concern. This audio-visual will teach our children respect and honor for their mother. Particularly for our sons, in this missing man society, honor and respect for women must be shown. I feel the expression "more things are caught than taught" has great validity. Husbands, love your wives is a command to action that requires a Holy Spirit filled and led life.

When we love our wives as Christ loves the church, *nourishing and cherishing it,* this is true servant love.

This word *nourishing* means providing resources for health and growth. The word to *cherish* means to protect and care for lovingly, to nurture. Serving our mates is to provide for them a resource-rich, secure environment of love, revenue, empathetic selflessness, affective listening, with lifting and edifying language. When our mates live with this God-ordained treatment, houses are transformed into loving lasting homes where sleep is sweet and two souls have lovingly became one.

Husbands, we are entrusted with a divinely designed helpmate. God made her to help us fulfill his will for our lives. We must admit, unfortunately, we don't always appreciate what God has blessed us with. A sobering question for us to ask our mates is, "Am I loving you as Christ loves the church?" You may want to sit down before you get the answer. Many men try to answer this question for their mates. Remember she is of age and her comments and countenance will tell it all. Therefore, I would like to encourage all the godly men to keep on demonstrating agape love. God is for us; he is on our side; we are blessed to be God's lover, leader, and lesson to a wife and watching world.

In Him,
Pastor Earl Whitaker

Epilogue

A Pastor's Wife by God's Design

Being a pastor's wife is not the biggest issue of life; living as God's child and handling circumstances in a manner pleasing to him is what matters.

—Dobson, *I'm More Than A Pastor's Wife*, 15

I don't know what your destiny will be, but one thing I do know: the only ones among you who will be really happy are those who have sought and found how to serve.

—Albert Schweitzer

When you were born, you cried and the world rejoiced. Live your life in such a manner than when you die the world cries and you rejoice.

—Old Indian Saying

My sisters, the journey to a godly satisfying marriage is never over. As pastors' wives, we do not live in a Pollyanna world shrouded in rose colored glasses, waiting for our prince charming to take us to a land where we will live happily ever. We are living in real world where God has entrusted us with the marvelous ministry of being a pastor's wife.

As we join with our husband as co-laborers for Jesus Christ we find that our ministry as pastors' wives is not predictable, but turbulent and fascinating. I pray that you will use the items in your success kit to make your journey easier. If not, maybe you can laugh more when you find yourself faced with the guts and glory of being a pastor's wife, or even cry without guilt. In the final analysis, you are not a pastor's wife by error or perhaps even by choice; you are a pastor's wife by God's design, and you are fearfully and wonderfully made. It's okay to be who you are, because God has made you to be uniquely you.

You can also rejoice knowing that God is not just with you on the journey; He planned the journey. Even though you are not perfect yet, God is carrying you from glory to glory. Some of you may fear you were never destined to be a pastor's wife, but God has given you everything you need to excel. By being the best "Me" that you can be, you will be a Spirit-filled wife that brings glory to God and honor to your husband—so much so that he can praise you in the gates.

You must recognize there will be times when your husband will disappoint you and not live up to your expectations, though fair. That does not nullify your commitment of fulfilling your role in marriage according to God's glorious design. At such moments, it is wise to remind yourself of the same advice Elisabeth Elliott gave to her daughter: You married a sinner who is subject to temptation and is in need of redemption just as you are:

> *First of all, who is it you marry? You marry a sinner. There's nobody else to marry. That might seem to be obvious enough, but when you love a man as you love yours it's easy to forget. You forget it for a while and then when something happens that ought to remind you, you find yourself wondering what's the matter, how could this happen, where did things go wrong? They went wrong back in the garden of Eden.*
>
> —*Elliott, 68-69*

You must also recognize that no one else in your life can satisfy you fully; only God can satisfy your every need. Joyce Meyer says it this way:

> *We all want to feel satisfied. We all want contentment. We all want to know we are loved and accepted for who we are. We may think acceptance and approval from people will make us feel complete. However, the Bible teaches us that when we trust in man to give us what only God can give, we live under a curse; but when we believe, trust in, and rely on the Lord, we are blessed. The joy, peace, and fulfillment we seek come from being filled with God, and nothing else. They do not come from having a certain person in our life, or from money, position, power, fame, accomplishments, or anything else.*
>
> — *Meyer, Approval Addiction, 246*

Knowing this, you must be a godly example to young and old alike. Disney has a saying, "Remember, you are always on show." In other words, someone is always watching you, so you have to walk in a manner that is pleasing to the Lord. If you have children, you should live a life before them that will cause them to rise up and call you blessed. You are also being watched outside of your family. If you are a seasoned saint, emulate the Titus 2 woman by teaching younger women how to live godly lives in reverence to God, and in submission to their husbands.

Perhaps, most importantly, realize that your worth and value are determined by your position, not your performance. I'm not referring to your position as a pastor's wife, but your position as a child of the living God. You are in an eternal blood covenant relationship with Jesus Christ, seated in heavenly places and are an heir and joint heir with Him. The exciting thing is that you are still work in progress and the Holy Spirit is molding you into what God destined you to be. So please be patient with yourself, God is not through with you yet. When God is through with you, you will come forth as pure gold; for He Who has begun a good work in you will perform it until the day of Jesus Christ.

May unspeakable joy rise up in your body, mind, soul, and spirit, as you manifest God's presence in your fascinating ministry as a pastor's wife.

From my heart to yours:

God Be With You Till We Meet Again

God be with you till we meet again;
loving counsels guide, uphold you,
with a shepherd's care enfold you:
God be with you till we meet again.

God be with you till we meet again;
unseen wings protecting, hide you,
daily manna still provide you:
God be with you till we meet again.

God be with you till we meet again;
when life's perils thick confound you,
put unfailing arms around you;
God be with you till we meet again.

God be with you till we meet again;
keep love's banner floating o'er you,
smite death's threatening wave before you:
God be with you till we meet again.

—*Jeremiah E. Rankin, pdmusic.org- public domain*

Peace and blessings to you in all you do, my sisters. I never cease to pray for you.

Now unto him that is able to keep you from falling, and to present you faultless before the presence of his glory with exceeding joy.

> *To the only wise God our Savior, be glory and majesty, dominion and power, both now and ever. Amen.*
>
> —*Jude 24–25, KJV*

Your fellow servant,

Sena

P. S. Let's keep in touch. I welcome your feedback about this book, and I hope you'll share some of your experiences with me. My e-mail address is earsen@att.net.

One last word for my writing sisters: "If anyone would ever write my life story, for whatever reason there might be; He'll be there between each line of pain and glory—Jesus is the best thing that ever happened to me!"

I told you I was a preacher…

Be a blessing!

Appendix A
From Sister to Sister

I sent surveys to approximately 75 pastors' wives asking the questions:

1. How long have you been a pastor's wife?
2. What is your greatest joy as a pastor's wife, and why is it your greatest joy?
3. What is your greatest challenge as a pastor's wife and why is it your greatest challenge?
4. How do you overcome this challenge?
5. What words of advice would you give to other pastors' wives?
6. What words of encouragement would you give to other pastors' wives?
7. Please list any books, organizations, or websites that would be helpful to other pastors' wives
8. Additional comments

Total responses received= 30

Contributors

I am grateful to the following women for participating in my survey and to those who chose to have their names listed anonymously:

Eldress Mary Adams
Billie M. Berry
Mary E. Brown
Sandra Burley
Veronica Y. Collins
Claudlene Duirden
Missionary Cynthia Elliott
Verlinda Flowers
Evangelist Lori Ann Blanton
Myrtle Harrison
Evangelist Claudine Tenelle Hines
Evangelist Barbara Lacy
Barbara Jones
Natasha Mitchell
Lisa Mitcham
Evelyn Morgan
Deloris Price
Janice W. Riggins

Carla Scurlock
Evangelist Sheree Tait
Katherine M. Tima
Missionary Carolyn Tyler
Evangelist Bernadine Ware
Evangelist Linda Hunter Wheat
Audrey White
Missionary Mary Kaye White
Anonymous (four)

Responses are grouped by number of years the respondents have been pastors' wives.

Of the thirty respondents, the number of year's breakdown is:
Less than 1 year = 2
1 to 5 years = 4
6 to 10 years = 7
11 to 20 years = 8
21 to 30 years = 5
31 to 44 years = 4
Range = 3 months to 44 years
Average number of years =18

Less Than One Year

What is your greatest joy as a pastor's wife, and why is it your greatest joy?

Witnessing the spiritual growth of my husband and the impact it's having on our family and marriage.

My greatest joy so far is being asked to agree with others in praying and seeing God work on their behalf.

What is your greatest challenge as a pastor's wife; why is it your greatest challenge, and how do you overcome this challenge?

Knowing that he has an obligation to help those who call upon him. And he never says no. He stretches himself way too thin. Overcome: I remind myself that he's working for a much higher authority. I keep my emotions and ego in check sometimes (smile). And remember it's *not about me!*

My greatest challenge is knowing how to be myself. This is my greatest challenge because I have seen where people put others on a pedestal because of a title in church. Overcome: I pray to God for guidance to be true to him, myself, and others.

What words of advice could you give to other pastors' wives?

I really don't feel like I have any advice to give, since I'm fairly new to this position.

I would advise others to pray.

What words of encouragement could you give to other pastors' wives?

I would encourage them that God has given them exactly what they need to complete the assignment he has given them.

Please list any books, organizations, and/or websites that would be helpful to pastors' wives.

The Power of a Praying Wife by Stormie Omartian
Managing Your Emotions by Joyce Meyer
Can You Stand To Be Blessed by Bishop by T. D. Jakes

One to Five Years

What is your greatest joy as a pastor's wife, and why is it your greatest joy?

Supporting my husband's ministry through my prayers and participation allows me to take part in the awesome responsibility he has as pastor.

The issues of life that I have overcome my husband will use as life applications in his preaching and teaching and people lives have been changed for the better.

Being his partner in spreading the Gospel through his vision. He gets so excited, and I really feel like I'm a part of something great developing.

That God has chosen me to be a pastor's wife because I know God's hand is upon me.

What is your greatest challenge as a pastor's wife; why is it your greatest challenge, and how do you overcome this challenge?

My greatest challenge is sharing my husband's time. He works a full-time joy and so do I. Our family time, away from church activities, is almost nonexistent. Overcome: By making the most of what we have and occupying myself with spiritually uplifting activities.

Wanting people to be submitted and dedicated to God and to the gifts and talents that he has given them. Overcome: I have to remember that it takes time for people to grow even when they know what is expected from them accord to the Word of God. I have to be patient, understanding, love, be in self-control, and pray always.

Addressing things he does in church or in regard to the church business. I know everyone watches my reactions and feeds on them. If I don't agree with his decision, I must remain silent and not display disgruntled. That can be difficult. Overcome: I get stoic and try to present my concerns in private from a questioning point. Example, when discussing vision statement I waited until we were on our way home and I say, "I thought? Never "I know!"

Being the best that I can be and to stay beside my husband 101 percent. And to know that I'm always there. Overcome: To stay read up, pray up, and suited up

What words of advice could you give to other pastors' wives?

Be yourself, you are not going to please everyone. Seek God's approval in all you do, the rest will follow.

Be willing to share your time. You cannot be jealous. Learn when to talk and to keep your mouth shut. Be willing to go places with your husband.

God becomes your best friend and the only one who maintains secrecy and doesn't hold anything against anyone. God won't repeat or judge either of you for it. You can be honest and expose yourself.

Trust in the Lord, never give up, to the pressures of the world. You're not two, you're one because when he hurts you hurt. So smile together.

What words of encouragement could you give to other pastors' wives?

God placed you in this position because he trusts you. You are called just as your husband, who God calls. He qualifies.

Support your husband. Encourage your husband. Have an open mind about your husband's callings.

People are usually angry at the situation not the person. They usually love you. Stand strong and know that God has left a comforter especially for you.

Weeping may endure for a night, but joy cometh in the morning.

Please list any books, organizations, and/or websites that would be helpful to pastors' wives.

God's Promise Book
Prayer for Your Every Need
Holy Bible
Power of a Praying Wife by Stormie Omartian

Additional comments

Being a pastor's wife has given me the time to see who I am in God. I have learned to look at people as individuals and have learned that we grow every day. I am learning to love and forgive people regardless of how they act and what they say. Die to flesh daily, renew the spirit of my mind daily, walking in the spirit, and asked God to take control of my life and the people who cross my pathway. Just because you wear the title "first lady," you should not act like you are better than the other ladies. Be down to earth, and the phony and fake will dissolve in others. God can heal the wounds and scars of others.

Six to Ten Years

What is your greatest joy as a pastor's wife, and why is it your greatest joy?

Fulfilling God's purpose for my life, serving people and seeing people's life changed by God's power

1. **Being co-laborers**: One of my greatest joys in life has been to labor side by side in ministry with my husband and to know that we're on the same team. It has been my heart's desire to help and support him, firstly through my life. People see more than they hear. I support him through prayer, encouragement, confrontation, respect, and unconditional love.
2. **The opportunity to model**: To be at the front of the pack and be able to say, "Follow me as I follow the Lord" (Corinthians 11:1) forces me to grow and keeps my own heart fresh with God.
3. **Seeing long-term fruit**: One of the greatest joys of my life has been to see spiritual fruit. Knowing that our labor has made a

difference in this life and throughout all eternity has made the trials worth it all.

My greatest joy as a pastor's wife is having a sense of holiness. I'm a part of a ministry that gives me the opportunity to serve freely.

To sense the presence of the Lord at home and at church through the leadership of my husband. Because I know that my pastor/husband loves the Lord and his people.

The greatest joy is hearing my pastor preach and grow in the Lord. Why? Simply, being a pastor is his (my pastor) calling and his joy. It's beautiful when you see someone you love glowing and growing at what they love. My joy is seeing and sharing his joy.

To have someone look to you as a mentor for life and to know that you can be trusted with it. It's a joy to be able to help those that ask and feel like you are capable of it.

Serving the people. By serving you are growing as well. You are learning patience, how to be humble, compassionate, love; all the many virtues it takes to be a pastor's wife.

What is your greatest challenge as a pastor's wife; why is it your greatest challenge, and how do you overcome this challenge?

Seeing people (believers) live lives that hurt or shame the body of Christ, because I know God expects and deserves better from his people. Overcome: Pray for people and work daily to live a holy, acceptable, and righteous life before God.

Unrealistic expectations: Every church is different, and every person in the church has different expectations of the pastor and his wife. We knew that no matter how we tried, we couldn't meet everyone's expectations as each person was different. We could only be true to the call that God had placed on our lives. We constantly had to remind ourselves to play to an audience of one, namely God himself. Overcome: Staying in truth and integrity, love and joy, reflecting God's grace, mercy and love on this earth is greater than any skill or talent that hides who you are created to be.

My greatest challenge as a Pastor's wife is dealing with the fact that my husband also is an evangelist. He has to travel frequently. So he is away from home. It's my greatest challenge because we have a daughter, and his presence is greatly missed. There are times when I think why can't we just live the simple life. Overcome: I overcame this challenge or shall I say I am *overcoming* it by realizing and understanding more of what my purpose is. I understand that he is called, and when you're called there is great responsibility placed on one's shoulders. I have to pray, stay, and focus and be supportive of his ministry.

Keeping myself walking in the spirit because my flesh still wants its own way in the people of God, through evil influences. Button pushing. It is a constant challenge to forgive and love my enemies. Overcome: worship and prayer—constant practice.

The greatest challenge is living up to the expectations of people. Why? Because it sometimes prevents me from being comfortable around people. I feel always on guard against the devil's people instead of being who I am, this wonderful person. Overcome: I pray that God continues to bless me with a calm spirit. I do a lot of listening and smiling, even when I want to frown.

To maintain humility and to get to know the people's personality so you can learn to treat each person as an individual rather than a group. Overcome: By maintaining my personality so that I will be looked at as an individual rather than "A pastor's wife" or "The pastor's wife" with respect.

Being submissive. Overcome: By releasing some anger, letting go of things in my past.

What words of advice could you give to other pastors' wives?

Be an example of holiness that members can be proud of. Always love, support, and encourage your husband; allow *him* to be the pastor and don't force your opinions on him (sometimes it's best to keep your mouth shut); you don't need to know everything, just pray. Be real, take off the masks.

1. A pastor's wife often finds it difficult to find other women who can relate to the struggles she faces—give advice how to seek a confidant. Know the caution signs—discerning spirit. I really have learned the lesson of not having close friends or best

friends within the congregation. It is best to have that outside the church-friendships with women who are not connected to my church. When you have a best friend, you share what is on your heart. If there are struggles going on in the church, you can't share them with people in the congregation because it reflects on them. They're part of the congregation, and they are biased. It is better to talk to somebody outside of the church to get a different perspective on things. And it's not good for the health of your relationships to talk about people in the church to a friend who is in the church.
2. A pastor's wife needs time alone with her husband. Nothing can replace time alone together.
3. We must have personal time with God, learning, growing in wisdom.

Be supportive! We all learn from Delilah. She gave Samson a place to rest his mind, his thoughts, and a safe haven after ministering and dealing with church work and church folk. It can be stressful. When all else fails, our husbands should be able to lay their heads in our lap. Our *spouse* is our ministry.

To stay encouraged and don't give up. Romans 8:28–31: All things work for our good. Stay in God's presence. The time we need God the most is when we think we can handle it on our own and when we don't feel like worshipping. That's when we need to draw near to him.

Be yourself and embrace the pastor's calling as he needs your help.

Never get involved in your husband's conversations that are not directed toward you in a meeting unless you are asked. Do not involve yourself in meetings that involve the church doing a *financial appreciation* for you (sometimes things are said you don't want to know). Do not allow yourself to be with a particular group of people we call *cliques*, spread yourself around with all the women of the church as much as you can. We never want to cater to one or two people. If you have friends you want to spend time with in a church, find another way outside of the church to do it, if it's not pertaining to church business. More than often people have a tendency to be close to the pastor's wife, but *sometimes* it's not for the right reason.

Pray daily, seeking God in everything you do, whether it's big or small. Learn to love the people for who they are.

What words of encouragement could you give to other pastors' wives?

Though this role can be lonely at times, take those lonely times as opportunities to grow closer to God.

Know that the Lord will supply all our needs, "God has not given us a spirit of fear, but of power, and of love and a sound mind" (2 Timothy 1:7 NKJ). We need not be afraid. If we trust God for everything, "God will supply all your needs according to his riches in Christ Jesus (Phil 4:19). We don't need to be fearful. We need to know that God is in control and depend on him. He is there! He will keep us in his grasp. We don't have to let anxiety take over; God has proven himself over the years to us that he is there, that he is faithful, and that he will look after us.

Know who you are in God first. Be confident because many women think they could do a much better job than you can, but God elected you.

You were handpicked and tailor-made for him. Be encouraged and *stay* prayerful and meditate on the word. Hold your peace. There will be many opportunities for you to speak or give your opinion. You will learn that timing is so important. Be graceful, and keep your *integrity!*

Because the devil would love to get you out of your character.

James 1:2–8. Praise God in good times and bad. Inquire of him often. Stay focused on God. Get off the fence. Meditate in Psalms and Proverbs daily. Get Psalm 27 embedded in your spirit. You have had trouble in the night, but joy comes in the morning.

Joy comes in the morning and it gets better as time goes by.

There will be times when you will feel that you are the least of all. Don't fret because little do they know that you are the driving force behind this man. So smile and keep smiling.

Look at being a pastor's wife as a test. You have to study God's word in order to face the many obstacles and overcome them.

Please list any books, organizations, and/or websites that would be helpful to pastors' wives.

The Bible
Power of a Praying Wife
Woman After God's Own Heart
Wife After God's Own Heart
The Lord is My Shepherd; Subtitle: Healing Wisdom of the Twenty-third Psalm by Harold S. Kushner
Don't Sweat the Small Stuff at Work: Simple Ways to Minimize Stress and Conflict While Bringing Out the Best in Yourself and Others by Richard Carlson
Women's Ministry in Smaller Churches by Becky Badry
Masterlife: Developing a Rich Personal Relationship with the Master by Avery T. Willis and Sherrie Willis-Brown
Experiencing God: Knowing and Doing the Will of God by Henry T. Blackaby and Claude V. King
Living by the Book by Howard Hendricks, William Hendricks
Women of the Bible
Disciplines of the Beautiful Women (with build-in study guide) by Anne Ortlund
Life Management for Busy Women by Elizabeth George
Bible Gateway

Additional comments

You may think that man or this world has you in a stranglehold, but just remember God's grip is tighter.

I believe that pastors' wives should be able to carry a service if it becomes necessary. I believe she should be able to carry on teaching the Bible in every capacity: Sunday school, mission, etc., especially in the absence of someone. Attitude is the best gift a pastor's wife should have (I mean a good attitude).

Eleven to Twenty Years

What is your greatest joy as a pastor's wife, and why is it your greatest joy?

My greatest joy is helping others and networking with people. I know that by helping others, I am doing the will of God, and I want to glorify him through my works.

My greatest joy as a pastor's wife is knowing that I have a God-fearing husband.

Knowing that I'm beside my husband as he carries the Gospel. I get joy knowing that his feet are blessed as well as beautiful. My husband loves to spread the word. I get joy in knowing this.

Just being supportive of my husband. I would never want to be a hindrance to a man of God.

Seeing people accept Christ. Because this is the will of God.

In my marriage: effectively working in union with my husband in ministry to restore the brokenness of God's people and then reconcile them back to Christ. In the church: witnessing to people and seeing lives transforms from a state of hopelessness to understanding their usefulness in God's kingdom.

What is your greatest challenge as a pastor's wife; why is it your greatest challenge, and how do you overcome this challenge?

My greatest challenge is supporting my husband as he performs his ministerial duties. I want to be able to give him 100 percent as his helpmate and keep him encouraged. Overcome: This requires total unselfishness on my part and I must keep my life balanced and I must please the Lord.

My greatest challenge is being sociable even when I am uncomfortable doing so. Overcome: I overcome this by asking God for guidance and putting myself out there regardless.

See him being hurt and mistreated by church folks and to have to listen to/watch members not get along as a body of Christ. Knowing that the members think you have all the answers to their why? Overcome: Staying prayerful, staying humble and fasting, treat everyone with love and respect.

The giving up of my personal desires to be able to always be available for the pastor. Overcome: Total submission to his needs.

Dealing with overheard criticism of the pastor. Wanting to squash it so he won't hear and be discouraged. Overcome: Pray, smile, and pray some more.

Getting the respect from the body as the Mother of the House/pastor's wife. Although I'm not the pastor (and have no desire to be), people don't realize the responsibilities and accountability that come with being in this position. There's little appreciation or concern for the pastor's wife (unless it's provoked by the pastor) or the balancing act of home, family, community, work, school, and church she performs every day. At times I have let the response of the body be a hindrance in how I have gone forth in ministry. My challenge has been to focus on the soul of the individual and not the face of the individual. Overcome: Pray, asking God to keep me humble, and then if God leads me to I'll talk about it with someone that will be in pray with me.

What words of advice could you give to other pastors' wives?

You must be saved and know the Lord. Because without him, we know we can do nothing. Now that you'll have trials and tribulations in many forms, but you must put all your trust in God and remain faithful to him.

Use the gift that God has given you to deal with people.

Stay prayed up, love those that mistreat you (and your family). Watch, fight, and pray. Keep your conversations with members at a safe level and most of all, keep them holy.

Always support your husband.

Stay faithful to God, study the word, be prayerful and be yourself, not what everyone expects.

Be who God created you to be. Don't conform to what others (including our husbands) think you should be or do. Remember that God created us just how he wanted us so that we can reach a particular group or population of people. If you like wearing your hair natural don't press/perm it because others want you to. If you like wearing nails, eyelashes, makeup, and weaves…wear it because that's what you want to do and it makes you feel good.

What words of encouragement could you give to other pastors' wives?

To love your husband, the church, and above all to love the Lord with all your heart, soul, and mind.

Continue to be supportive to your husband.

"Know that your labor is not in vain." "Only what you do for Christ will last."

Remain humble during the hard times that are surely to come in the most critical ways.

Always put God first, be yourself. Use the gift God gave you. Pray for, love, and take care of your husband and family.

The tests and trials do make you strong. Don't believe for one moment that no one else has gone through what you've gone through, no matter how embarrassing, ashamed, or terrible it might be. Pick yourself up; learn the lesson from your trial and move forward.

Please list any books, organizations, and/or websites that would be helpful to pastors' wives.

The Bible
Church Constitution
The Purpose-Driven Life

Additional comments

Life as a pastor's wife. It takes someone special to be a pastor's wife. First of all, one must be sensitive to the needs of people, a true people person. In order to love people you must be real, sociable, prayerful, and dedicated. One must be able to show the same love and respect for all the children of God equally. You must be a well-rounded person, trustworthy, strong in the word, body, soul, and spirit. Able to tell everybody the truth, whether it hurts their feelings or makes them a better person. We may not be the pastor, but we bear a lot of responsibility. As a wife, we are their helpmates in all things. However, some feel that if the husband has been called by God, "that's him not me." Once twain became one, she's automatically included, want it or not.

Yes, some pastors' wives just go with the flow, especially if money is involved. A lot of times pastors' wives have to take the backseat to a lot of things, because the pastor is doing church work. Who's taking care of the house while he's gone? Yes, the wife. Well now, she has the church to make sure things are operating properly and take care of her personal house. If there's children involved, she has to make sure they go to school, get home work done, take them to doctor appointments, handle problems that arrive from: home, school, church, and work. If she works outside of the house. With all these things going on, she becomes frustrated. When pastor arrives home, the wife is tired. She wants "Me Time" from the pastor.

Pastor gets back in town, tries to have some "Me Time" with his wife. Telephone rings, his favorite show is on, or a friend calls wanting him to go play pool, or something, and guess what? There goes her "Me Time," because he feels they need him. Okay, the pastor's wife is crying out "what about me?" A lot of times, the pastors' wives are hurting and not able to communicate with the lay members for fear of destroying the pastor, of whom they look up to.

Not all, but some pastors' wives are not sociable with the church members. They'd rather not be bothered. I'm not gonna say anything, 'cause if I say something it might be wrong or it might not come across the right way. There's some pastors' wives who feel "I'm the pastor's wife; I'm not talking to those crazy people. He can deal with them. I'm just here to meet his needs." When you find this type of attitude from the Pastors' wives, it has a bad reflection on the pastor. If that's the way she feels, I'm sure the church is saying the same thing about her. One must be willing to adapt to change.

It's really not an easy task to be a pastor's wife. A lot of women desire to be a pastor's wife, and some women go to church to see if they can get the pastor. That's why it takes a strong, matured person in the Lord to pray for her husband, fulfill his needs, as he fulfills hers. It's not a one-sided deal. If the pastor and wife are taking care of one another at home, like Christ took care of the church, he wouldn't even entertain these type women. Sometime, I think the pastors play naive, but you can't play with the devil. These type of women are the ones with the Jezebel spirit. So as a helpmate, a pastor's wife must be alert at all times.

When the pastor has completed his daily task, whether a good or bad day, the pastor's wife has to be there for him. Whether it's just listening to him vent his frustrations or whatever his need maybe. Although we have our issues, as a woman, we're able to balance more things than the man. Of course, nobody knows what goes on behind closed doors, but they sure can tell by your reactions to certain things. Folk watch the pastor's wife like a hawk. They know when your nails aren't manicured. Some may not say anything but trust me, they know. Sometimes, we talk too much about the pastor to make them desire him more—especially talking to single, divorce, or unhappy women. So be careful for nothing as the scripture has said.

Twenty-one to Thirty years

What is your greatest joy as a pastor's wife, and why is it your greatest joy?

Helping my husband fulfill his calling.

Pastor's wife: learning what makes him tick. To tell the truth I have not really thoughts about it. Because of my first experiences when I married him with the members.

Seeing the Holy Spirit take control of every aspect of the service… from praise and worship to taking pastor out of "self" and using him to proclaim the pure gospel. I feel that with each of these experiences it brings us closer to God or helps all of us grow spiritually.

Knowing that I'm being supportive and being by my husband's side.

Serving God's people. It allows me to share what God has given me and help someone along the way.

Watching my husband minister and encourage the downtrodden and discouraged of this world. The joy is knowing it's on a personal level (we have been there).

What is your greatest challenge as a pastor's wife; why is it your greatest challenge, and how do you overcome this challenge?

Watching and observing others. Learning what to keep and what not. Overcome: Praying and asking God's help.

Not feeling worthy or feeling inadequate in that position. In addition, I don't like the added pressure of being a first lady with all the expectations (real or perceived). I don't enjoy the spotlight. Overcome: I try to minimize the pressure I put on myself and that I feel coming from other sources by meditating and just trying to be me.

Church folks being so mean and messy. Overcome: I try to respect all, but at the same time stay away from "clicks." I try to show love to all, but not really *hang* with anyone. I've never attended a business meeting.

Understanding people. Because God is giving us time to get it right with him. And so many of our people, i.e. God's people are missing the opportunity; continuing to live like they have all the time in the world to get it right with him. Overcome: Continue to give them the word of God every opportunity that becomes available to me. Let them know God is on his way back and time is winding up.

Pretending that I don't hear when snide remarks are targeted at him as a minister. Challenge is to hold my peace because of the love I have for him. Overcome: By consoling myself that these people are "small," they don't know from whence he came.

What words of advice could you give to other pastors' wives?

Be sure that this is what you want.

Never allow anyone to speak against your husband in your presence. When they start, put a stop to it ASAP. Always stay neutral with the members of the church so it won't be said you are in favor with anyone.

Don't let the possible negative things you hear or see directed toward your husband sow seeds of bitterness in you. Always be forgiving and gracious. Don't always say what you think (smile). Also, be as supportive and as encouraging as possible toward your husband. Pray and continue to ask God for help and guidance.

To remain prayerful, fast and stand by your husband. When he needs an ear to listen or a shoulder to cry on, be there.

Let Christ lead you in every aspect of your life. Make sure you are for real. Find yourself a mentor; someone you can trust. Make sure you are taken care of if something happens to your husband. Make sure your future is made beyond the church. Know the financial affairs of your household. Have an education so you can live afterward.

Support your husband in his endeavors, even though you may not see the vision. Remember, he was called, you were not.

What words of encouragement could you give to other pastors' wives?

You must be confident of yourself or you will not be a happy minister's wife.

Always be a cheerleader for your husband when he is preaching. Be the first to give support and others will follow.

Stay strong and positive. Be the best you you can be.

Remember only what we do for Christ will last. If we keep our focus on Christ, we can reach the mark.

Know that you are chosen by God to lead and guide every person that you come in contact with. Always remember only what you do for Christ will last.

Know that you are a person in your own right and not just your husband's shadow.

Please list any books, organizations, and/or websites that would be helpful to pastors' wives.

Reviveourhearts.org
A Woman After God's Own Heart
A Praying Wife
The Battle of the Mind
A Heart Like David's
The Purpose Driven Life

Additional comments

Being a pastor's wife is a challenge in itself. There are times I just want to relax and not worry about other problems or needs, but that is rarely the case. I have to put my needs aside and go after the one that is hurting or in need. Sometimes I feel the need to talk with someone about my struggles being a minister's wife, but who can you confide in within the congregation or elsewhere?

Thirty-one to Forty-four...

What is your greatest joy as a pastor's wife, and why is it your greatest joy?

My greatest joy has been in knowing that I have been in a position to help some of the lives come to the Lord. After thirty-one years of serving at eight different church locations, and knowing that many times I may have been "in my sister's shadow," I am yet surviving and trusting in the Lord.

A closer walk with God.

Joy comes after many years of hardships, when you are an overcomer.

My greatest joy is searching the scriptures and learning more about God. This is my greatest joy because it is one of the most important things I can do and because it makes me feel close to God.

I have so many things. Being a pastor's wife isn't easy because there are ups and downs, but just loving my husband and knowing that he is following God is a great joy. This is not always easy for me, but the Lord brings it to pass where I understand.

What is your greatest challenge as a pastor's wife; why is it your greatest challenge, and how do you overcome this challenge?

My greatest challenge is to keep from being pulled into the middle of a pastor versus lay member dispute or shall I say correction of a member.

Overcome: I have to realize that I am not the pastor who must correct even me when I am wrong, so I try my best to not get in the crossfire by remaining in my place as a wife and help for the pastor.

Since I've been a wife for thirty-seven years there is no challenge God can't take me through. Overcome: With prayer, steadfastness, meditation, fasting

A call to fight. Learning to fight spiritually. The battle is not yours, it's the Lord's. Overcome: By humbling oneself unto the Lord, seek him only, and pray.

My greatest challenge is trying to understand the members of the church. It is my greatest challenge because I really want to understand people more, and a lot of times they don't want me to understand them. Overcome: By praying about it.

My greatest challenge is missing my husband. He has many things to do, and I am left out. I know what it is, but I'm kind of jealous. I won't say that I'm not. I need him and his touch, and after a busy day he goes straight to sleep or whatever, but I really miss him as my husband. Overcome: By staying prayerful. I also meditate on Philippians 4:13: "I can do all things through Christ who strengthens me," because there are many things I come in contact with that I don't like to do but have to do, so I stay prayerful.

What words of advice could you give to other pastors' wives?

Keep your personal feelings to yourself. Never discuss your sexual life or marital problems with church women. Keep them private. Never try to correct your pastor in the public. Talk to him at home or in seclusion in a pleasant atmosphere.

Love the Lord with all your heart. Keep an open mind to your husband's needs: moods, clothes, his health. Encourage him—praise God for his calling.

Do not become a buddy or a pal. Be the pastor's wife (at home) and helper (wife) watchman.

Stand with your husband, not in front of him or behind him, but beside him. Whatever you have to say to him, say it at home. Do a lot of meditating and studying the word of God.

Pray and pray mightily for your husband and understand where he is. Talk to him and let him know where you are and what you need from him; we need more than just a pastor, we need a husband, which God has given. Also, block out space for yourself and maintain your space.

What words of encouragement could you give to other pastors' wives?

To be strong in the Lord and in the power of his might. Put on the whole armor of God…and having done all to stand, stand for whatever you may be going through, remember, that this, too, shall pass.

Pray. Love people (congregation). Last but not least love the word of God.

Be prayerful at all times. Remember: this pastor is your husband at home.

Seek the Lord first and he will direct your path. All other things will be added unto you.

Seek the Lord for yourself and read, read, read. A pastor's wife has to be understanding and patient. Seeking the Lord and reading helps you to understand where your husband is coming from. Also, you don't know what the Lord is telling him, so you have to understand that he still loves you. You also have to understand that there will be times when you are lonely just like other women who are not pastors' wives.

Please list any books, organizations, and/or websites that would be helpful to pastors' wives.

The Bible
Mrs. Billy Graham's book
King James Version of The Bible

The Power of a Praying Woman by Stormie O'Martian
The Daily Word
Power of a Praying Wife
Books about learning how to be a pastor's wife
Books that help you to understand where our husbands are coming from in their position, and when we are as pastors' wives

Additional comments

A pastor's wife should remain in control of her speech (tongue) at all times. There are those who will twist your words completely around. So always think before making a hasty remark. Keep your tongue with grace.

Be willing to do anything for the furtherance of the kingdom. "A soul winner is wise." (Proverbs 11:30)

"Supporting" is another word for love, and love is woman's métier. Your helping and supportive relationship with your minister husband can be whatever you and he wish to make it. But if you have never quite found your special place of usefulness in the body of Christ, it may be that teaming up with your husband in his ministries will be the most satisfying and productive way you can give time and energy in the Lord's service.

Pray for your husband, yourself, and the congregation. Keep your hand in Jesus' hand. If you don't, you will become discouraged.

Stay prayerful. Understand your husband and where he is and love him.

First be a woman of dignity; one who has poise and self-respect and who inspires the respect of others. Homes, church, and communities need women of dignity.

Second, recognize your need to grow. Every Christian needs to grow. Until she does she'll remain wrapped in a cocoon. Growth takes effort, too. God waits upon you to do your part.

Finally, be faithful in all things. A man in a position of spiritual leadership is hampered by a fickle and frivolous girl for a wife. None of us can be all things to all people. There is a definite limit to the number of people whom we can genuinely help at any given time. But each of us can do something. Together you have something to offer that no other partnership ever could.

Appendix B

From Female Pastor to First Lady

Contributors

I am grateful to the following eleven pastors for completing the surveys:

Prophetess Dorri Burrell
Bishop Annell Castille-Haney
Eldress Dr. Gloria Collins
Pastor Mary Henderson
Apostle Gwendolyn Hollins
Evangelist Doris Jean Johnson
Reverend Bettie R. Kennedy
Pastor Barbara Linton
Pastor Patrina R. Mitchell
Pastor Valetta Shaw
Evangelist Lillian Windom

What words of advice could you give to pastors' wives?

The words of advice I would give to pastors' wives are to pray without ceasing for themselves, their husband, and the church. Secondly, to recognize the difference between their husband and "the Man of God." Live selflessly and be secure in who God made them.

What words of encouragement could you give to pastors' wives?

Words of encouragement I would give to pastors' wives are to know that they are special to God and especially chosen, and made to be a pastor's wife. A woman can't be a pastor's wife, she must be a "Woman of God." A pastor's wife can't be a woman, she must be a woman of God.

Additional comments

None

Pastor Dorri Burrell

What words of advice could you give to pastors' wives?

Learn to prioritize your everyday life. It is so easy to get caught up in what everyone else thinks you should be doing. Don't allow others to determine your priorities.

What words of encouragement could you give to pastors' wives?

Seek God first in *all* things to direct and guide your steps; then obey him first.

Additional comments

None

Overseer Gwendolyn Hollins

What words of advice could you give to pastors' wives?

Know who you are in Christ and lean, depend, and trust in who he says you are.

What words of encouragement could you give to pastors' wives?

In the midst of the hustle and bustle of ministry remember ministry starts at home and then spreads abroad.

Additional comments

None
Pastor Patrina Mitchell

What words of advice could you give to pastors' wives?

People see more than they hear—watch our body language. Adhere to the scripture and become the perfect wife, friend, mother, first lady. Know who you are in Christ—please him!

What words of encouragement could you give to pastors' wives?

There is no room for headiness, jealousy, etc. Develop good communication skills. Encourage, support, and give unconditional love to your spouse.

3. Additional comments

None

Pastor Eldress Mary Henderson

What words of advice could you give to pastors' wives?

Never assume the role as just a pastor's wife, but a man filled with God's spirit, and most of all *a man* who can be your friend as well as your husband.

What words of encouragement could you give to pastors' wives?

Trust your husband as he trusts in God for direction in marriage as well as in his pastoral position.

Additional comments

None

Evangelist Lillian L. Windom

What words of advice could you give to pastors' wives?

A wife can help her husband to be a more effective pastor by recognizing that he is the pastor and willingness to listen to his problems. She should refrain from passing judgment until he expresses his opinions. She should avoid betraying the confidence of home to outsiders.

What words of encouragement could you give to pastors' wives?

Be the best wife you can be. Sing in the choir but don't hold an office in the church; teach a Bible class some time.

Additional comments

None.
Bishop Annell Castille-Haney

What words of advice could you give to pastors' wives?

First you must always acknowledge you are helper to a servant of God. That means you will give support and help your spouse in church activities. Sometimes the spouse is the only earthly support a pastor has beside God almighty. I advise all pastors' wives to read St. Matthew 12:25, which says to all Christians that divided homes or cities divided against themselves shall not stand. Being called "first lady" does not mean you make decisions concerning the church for your spouse; even if you are an "Associate Minister," the pastor is the one responsible for the church's welfare.

What words of encouragement could you give to pastors' wives?

Just as Paul said in Ephesians 5:25, "Husbands, love your wives, even as Christ also loved the church and gave himself for it." This means husbands are to love their wives, lead them, nurture them in the things of Christ, and live with them faithfully until death (Matthew 19:3–4). These same rules are also for the wives to submit to their husbands. Ephesians 5:22 says, "Wives submit yourselves unto your own husbands, as unto the Lord." It did not say you are to lead your husbands, so be wise and don't be a partaker of gossip in any form or fashion.

Additional comments.

None.

Pastor Evangelist Ila P. Warren

What words of advice could you give to pastors' wives?

Exodus 14:13: "Fear not, stand firm, and see the salvation of the Lord, which he will work for you." Today, my advice to a pastor's wife is The Seven Ups: Stand up, Pick up, Shut up, Wake Up, Look Up, Stay Up, and Pray Up

What words of encouragement could you give to pastors' wives?

Luke 6:18: "Give and it will be given to you a good measure pressed down shaken together and running over." In all things, thank God for everything in your life. Habakkuk 2:3: "The vision is for an appointed time. Though it tarry, wait earnestly for it, for it will surely come." As a pastor's wife you have many hats to wear, but wear them well. Be patient, be alert, stay steadfast, and always pray for guidance.

Additional comments.

None.

Pastor Eldress Barbara J. Linton

What words of advice could you give to pastors' wives?

Keep working for the Lord; he will pay you. God gave you gifts that no one else has. Never stop, for pay is coming.

What words of encouragement could you give to pastors' wives?

Know who you are, who made you, and gave you gifts. He knows you and where you are. You are his child.

Additional comments

None

Reverend Bettie R. Kennedy

What words of advice could you give to pastors' wives?

Love, encourage, support your husband in his ministry. Bear and wear the qualities of love in I Corinthians 13:4–13. In the midst of your lonely moments when he is away, never cease to cover him in prayer.

What words of encouragement could you give to pastors' wives?

Thank God that you were chosen to be a pastor's wife. Not everyone can handle the people they have to deal with sometime. Be sure to praise him as in Song of Solomon 5:10–16.

Additional comments

None

Evangelist Doris Jean Johnson

What words of advice could you give to pastors' wives?

- Be yourself
- Develop a prayer life that covers all areas of your ministry—home, church, and husband
- Never take sides or show favoritism in your church family.
- Always have an open mind and know your husband is not always right nor you, either. Seek God for wisdom in how to approach this issue and all other issues.
- Realize that when opposition and adversity comes put the blame where it belongs, the devil and not the person. Deal with it through the spirit and not the flesh.

- Remember that with more territory and blessings come more responsibility, accountability, and accessibility. Get ready to work and to serve, not be served.
- Many don't agree, but your husband's ministry is also your ministry. Marriage made you one in everything.
- Establish what your role will be in your ministry with your husband at the start. This will prevent problems before they start.
- Everybody is not going to like you and be your friend. So love unconditionally and put your armor on.

What words of encouragement could you give to pastors' wives?

Know you have been chosen for an important ministry and your mission is as important as your husband's. "Many are called but few are chosen." So take a deep breath and enjoy your marriage and your ministry. You have been blessed with a blessing that many women desire and don't have.

Additional comments

Sena,

You are so special to me! I think of you often and pray for you. To have a sister like you has been the greatest gift ever, and I pray one day I will be able to show you just how much I love and appreciate you. If I have been a disappointment to you in any way, please charge it to my head and not my heart. I wish there were more I could do for you. Praying for the success of your book, and I know it will be a blessing to many, many women.

Much Love!

Pastor Valetta Ann Shaw

What words of advice could you give to pastors' wives?

1. Always remember who was called to pastor.
2. Never let your ambitions or ideas for a project be forced on the congregation because of your position.
3. Don't give members advice based on your opinions; be led by the spirit of god and use god's word.
4. Don't be pulled into clicks, treat all members as if they are a part of the body, leave your personal feelings home.

What words of encouragement could you give to pastors' wives?

1. Know who you are in Christ, not as a pastor's wife.
2. Stay prayerful and in the word.
3. Always remember who you represent so carry yourself with respect in appearance and your lifestyle.

Additional comments

None.
Eldress Dr. Gloria Collins

Appendix C

From Congregation to Pastors' Wives (a.k.a. First Lady)

I am grateful to the following women and men and to those who chose to have their names listed anonymously for their candid response to my survey question, "In general, what is your opinion of pastors' wives (a.k.a. First Ladies)?"

Jamina Agnew
Julia Anderson
Ingrid Baker
M. V. Black
Courtney Blanton
Carolyn Brooks
Mother Lillie Mae Brown
Meranda Bryant
Josalyn Buchanan
Minister Sheila Burns
Trina M. Chatmon
Donna Sher'ronn Christwell

Evangelist Cecilia Darden
Mother Dorothy Davis
Wanda Davis
Velma Douglas
Andrea Dunn
Marian Easley
Domingo Forney
Angel Gooden
Pastor Dan E. Goodman Jr.
Mother Wilhelmenia Hardy
Susan Hildreth
Evangelist Patricia Hudson
Minister James Jackson
Wilma Johnson
LaFonya Jones
Missionary Sherri Levine
Shon Levine
Evangelist Ruby Lewis
Frances Money
Ladonna Lewis-Palmer
Glenda Mapps
Bonnie Mask
Tammie Mask
Stacy Page
Jessie Parks
Avis Phillips
Bettye E. Ray
Chirlanda Richardson
Elizabeth Roaches
Vanessa Roberts
Elaine Rogers
Helen R. Sanders
Evangelist Agnes Scott Taylor
Evangelist Cathy Thompson
Maxine Turner
Kanesha Davis Waites, Psy.D
Carolyn White

Evangelist Deborah R. Whitaker
Maxie Williams
Amelia P. Young
Debra Washington
Joan Weathersbee, Ph.D, LPC
Ruth E. Williams
Anonymous (four)

Proverbs 31 describes what a pastor's wife should be. The white rose is the queen of the roses. To the congregation I think the pastor's wife should be as a white rose—not in words only, but in words and deeds. She should be an example for the congregation; someone the congregation would like to emulate. The pastor is her husband as well as the pastor. She should have a special place in the congregation among the people, because she can contribute so much to the church and congregation—especially to young people. A lot of things that arise could have been prevented by giving her an opportunity to contribute. She should and will have favorites, but in the church she must treat everyone alike. I don't think the congregation should expect more of the pastor's wife than we are will to do and give. Some scriptures the pastor's wife can meditate on are:

> *Let your speech be always with grace, seasoned with salt, that ye may know how ye ought to answer every man.*
>
> —*Colossians 4:6 (KJV)*

> *Let no corrupt communication proceed out of your mouth, but that which is good to the use of edifying, that it may minister grace unto the hearers.*
>
> —*Ephesians 4:29 (KJV)*

> *But there is a spirit in man: and the inspiration of the almighty giveth them understanding.*
>
> —Job 32:8 *(KJV)*

—*Mother Wilhelmenia Hardy*

A lot that goes on about pastors' wives. They are second to the pastor. As soon as they see the pastors, they want to know who their wives are. She has a lot to live up to, a standard to uphold, a mother to the whole church. We as the people make it harder on the pastors' wives than we should. Everything that the pastor has to deal with she has to deal with, too. Every pastor needs someone to minister to them; that's the role of a pastor's wife. I believe in first ladies. They will have to take care of us when the pastor is not here.—*Minister James Jackson*

The pastor's wife has a great responsibility. The wife is there when the members are not there. She has to console the pastor about what he has to put up with the members. Pastoring is a hard job; he has to deal with all kinds of personalities. When we are asleep, she and the pastor are thinking about the sheep and are responsibility for the sheep when they stray.—*Mother Dorothy Davis, Mother of Her Church*

Remember the country song, "Stand by Your Man"? They see a lot of that in the first lady regardless of whatever they are doing—even though they get into scandals. Even those who go through abusive situations they stand by their man. Pastors' wives come in all different forms. Some are nice, but some are stuck up and are ones to be reckoned with.—*Chirlanda Richardson*

The pastor's wife I encountered is really nice. She's down to earth. Even though she carries herself at a different level, she's grounded and personable, and don't feel like I'm being offensive. You can't have a true conversation with some pastor's wives. Sometimes you have to be guarded about you say or how you say things because of the way they portray themselves at a different level. We look up to them. Sometimes a pastor's wife forgets where she came from and what it took to get there. She thinks she's arrived and doesn't remember what she's been through.—*Andrea Dunn*

Funny question, in the way that my late mother, to whom you were so kind to, used to dislike that term, because she said she met too many pastors' wives that acted like they were married to the president of the United States, and even as that "first lady," it was no excuse to think or feel "better" or loftier than other of God's children. She said we are all held to a status of helping one another. Then I met you, then I met Mrs. Landrew, and I think you should both be "poster wives of the men appointed by God" to do the most difficult job. A man appointed by God cannot just have anybody by his side; there is no time clock, the "sheep" of your flock will always, if just for a moment, creep into your mind, and the "signals" you feel when danger is real and very near can shut you down, if you cannot focus on the greater good for so many people. "Never have so few owed so much to so many," type of life. Bless you all! Love you all!—*Josalyn Buchanan*

P.S. I would never marry a minister. I get in trouble for saying exactly what I think; got me spanked since age five.

My pastor's wife is graceful, considerate, encouraging, and lovely. A woman that loves God and her husband.—*Helen R. Sanders*

A pastor's wife is a woman of elegance, class, and is self-controlled. A woman who is of grace and character.—*Courtney Blanton*

First and foremost a pastor's wife should be a true child of God, able to stand the test when her husband has to minister away from home a lot. Be steadfast and unmoveable, always willing to work with the women of her church, and give sound advice.—*Carolyn White*

Pastor's wives are important in many ways in the church. She is an asset to her husband, by being friendly to members and showing them that she cares. Sometimes she might have to pull his coat, concerning some things.—*Anonymous*

A pastor's wife to me is like the first lady of the president. She's his helpmate and stands beside him. She walks with him. Her attributes and spirit are positive and inspiriting. She has a spirit that glows from within and has a caring spirit.—*Anonymous*

To just sum it up. They are angels sent to not just their husbands but to everyone they meet. We need them as much as the pastor. Love them all.—*Trina M. Chatmon*

Pastors' wives are like mother hens keeping the little chicks in the word so that the hawk won't get them.—*Minister Sheila Burns*

I think it is a great honor to be a pastor's wife. A pastor's wife has to be a woman of God. She should be patient and understanding and ready and willing to help in any way.—*Maxie Williams*

Pastors' wives have to endure a lot, and they are to be commended.—*Maxine Turner*

Our pastor's wife is very caring, soft-spoken, and dedicated to serving God. She welcomes everyone she meets and served on several committees at church. Pastors' wives show a dedication to God and their church families. They enjoy people and have a knowledge of the Bible. They are willing to serve in any capacity they are asked to. They are always willing to help the church membership grow.—*Anonymous*

My pastor's wife is very free-hearted and caring. She does not like the spotlight, but will give you her last. But she is very strong in the Lord.—*Elizabeth Roaches*

I think the most effective first ladies are those that are comfortable in their own skin and know *who* they are. It is then and only then that they can minister without being ruled by popular opinion or the *fod du jour*. I have always looked to my first ladies as an example of what to aspire to. This example included more of what was done rather than what was said because a pair of lips will say anything, but a person's actions, even when she thinks no one is looking, reveals the true heart of a man. One of the things that has stood out the most for me was the love the three first ladies I fellowshipped under showed for their husband and their children and the children of the church. Another thing I admired is how regardless of what was going on they always exhibited grace under fire. A first lady can make or break a church and I have been fortunate to have someone who has latched hold to and nurtured the vision for their respective congregation.—*Ingrid Baker*

I think pastors' wives have to be understanding, loving, and humble. When the pastor goes through different things the wives do, too. They have to be able to put flesh in order, because women will be after their husbands. I love it when I can see the love of God in a pastor's wife. Now on a personal note, I have the best first lady ever. I love her so much, all first ladies should be like Sena Whitaker, Praise God!—*Missionary Sherri Levine*

The pastors' wives that I have met are very warming, with love, caring, etc. They didn't mind sitting among other sisters in the church.—*Avis Phillips*

My pastor's wife is a lover of God, helpful to her husband and always stands by her husband. She's giving to others, and helpful. —*M. V. Black*

The pastors' wives I have encountered first of all love God. They are godly women who loved their husbands because they stand beside him, too. They respect his leadership and reach out and embrace the body of God. They are lovers of God then lovers of man.—*Elaine Rogers*

Pastors' wives are special ones. As far as I know they have been kind to me. They were respectable. It seemed as though they obeyed their husbands well.—*Mother Lillie Mae Brown*

I believe that pastors' wives need much prayer and should be commended for their strength. Pastors' wives have to hear what the pastor does not hear, as well as put up with so many things she cannot share with her husband. Bless you all pastors' wives! Remain constant in prayer for your husbands, and we are praying for you all.—*Evangelist Ruby Lewis*

My experiences with pastors' wives (first ladies) have been positive thus far. They seem to be very open and genuine. However, they all presented this openness and genuineness differently. When they speak it's with care and love, you feel their empathy for the situation. They all seem to be fair women looking at both sides of a situation and helpful in creating a solution. They present themselves before the congregation as classy women with passion for her husband and compassion for his flock. Most first ladies are bold and tactfully outspoken and are not afraid of disclosing their faults in the right setting.—*LaFonya Jones*

I have good experiences with pastors' wives thus far. Most were in general friendly and empathetic. Most appeared to be introverted but could be extroverted (more outgoing) when necessary. Some of the wives were reserved and cordial. Most of them were helpful and willing to listen and help others or refer them to someone who could assist them with their issue/problem.—*Stacy Page*

Meeting the needs of the members of the church:

1. Organizing drivers for donations for food/clothes.
2. Organizing social events.
3. Visiting shut-ins or individuals in the hospital to assist pastor.
4. Setting the tone for women members to mirror how to walk in faith.
5. Modeling an opposing perspective as a woman of faith.—*Anonymous*

I'm a member of the St. John Church of Greenville, Texas, and our first lady is Sister Sandra Jolla. She's what a Christian should be. Sister Jolla stays in Coppell, Texas, out by DFW, but on Sundays she's here for church, and Mondays she's here for choir practice and Wednesday for Bible study. Sister Jolla is a very active first lady in church, Mission Dept., Ushers Dept, choir, and teaches a Sunday school class. We have opportunities to spend time with them at their home a day before Christmas, and it's just a blessing to be there. We sing songs, play games, and we leave. Everyone that goes has left with a blessing. I remember when my mom died and Sister Jolla had to go to Washington for her job. The day of my mom's funeral, I was so upset and was crying and someone opened the door of the lady's room, and in came Sister Jolla. She said smiling, "I just couldn't leave you here" grabbed me and said, "I'm here for you," and started praying in my ear that everything would be well with me. That's the kind of first lady we have at St. John. She is always concerned about us. She's just not my first lady, she is my best friend. The ladies at St. John have a women's day where we all get together and spend the day out and our first lady is always there. She wears so many different hats but she's always the same. She always tells us to put God first and there is nothing we can't do as black women. She says doesn't settle for less. I can say a lot more, but I know you didn't ask for a book so I'll stop, because when I talk about my first lady Sister Jolla my heart is full.—*Glenda Mapps*

My assessment of pastors' wives is of respect, appreciative, and honor. They are special people. They are the ones that encourage the pastor in his ministry by walking in faith, praying, and willing to follow him. My opinion is the first lady is really the armor bearer. The price of a first lady is far above rubies. So many times pastors' wives are in a fish bowl. First ladies are precious, they are to be honored. May God Bless them.—*Julia Anderson*

To the Pastor's wife:

The pastor was created from God to minister and assist others in their time of need. I believe the pastor's wife should lend a helping hand to those in need of spiritual guidance and comfort. I am a member of the congregation who wants to be loved for who I am. Unfortunately, the media and society are the ones telling us how we should live, and we have lost out on who God created us to be. My thoughts about what a pastor's wife should be are respectful towards others and love without changing their personality for the role at hand (pastor's wife). I don't expect pastor's wives to be perfect in meeting my relational needs, whether they be in regards to my spouse, parents, friends, colleagues, or pastor. As a member of the congregation, I appreciate individuals who are whole as an individual, good or bad, and not for what they can give to me or how they behave. I expect the pastor's wife to take responsibility for her own thoughts, feelings, goals, and actions such as myself. I expect the pastor's wife to not fall into a victim mentality or blame game in times of distress. I expect the pastor's wife to state her own beliefs and values, as I would as a member, and be able to except the members who may disagree without becoming adversarial. As a member, if I am able to accurately self-assess my limits, strengths, and weaknesses and freely discuss them with others in the form of a testimony, I expect the pastor's wife to as behold this gift of sharing. I am deeply convinced that I am absolutely loved by Jesus Christ, and I have nothing to prove and nor should the pastor's wife. Why? Because we are all human (the pastor, pastor wife and members of the congregation), and we are expected to make mistakes and errors; however, it's what we do with those human errors that determines if we've past God's test.—*Kanesha Davis Waites, Psy.D.*

My pastor's wife is very caring person; she loves the Lord with all her heart. You can see that just by look at her face, always willing to work in the church if needed. If you need to talk to her about anything she there with good advice.—*Vanessa Roberts*

I feel pastors' wives are strong and loving women that have to be hand pick by God. Growing up in a family where my mother was a pastor's wife, I saw firsthand all a wife has to endure—from tirelessly going, going, and going to a husband having to spend so much time encouraging others—which that takes away from the family. One thing I never understood is why so many women in the congregation are so obsessed with preachers, especially knowing they are married, and that's another issue that wives have to deal with. Something I have wanted to say for a long time, ladies stay in your lane and respect the pastors' wives/first ladies. As a teenager I said I will never marry a preacher because it came with so much responsibility, and most people fail to realize what the wife has to endure.

Some think it is the ideal life and that the wife's role is simple (just sit there and look pretty), but ladies it's not that simple. Hats off to pastors' wives/first ladies. I have the upmost respect for pastors' wives/ first ladies.—*Tammie Mask*

Pastor's Wives...hummmmm what can I say? Well there are several words I can use to describe them on both ends of the spectrum:

Unappreciated: People not understanding the responsibilities of them having to care for the families the husband and other people and still have to be at the church for every service, people expect them to be at their every time they call, some people underestimate what a pastor's wife has to go through.

Discouraged: I'm putting myself in their shoes, being that I have been around a lot of pastors' wives, and I can only imagine what they go through, being at the church from sun up to sun down sometimes, having to put up with some of the comments and the mess that are being said to them and about them, and yet some remain meek and humble. I'm sure they feel like throwing in the towel many times; I'm sure they feel overworked and underpaid from constantly going and going and going, and yet they are still Women of God.

These same women who are unappreciated and discouraged are still **P**recious, **A**nointed, **S**aved, **T**rusted, **O**verlooked, **R**espected, **S**anctified**,** **W**orshiping, **I**ntelligent, **F**orgiving, **E**ncouraging, Women of God."—*Evangelist Deborah R. Whitaker*

I believe pastors' wives are very essential to the body of Christ. Especially those that live above reproach and who follow the mandates of Christ and his word. Because of the monumental responsibility of pastors, having a godly wife is most important. It ensures harmony in the home, church, and community. Because her priority is Christ, she will do all that she needs to do to advance the ministry of her husband, marriage, and family.—*Amelia P. Young*

A couple of the more important things to me are:

1. Confidentiality
2. Support but, allowing the pastor to take care of the business of the church.
3. Staying out of member politics.

First lady Mitcham does a great job in these areas.—*Bettye E. Ray*

My ideal first lady is one that can hear the voice of a broken soul whether male or female. She feels the inner tension of her members from their outward reactions. Because she is a prayer warrior, one with a connection to God that affords her the benefit of being able to know why they act, why they say, why they reject her, and why pastors do not understand how you have the best advice to correct or apply to said situations. When first lady and pastor are working to make themselves one in Christ Jesus, they are prepared to face the uglies that the church members will throw at them. Since they know it's coming, as a team they work to stay one in every area of their lives, so that the devil can not divide and conquer. When the first lady knows who she is, she can draw the unlovable in the church, she can speak the word to a hurting soul without quoting scripture because of her personal love relationship with God. First ladies more times than not are put to test that no other woman has to deal with. To me tears are her frequent companion; being accused of trying to take over or not doing enough. First ladies must find that friend who can and will be truthful with them so that they can verbalize unsolved issues that they and pastor cannot agree upon. Then consult the great problem solver for wisdom, understanding and peace. A first lady is like a mother with adult children who knows everything yet asks you for your opinion only to reject whatever you say. You are expected to be at church every time the door opens; you are expected to spend and lend at the drop of a hat. I guess what I am saying is that a first lady will know God like she never thought she would in order to serve as the helpmate to her husband. May God truly bless and keep the first lady of any church.—*Evangelist Cathy Thompson*

From the outside looking in, a pastor's wife is an understanding, loving, and giving person. She has to deal with the unsaved people as well as the saved. She follows God just as the pastor does. Be there for the pastor to encourage, respect him, love and support his ministry as he follows God.—*Bonnie Mask*

The first lady is a God-fearing Christian woman who is loyal and faithful to God, her husband and the church body. The first lady should be kind hearted and easy to love. She should be filled with encouragement and always there to lend a helping hand in any capacity. The first lady is someone you should be able to call your friend. Above all, the first lady must be blameless. To act as a spiritual leader, one must be above reproach, avoiding all hypocrisies.—*Wanda Davis*

Pastor's wives should exemplify the beauty of holiness: (1) A gracious woman of God who is approachable, courageous, friendly, and humble; (2) respectable and full of wisdom, a teacher in knowledge in the word of God and a devout prayer warrior; (3) always beside the man of God as a source of strength, naturally and spiritually so that he always stays focused and balanced on what God has bestowed on his life for edification to the body of Christ. Love in Christ.—*Ruth E. Williams*

The wife of a pastor carries many burdens and also wears many hats. She is often asked to fill the vacant classroom, empty choir chair, or cook the extra dish for a pot-luck dinner. She is kept in the dark about confidential conversations that go on between her husband and others in the church. To be the wife of a pastor takes a special God-called woman who is of noble character with the patience of Job. There are many obligations in which she should attend as her husband shepherds the flock:

1. She should be helpmate and biggest supporter of her husband.
2. She should be a Godly mother.
3. She should be a mentor to younger women.
4. She should be an example to all.—*Domingo Forney*

First of all, I do not put all pastors' wives in the same category. There are different personalities, upbringing, and understandings. It depends on who she is. I expect her to be a lover of God, lover of her husband, lover of people, supportive of her husband, supportive of the congregation, prayerful, kind and humble. If she possesses these characteristics she can make it as a pastor's wife.—*Marian Easley*

Pastors' wives are unique. They have the responsibilities of caring for their families and expected to be a role model. Pastors' wives are also helpers to their husbands. Most often they are not involved in the business-decision making of the church. Some may feel left out often not knowing what the congregation expects of them.—*Susan Hildreth*

I think pastors' wives have to be some of the most patient, understanding, supportive, trustworthy people in the world. She's the best kept secret. She has to do more than smile, she has a leadership role in the church. She is a kind of a symbol of the church, being the first lady. She is expected to be an extension of her husband in the church, by providing emotional and physical support for her husband and the congregation.

Pastors' wives are also women who have the ability to *hear* and know what buttons to push so the pastor can minister. She has to deal with what the pastor has to deal with from a different perspective. She sees everything the pastor does, including when he is under stress. She shores him up and gives him the support and additional strength he needs to enable him to deal with the pressures and his added responsibilities.

As of 2011, pastors' wives roles are taking on a different format. Some first ladies work hard and behind the scenes. Others are out front overseeing ministries in a more visible role. Then you have the ultimate first ladies who are co-pastors (exceptions to the rule) because a lot of pastors let their wives operate as co-pastors (primarily Charismatic movement). I cannot justify this biblically, unless she has been called into the ministry. Then she can be over the Women's Ministry.—*Pastor Dan E. Goodman Jr.*

I have found that pastors' wives are different depending on the type of church, the size, etc. The larger church pastors' wives tend to be nice but not very warm or friendly. Some even come across as being fake. They are not easy to get to know and appear guarded. Small to medium churches are totally different; their wives tend to be more spiritual; they tend to create a warmer atmosphere and are approachable. I am not saying they all are, but the majority of them are. I feel that some of it is insecurity and not knowing how to fit in with their congregation. Some of them feel that getting to close makes them vulnerable somehow. Overall, I would prefer a first lady that is warm, full of the spirit, know who she is in the Christ and is comfortable with herself and that way she is also comfortable with others.—*Evangelist Patricia Hudson*

When I think about a pastor's wife, I automatically think of my mom. A strong, caring, respectful, and unique individual. Anyone can be a pastor's wife; however, it takes a unique, God-fearing woman to truly take over all the headaches, pain, and responsibilities that come along with it. I believe that is one of the hardest titles to uphold.

But if you are really called by God all things are possible.—*Ladonna Lewis-Palmer*

It's hard for me to speak about them in general, because I'm really only familiar with few. That said, it has been my impression that they fulfill a background role of primarily supporting the pastor. In addition, I view them as somewhat of a role model for a wife and a Christian woman. It may be unfair, but I expect them to fulfill those roles. I think they have an incredibly important job of encouraging the pastor, being a good wife, raising a family, and fulfilling the role of being the pastor's wife. I would argue that their job is just as demanding, if not more, than the pastor's, but their importance can be missed.—*Angel Gooden*

I have not been a pastor's wife, however, by speaking to others in the ministry and having a family member who was a missionary, it became apparent that congregation members typically do not realize that pastors and their wives have needs and feel vulnerable also. There is an unfortunate expectation for them to primarily be on the giving end of the dynamic, rather than on the receiving end. We need to remember to take care of those who take care of us. It is also common for pastors and their wives to feel pressured to not set firm boundaries, which leads them to become depleted and neglect opportunities to have, what I call, "Elijah in the Desert" moments for rest and relaxation and re-charge, allowing them to continue God's work fully.—*Joan Weathersbee, Ph.D, LPC*

It's hard to generalize about pastors' wives because first ladies are different. There are those who are stuck up, "I'm the first lady, I don't have to talk to you, be your friend, because I'm the pastor's wife, I'm going to be here regardless." Then there are those who are "get involved" first ladies. They are real, they are not fake, they are helpful, they love the church and the people in the church from their heart—not because I'm the pastor's wife, but because I love God and my brothers and sisters.—*Jamina Agnew*

What most people fail to realize is that a pastor's wife is human just like we are. People tend to put the pastor's wife on a pedestal. When she makes a mistake or if something is not right, they tend to look down on her. She is entitled to mistakes just as we are, although she has a certain image to uphold since she is a Christian lady and a pastor's wife, but the people should not pass judgment on her. If she's living a godly life the people in the public are trying to pattern their lives after her.—*Velma Douglas*

I love them. I play the pastor's wife in a play, *I Plead the Blood.* —*Shon Levine*

Our pastor's wife is a strong, devoted, and caring—she endures much! Very misunderstood for not being part of the flow, but she yet stands on God's word, where she is rooted and grounded.—*Wilma Johnson*

She should be an example for the younger women.—*Jessie Parks*

No respect by most members; willing worker; always with a smile, with a broken heart; good listener; loving heart; praying woman of God; well dressed.—*Evangelist Cecilia Darden*

First of all, giving all glory and honor to our heavenly father, Dr. Sena Whitaker, and readers of this great blessing. I am still a single Proverbs 31 lady; however, I truly believe that my mother, the late Alice Marie Christwell, was an excellent role model as a pastor's wife for my father, Elder Clinton Christwell, Jr. She was a devoted wife who listened more than she spoke, but when she did speak, she would try to be encouraging to the person before her. She was also a "praying" warrior whom I knew for praying on her knees before God on a daily basis. During church ministry services, she assisted my father with all of his duties whether secretarial, assisting with the choir, environmental services, or first lady extraordinaire. Through the teaching of God's word, I believe that both of my parents worked as one to exemplify the roles of being God-centered, humble, and meek. She was careful to respect the position of the man of God, and she complemented his role as a pastor's wife. This reminds me of the same help meet role that Eve was created to display in biblical times. My mother ensured that my father had everything that he needed to lead his congregation(s) from spiritual to natural support. She also made herself available to the congregation and visitors as a mentor for life's personal challenges without idle gossip. She was a great mother to her natural children, and, in addition to that, she was a mother figure to several people. My mother shared my father openly with his congregation, and she didn't interfere with any saint or sinner, she just prayed that God would "move" and "he did." All praises go to God! Hallelujah!—*Donna Sher'ronn Christwell*

I think the role of a pastor's wife is complex especially because a pastor's wife has to wear many hats at times and people have many expectations from the pastor's wife. I want to say that my pastor's wife is the greatest. She is loved and respected by everyone. She is genuine and honest...she listens and she cares. She is the most real person you could ever know. She is a perfect example of a pastor's wife. A pastor's wife is significant in the church...she is the woman that Christian women look up to; a role model, and she encourages other women to strive to be all that God calls them to be.—*Meranda Bryant*

I believe a pastor's wife is a special person with a special gift for loving people. A pastor's wife has to take on the frustrations of her husband without being seen and most of the time being heard. Most of the congregation love their pastor and ignore their wives. If a pastor is called by God surely his wife will need to be called also.—*Carolyn Brooks*

I really do not like the term "first lady," and naturally you won't hear me use that term because I believe all of us are "first." But I believe the pastor's wife is a woman who is worthy to receive praise and honor because of her actions, her smiles, and just being who she is—a real person. We all have problems and difficulties we face and have to endure. I just believe that the pastor's wife, one of the ladies of the church, should be engulfed in the Holy Ghost.—*Evangelist Agnes Scott Taylor*

Pastors' wives need to be born again so they can endure. They should be multifaceted and wear a lot of different hats and roles. They also need to work well where needed, whether in the background or forefront, and have the discretion when to do what. They should be a people person and all-around role model for adults, children, whomever. Most importantly, they need to have the pastor's back: be a prayer warrior, uplift him at all times, and be there for him.—*Frances Money*

Pastors' wives are helpful and an encouragement. They actually allow you to see what a holy bond should look on this side of glory. My personal experience of pastors' wives is that they can be friends, mentors, and spiritual leaders and are a great asset to ministry, as they can help the pastor in areas where he is not comfortable or does not have knowledge. She can be as iron sharpening iron for her husband so that he can be ready to bring the bread of life to people who are starving. Pastors' wives can also be comforters and give incredible words of knowledge. When you are at your lowest they can give you just what you need to hear to lift your spirit. In addition, they can be attuned to the congregation and can allow the pastor to become aware of ministries that are needed, such as Outreach.—*Debra Washington*

Appendix D
Prayers and Affirmations

Prayers and Affirmations

Source: *Prayers*, Christian Word Ministries, Lexington, Kentucky
Reprinted with Permission.

Praise the Lord Prayer

Heavenly father, in the name of Jesus Christ, I praise your holy name. Thank you, Lord O Lord, you are my God; I will exalt you. I will give thanks to your name, for you have worked wonders, plans formed long ago, with perfect faithfulness according to Isaiah 25:1. Thank you, Lord, that you are my strength and my song and you have become my salvation. You are my God, and I will exalt you according to Exodus 15:2–3. Thank you, Lord, that our mouths will speak the praise of the Lord, all flesh will bless your holy name forever and ever according to Psalm 145:1. Praise be to your glorious name forever; and may the whole earth be filled with your glory according to Psalms 72:19. The Lord lives, praise be to my rock; exalted be God my savior according to Psalms 18:46. Thank you, Lord, that we will praise you from the rising of the sun to the place where it sets, the name of the Lord be praised according to Psalms 113:3. In Jesus's holy name I pray. Amen.

For Hearing God's Voice

Heavenly Father, I come to you now in the name of my lord and savior Christ Jesus. It is written in your word, according to John chapter ten that your sheep know your voice. Heavenly Father, I am one of your sheep. I ask you heavenly father to teach me to hear your voice distinctly and clearly according to John chapter ten. I ask you to increase your anointing on me to clearly hear and know your voice and not that of a stranger. I ask you to do this is in the name of Jesus Christ of Nazareth. Amen.

For Surrender to God

Heavenly Father, I come to you in Jesus Christ's holy name. I surrender myself to you, Heavenly Father, Son, and Holy Spirit. Your word says in Jeremiah 33 verse three to call upon you and you will show me great and mighty things that I do not know. Lord God, I come to you and cry out. I call unto you creator of the universe. I ask you to show me great and mighty things, of the unfathomable riches of your glory and splendor, all that you are. Help me to plumb the depth of your being and know you. I worship you. I praise your holy name. In Jesus's blessed and holy name, amen.

For Victory in Jesus

Heavenly Father, I thank you that we have received from Jesus Christ the victory over all diseases, afflictions, infirmities, hindrances, persecutions, torments and lies that the enemy is trying to send our way now or in the future. We claim victory and deliverance from all demonic spirits, curses, hexes, vexes, enchantments, witchcraft prayers, psychic prayers, or spells.

We thank you that Jesus Christ is victorious through the power of his might against all the wiles of the devil, against principalities and powers and rulers of darkness of this world and against spiritual wickedness in high places (Ephesians 6:10–12). We claim our victory in faith through our salvation and his shed blood of all these things now. We declare according to Job 22:27–28 that we are victorious through the shed blood of Jesus Christ. In his holy name we pray. Amen.

For Baptism of the Holy Spirit

Heavenly Father, I plead the blood of our lord and savior Jesus Christ over us and I thank you for the most wonderful gift of salvation. Lord Jesus, you promised me another gift, the gift of the Holy Spirit. So I ask you Lord Jesus, to baptize and fill me in and with your holy spirit, just as You filled your disciples on the day of Pentecost. I want to be a disciple of yours, filled with the Holy Spirit just as your disciples were. I will try to do what you tell me to do. I forgive all those who have ever caused me pain, trauma, shock, harm, rejection, or shame, and I ask you to forgive them. I also ask you to forgive me for holding a judgment against me.
Christ Jesus, breathe in me your holy spirit. Thank you, Lord, for hearing my prayer. I lift up my hands unto you, worshipping and praising you in the spirit. I give thanks praise, and glory to you forever with all my heart. In Jesus's name, amen.

For Restoration of Marriage

Heavenly Father, I thank you that you will hear my prayer, for I come in the name of Jesus and on the authority of your word. I come boldly to the throne of grace to receive mercy and find grace for your help in restoring my marriage. I take my place standing in the gap for my husband against the devil and his demons until the salvation of God is manifested in her life.
Father, I have forgiven them of their sins and transgressions, just as you have forgiven them. I stand firm knowing that the Holy Spirit will convict and convince him of his sin, unrighteousness and judgment. Help me, Lord, to remain sane and sober-minded, temperate and disciplined

because I love my husband and I commit myself to him. May I steadfastly remain self-controlled, chaste, good-natured, and kindhearted, adapting myself so the word of God may not be exposed to reproach, blasphemed, or discredited. May our family know that you are Lord, spirit soul and body and that you watch your word of perform it. In Jesus's name we pray (Acts 16:31), amen.

Against Divorce and Separation

Heavenly Father, we render Satan helpless in his activities against our marriage. We come against the spirit of separation and divorce, and we loose him from his assignment against our marriages. His power is broken from our marriage in the name of Jesus (2 Timothy 2:26). We thank you, Father, that our marriages will be constantly renewed in the spirit of our minds, having a fresh mention and spiritual attitude. We have put on the new nature and are created in your image in the true righteousness and holiness (Ephesians 4:23).

Lord, I pray that we will love each other with the God-kind of love, united in total peace and harmony and happiness. We know that whatever you forbid and declare to be improper and unlawful on Earth must be what is already forbidden in heaven, and whenever you permit and declare proper and lawful on earth must be what is already permitted in heaven (Matthew 18:18). Therefore, Lord, I ask you to speak to our hearts and heal our hurts so we may be reconciled in making this marriage work. In Jesus's name we pray, Amen.

For Our Children

Heavenly Father, in the name of Jesus, we affirm your word over our children and grandchildren. We commit them to you and affirm your word of them in Isaiah 54:13 that tells me my children shall be taught by the Lord and great shall be the peace of my children. I thank you that you have delivered them out of rebellion into right relationship with us and their parents.

Your word teaches us that the ffirst Commandment with a promise is to the child who obeys his/her parents in the lord. And Father, you say in

Deuteronomy 5:16 that all will be well with my child/children and they will live long on the earth. I affirm this promise on behalf of my child/ children, asking you to give them an obedient spirit that they may honor his/her father and mother.

Father, forgive me for mistakes made out of my own hurts or selfishness, which may have caused my child hurt. I ask full and true repentance for the mistakes I have made in raising my children. I release the anointing that is upon Jesus to bind up and heal our broken hearts and the broken hearts of our children. Give us the ability to understand and forgive one another as God has forgiven us.

Thank you for the Holy Spirit who leads us into all truth and corrects any wrong perceptions about past or present situations. Father, I promise to train and teach my children in the way that he//she is to go and when they are old they will not depart from you, Lord, but will follow you all of the days of his/her life.

In the name of Jesus, I command the spirit of rebellion to be far from the heart of my child and confess that he/she is willing and obedient, free to enjoy the reward of your promises. I ask that they shall be peaceful and a blessing to others. I refuse to provoke, irritate, or belittle my child; I will not be hard on him/her or require perfection, lest he/she becomes discouraged, feeling inferior and frustrated. I will not break his/her spirit, in the name of Jesus and by the power of the Holy Spirit.

Father, I forgive my child for the wrongs that he/she has done and stand in the gap until he/she begins to understand your love and your grace causes them to come out of the spirit of rebellion which is the name of the enemy. We will not abandon hope in your love and commitment to all your creation. We know you, Jesus, died for our children, even before they were born. Although it may seem to us that our children's journey into selfishness, self-destruction, and the world is never-ending, God we know you are at work in our children's lives in ways we may never understand.

We ask you, Heavenly Father, for a quiet assurance that this process of conversion will take place and the inner peace that only you, Lord Jesus can give us, will now manifest in our lives, in the name of Jesus. Help us also to know and understand that we must let God control difficult situations and always be mindful to trust you. Heavenly Father, help us to remember always that our children have belonged to you from the

beginning. Help us, Lord, to understand that we are here to nurture them and guide them in your ways while they are in our care.
In the name of Jesus Christ of Nazareth, I ask you to destroy any assignments or plans that Satan or our spiritual enemies have against us, against anyone we have prayed for today, against our children, or grandchildren, our marriages, our homes. In Jesus's name, amen.

For One Another

Heavenly Father, in the name of Jesus, we bring our marriage before you. We pray and confess your word over it, and as we do, we use our faith, believing that your word will come to pass. Therefore, we stand in the gap for our marriage and we pray and confess that we will let all bitterness, indignation, wrath, rage, bad temper, resentment, brawling, clamor, contention, slander, abuse, evil speaking of blasphemous language, all marriage, spite, and ill will be banished for us. We pray that we will become useful and helpful and kind to each other, tenderhearted, compassionate, understanding, loving-hearted, forgiving one another readily and freely as you, Father, in Christ forgave us (Ephesians 4:31).
We ask, Lord, that we will walk in love, esteeming and delighting in one another as Christ loved us and gave himself up for us, a slain offering and sacrifice to you, God, so that is becomes a sweet fragrance. In Jesus's name we pray, amen.

Prayer for a Person Who is Grieving Over the Loss of a Loved One

Father, please help me in this time of loss of my loved one. I seem to be frozen with this overwhelming grief. I don't understand why my life is filled with this pain and heartache. But I turn my eyes to you as I seek to find the strength to trust in your faithfulness. You, Lord, are a God of comfort and love, and I ask you to help me to patiently wait on you and not despair; I will quietly wait for your salvation. My heart is crushed, but I know that you will not abandon me. Please show me your compassion, Lord. Help me through the pain so that I will hope in you again. I believe the promise in your word to send me fresh mercy each day. Though I can't see past today, I trust your love will never fail me. In Jesus's name I pray, amen.

To Break Strongholds of Anger, Pride, Bitterness, Resentment

Lord Jesus, I truly regret my sin of anger. I come to you in humility and lowliness of mind. I acknowledge my sin of anger and repent. I turn from that way to walk in your chosen paths of righteousness. I ask You to forgive and cleanse me of all unrighteousness, pride, self centeredness, hate, rage, bitterness, resentment, strife, contention, taking offense, giving offense, misplaced hostility, indifference and all forms of anger in my life.

Lord Jesus, your word sys that your anointing destroys all yokes of bondage (Isaiah 10:27), so I ask you now to use your anointing to break and destroy any yokes and strongholds of pride, self-centeredness, hate, rage, bitterness, resentment, strife, contention, taking offense, giving offense, misplaced hostility, indifference, and all forms of anger in my life along with all of their works, roots, fruits, tentacles and links that are in my life, the lives of anyone that I have prayed for today.

I ask you, Lord, to force out all spirits of pride, bound till they are judged and thrown into the Lake of Fire. Lord Jesus fill me in all these areas that were set free with your love and your holy spirit, according to John 14:14, in the name of the Lord Jesus Christ, amen! (Extra reading, Psalms 37.)

For Forgiveness of Others

Heavenly Father, I forgive anyone who has ever wronged me or hurt me or cursed me or lied to me or prayed witchcraft prayers over me and I bless them in the name of Jesus Christ. I ask you to forgive me for any unforgiveness, any bitterness, any anger, any strife, any animosity, and any resentment that I have in my heart toward anyone at this time. In Jesus's name I pray, amen.

Repentance for a Wrong Attitude

Lord Jesus, I ask you to forgive me for the sin of grumbling and complaining, for not walking in faith, and living to the destiny that I have. My whining attitude is a thing of the past; I am going to rejoice in the Lord; I am going to accept the mind of Christ; I am going to talk about good things; glorious things, God's things. I am going to live with joy unspeakable, and full of glory, and it is going to begin today. In Jesus's name, amen.

For Bitterness and Resentment

Heavenly Father, I come to you now in the name of our lord and savior Christ Jesus. Help me to let go of all bitterness and resentment. You are the one who binds up and heals the brokenhearted. I receive your anointing that breaks and destroys every yoke of bondage. I receive healing by faith according to your word in Isaiah 53:5, "And with his stripes we are healed." Thank you for sending me your holy spirit. I acknowledge the holy spirit as my wonderful counselor! Thank you for helping me work out my salvation with fear and trembling, for it is you, Father, who works in me to will and act according to your good purpose. In Jesus's name, amen.

Forgiveness

Heavenly Father, I come to you now in the name of my lord and savior Christ Jesus. I forgive everyone for anything that they have ever done or said to me. I bless them in the name of Jesus Christ, and I ask you to forgive and bless them in the name of Jesus Christ according to John 14:14.

Father, I ask you to forgive me for any hard feelings I had toward them and fill me with your love. Jesus, I come to you now, in your precious name, and I ask you to forgive them for any unforgiveness they have in their heart toward me or others. I ask you to bless them and forgive them for this unforgiveness. In the name of Jesus Christ of Nazareth according to John 14:13–14, amen.

Receive Forgiveness and Cleaning for my Sins

Heavenly Father, I come to you now in the name of my lord and savior Jesus Christ. Holy Spirit, I pray that you will quicken me to hear my heavenly father's voice and lead me in prayer. Father, I bow and worship before you. I come to you with praise and with thanksgiving. I come to you in humility, in fear, and in trembling. I come to you in gratitude, in love, and through the precious blood of your son, Jesus Christ of Nazareth. Lord Jesus Christ, according to your word in 1 John 1:9, you said if I confess my sins you are faithful and just to forgive me of my sins and cleanse me from all unrighteousness. So Lord Jesus Christ, I come to you now. I receive my forgiveness and cleansing from all unrighteousness: spot, wrinkle and blemish. I am free, totally blameless, from the top of my head to the soles of my feet, in Jesus Christ's holy name, amen.

Your Divine Purpose

Dear Lord, help me, oh gracious Father to not be caught up in religion, but to be caught up in spirit; your holy spirit that I might be more effectual in my prayers and be obedient to You (Jeremiah 1:5). I want to serve your divine purpose, Lord; and do what is good and right in your sight. Allow me, Dear Lord, to live in your light and the love that you have for me. Show me how to be helpful to your kingdom. Show me how to live a life of constant praise to you (Jeremiah 29:11). Bless Jesus Christ's holy name. Amen!

Spiritual Doors Opened

Heavenly Father, I come to you now in the name of our lord and savior Christ Jesus. I ask that you shut any doors that need to be shut in our lives and open any doors that need to be opened, in the spiritual and natural realms of our lives.

We plead the blood of Jesus over those doorways and ask that the enemy be rendered powerfulness and harmless so they cannot come back through those doorways ever again to our home, business, finances, ministry, my spouse, spouse's work place, or children, their schools, their work places, or friends and loves ones. In Jesus Christ's holy name, we pray with thanksgiving. Amen.

Blood of Jesus Covering

Heavenly Father, I come to you now in the name of my lord and savior Christ Jesus. I plead the blood of Jesus, the Blood Covenant, and Psalms 91 over, through, around and about me: my spirit, mind, will, emotions, ego, libido, imaginations, thoughts, and all subconscious areas and physical beings. All spiritual and natural doors and openings coming in my life and properties. The atmosphere above, around about me and my home, possessions, animals, and work places. In Jesus's name, amen!

Finances

Heavenly Father, in Jesus Christ's holy name, I pray your word over my finances, and I thank you for manifesting your word in my life according to 3 John 2, which says you desire that I be in health and prosper as my soul prospers. On the authority of your word, I now declare that all my debts, mortgages, and notes are paid in full, cancelled, or dissolved. I pray in Jesus's holy name with thanksgiving, amen!

Bedroom Blessing

I bless you doorway to this bedroom as the gate of security of this room.
Bed, I bless you with serenity and peace.
I bless you as a place of dreams and the presence of our God.
I bless you with the blessings of rest and refreshment.
I bless you bed, as a gentle invitation to slumber and sleep, to regenerate.
Bedroom, I bless you with quietness.
I bless you to be a haven that angels watch over.
I bless you as a private place, leaving all the care of the day at the gate.
I bless you as the place where we awake, fresh and alive to begin each day.
I bless you as a place of beauty.
I do this blessing in the Name of Jesus, who neither slumbers nor sleeps,

but gives to us, as his beloved, even in our sleep.

Affirmations for Daily Living

I declare God the battle is already won. God is removing the enemy.
I declare that my God will take care of the enemy that has come against what God has ordained for me.
I declare that my God is preserving me for what he has ordained for me.
I declare that we have won the victory!
I believe God has sent his word and it will not return void.
I declare that God has anointed us to do his will.
I declare that God has given us divine healing and divine life.
I expect the victory that Jesus has won for us on the cross.
God's favor and blessings are on me today.
I expect God's mercy and grace on me today.
I expect God's favor on me today.
I expect God to extend my life to the rapture.
I declare that God is going to give me supernatural increase till the rapture.
I will live and not die, but declare the word of the Lord.
I declare that God's favor is on me, that he has given me his strength, wisdom, blessings, and peace.
I expect God's blessings in my life today.
I believe God has give me his abundant life.

Affirmations for our Children

Heavenly Father, in the name of Jesus Christ of Nazareth, I thank you and praise you for the promises in your word concerning our children and grandchildren. I affirm now that all my children and grandchildren shall be taught of the Lord and great shall be the peace of our children and grandchildren according to Isaiah 54:13.
I thank you and praise you for the salvation of our children and grandchildren and pray that they will love you with all their heart, with all their soul and with all their mind, might and strength and love their neighbor as thyself; according to your word in Deuteronomy 6:5, Mark 120 and Matthew 22:37–39.

According to your word in 2 Corinthians 5:21, our children are the righteousness of God in him. And they are the head and not the tail as promised in Deuteronomy 28:13.
We thank you that our children honor their fathers and mothers according to Deuteronomy 5:16.
We pray that nothing will be done by our children through selfish ambition or conceit.
As written in Ephesians 5:17, our children are not unwise but understanding what the will of the Lord is.
Their speech is always seasoned with grace (Colossians 4:6)
According to Psalm 34:10, they seek the Lord and shall not lack any good thing.
Thank you, Heavenly Father, that our children and grandchildren are kindly affectionate to another with brotherly love, in honor giving preference to one another as promised in your word in Romans 12:10.
Our children have an anointing form the Holy One and they know all things (1 John 2:20).
To God be the glory, amen!

Affirmations About Finances

As I give, it is given unto me, good measure, pressed down, shaken together, and running over. Luke 6:38
My God makes all grace abound toward me in every favor and earthly blessing, so that I have all sufficiency for all things and I abound to every good work. 2 Corinthians 9:8.
I am blessed in the city blessed in the field, blessed coming in, and blessed going out, my laying down, my rising up. I am blessed in the basket and blessed in my bank accounts, investments, health, and relationships; they flourish. The blessings of the Lord overtake me in all areas of my life and I receive them. Deuteronomy 28:1–14.
The blessings of the Lord makes us truly rich, and he adds no sorrow with it. Proverbs 10:22.
God delights in my prosperity. He gives me power to get wealth that he may establish his covenant upon the earth. Deuteronomy 8:18, 11:12.

God has given me all things that pertain to life and godliness, and I am well able to possess all that God has provided for me. Numbers 13:30, 2 Peter 1:3–4.
I delight myself in the Lord, and he gives me the desires of my heart. Psalms 37:4.
The Lord rebukes the devourer for my sake, and no weapon that is formed against me will prosper. All obstacles and hindrances to true prosperity are now dissolved. Malachi 3:10–11; Isaiah 54:17.
The Lord is my shepherd, and I do not want. Jesus came that I may have life and have it more abundantly. Psalms 23:1; John 10:10.

Source: Prayers, Christian Word Ministries, Edition 10. Lexington, KY. Reprinted with permission.

Appendix E
Additional Resources

Conferences

Family Life Conferences: 1-800-358-6329, Annual Conferences to Strengthen Your Marriage and Family, www.familylife.com

Marriage and Family Resources

America's Family Coaches, 2540 106th St., Ste. 101, Des Moines, IA 50322. 888-ROSBERG. www.afclive.com.

Breakthrough World Harvest Church, P.O. Box 32903, 4595 Gender Road, Columbus, OH 43232. 614-837-1990.

Concerned Women for America, 1015 Fifteenth Street, N.W., Suite 1100, Washington, D.C. 20005. 202-488-7000, www.cwfa.org

Family Life: Lifting My Husband Through Prayer, 2000. ID #5724, 1-800- FL-TODAY. Includes a ten petition prayer for husbands and excerpts from *The Power of a Praying Woman* by Stormie Omarian.

Works Cited

Adams, A. Dana. *4000 questions & answers on the Bible*. Nashville, Tn.: Broadman & Holman, 1996.

Anguished Repose. " Anguished Repose." It's Not The Stress That Gets You, But How You Respond To It!. http://anguishedrepose.com (accessed December 29, 2011).

Arthritis Foundation. "Arthritis Foundation | Symptoms Treatments | Prevention Tips | Pain Relief Advice." Types of Exercises, Top Three Types of Exercise. http://arthritis.org (accessed January 1, 2012).

Attig, Thomas. *The heart of grief: death and the search for lasting love*. New York: Oxford University Press, 2000.

Ator, Jen. "Sponsored Listings." Stress Relief Tips. http://womenhealth-mag.com (accessed December 31, 2011).

Barna Group. "The Barna Group - Barna Update." Born Again Christians Just As Likely to Divorce As Non-Christians Are . http://barna.org (accessed December 29, 2011).

Barnes, Bob. *What makes a man feel loved*. Eugene, Or.: Harvest House, 1998.

Benenate, Becky, and Joseph Durepos. *No greater love*. Novato, Calif.: New World Library, 1997.

Blackaby, Henry T., and Richard Blackaby. *Experiencing God Day by Day Devotional and Journal*. Nashville, TN: Broadman and Holman, 1998.

BrainyQuote/BookRags Media Network. "Famous Quotes at BrainyQuote." Ranier Maria Rilke Quotes. http://brainyquote.com (accessed January 5, 2012).

Brantley, Garry. "Focus on the Family: Helping Families Thrive." Marriage: A Sacred Dance. http://focusonthefamily.org (accessed December 29, 2011).

Briscoe, Jill, and D. Stuart Briscoe. *In a quiet place: daily devotions with Jill & Stuart Briscoe.*. Wheaton, Ill.: H. Shaw, 1997.

Campbell, Susan M.. *Saying what's real: 7 keys to authentic communication and relationship success*. Novato, Calif.: New World Library, 2005.

Carter, Norvella. *Women to women: perspectives of fifteen African-American Christian women*. Grand Rapids, Mich.: Zondervan Pub. House, 1996.

Central Source LLC. "Official Site to Help Consumers Obtain Their Free Credit Report." Request your free credit report. It's Quick, Easy, and Secure. annualcreditreport.com (accessed December 29, 2011).

Chandler, Brynne. "eHow | How to Videos, Articles & More - Discover the expert in you. | eHow.com." How To Remove Earthquake Wax. http://ehow.com (accessed December 28, 2011).

Chapman, Gary . *The Five Love Languages*. Chicago, IL: Moody Publishers, 1995.

"christianjokes.net: The Leading Christian Joke Site on the Net.". http://christianjokes.net (accessed December 28, 2011).

Cloud, Henry, and John Sims Townsend. *Boundaries in marriage*. Grand Rapids, MI: ZondervanPublishingHouse, 1999.

Clowers, Don . *Right & Wrong Expectations in Friendship*. Coppell, TX: Don Clowers Ministries, 2000.

Colbert, MD, Don. *The Seven Pillars of Health: The Natural Way to Better Health for Life*. Lake Mary, FL: Siloam Press, 1999.

Cook, Suzan D. *Too blessed to be stressed*. Nashville, Tenn.: T. Nelson, 1998.

Cottrell, David. *Monday Morning Choices*. New York, NY: HarperCollins Publishers, Inc., 2007.

Coughlin, Paul T., and Sandy Coughlin. *Married but not engaged*. Minneapolis, Minn.: Bethany House, 2006.

Covey, Stephen R.. *The 7 habits of highly effective people*. New York: Simon & Schuster, 1989.

Curtis, Brent, and John Eldredge. *The sacred romance: drawing closer to the heart of God*. Nashville: Thomas Nelson, 1997.

Driftword Creative Services, LLC. "Advice From The Blender Home." Help for Stepfamilies with a Christian Twist. http://www.advicefromtheblender.com (accessed December 28, 2011).

Dalrymple, Byron W. *Survival in the outdoors*. New York: Outdoor Life, 1972.

DeMoss, Nancy Leigh. *Lies women believe and the truth that sets them free*. Chicago: Moody Press, 2001.

Dillow, Linda. *What's it like to be married to me?: and other dangerous questions*. Colorado Springs, CO: David C Cook, 2011.

Dobson, James C.. *Marriage under fire: why we must win this war*. Sisters, Or.: Multnomah Publishers, 2004.

Dobson, Lorna. *I'm more than the pastor's wife: authentic living in a fishbowl world*. Rev. ed. Grand Rapids, Mich.: Zondervan, 2003.

Eggerichs, Emerson. *Love & respect: the love she most desires, the respect he desperately needs*. Nashville, TN: Integrity Publishers ;, 2004.

Elliot, Elisabeth. *Let me be a woman: notes to my daughter on the meaning of womanhood*. Living Books ed. Wheaton, Ill.: Tyndale House Publishers, 1976.

Ethridge, Shannon, and Stephen Arterburn. *Every young woman's battle workbook: how to pursue purity in a sex-saturated world*. Colorado Springs, Colo.: Waterbrook Press, 2004.

Exley, Richard, and Mark Galli. *Dangers, toils & snares: resisting the hidden temptations of ministry*. Sisters, Or.: Multnomah Books, 1994.

Gallagher, Kathy. *When HIs Secret Sin Breaks Your Heart*. Dry Ridge, KY: Pure Life Ministries, 2003.

Gass, Bob. *A fresh word for today*. North Brunswick, NJ: Bridge-Logos, 1998.

Gentle-Stress-Relief.com. "Gentle Stress Relief Tips for Peace Health & Happiness." Use Aromatherapy Stress Relief to Gently Remove

Tension. http://gentle-stress-relief.com (accessed December 31, 2011).

Gillogly, Harold, and Bette Gillogly. *Experiencing Oneness*. Fountain Valley, CA : Joy Publishing, 1995.

God Calling. New York, NY: Barnes & Nobles, 1977.

Goldstein, Scott. "Dallas-Fort Worth News, Sports, Entertainment, Weather and Traffic - The Dallas Morning News." Men arrested in Arlington pastor's death laughed and bragged, court papers say. http://dallasnews.com (accessed December 29, 2011).

Got Questions Ministries. "Bible Questions Answered." What's the Difference Between the Soul and the Spirit of Man?. http://gotquestions.org (accessed December 28, 2011).

Graham, Billy, Franklin Graham, and Donna Lee Toney. *Billy Graham in quotes*. Nashville, Tenn.: Thomas Nelson, 2011.

Gray, Alice. *Lists to live by: the fourth collection, for everything that really matters*. Sisters, OR: Multnomah Publishers, 2002.

Gressett, J. K. . "Take Courage." *Pentecostal Evangel*, April 30, 1989.

Groeschel, Craig. *The Christian atheist: believing in God but living as if he doesn't exist*. Grand Rapids, Mich.: Zondervan, 2010.

Harley, Willard F., and Jennifer Harley Chalmers. *Surviving an affair*. Grand Rapids, Mich.: Fleming H. Revell, 1998.

Harley, Willard F. *Love busters: overcoming habits that destroy romantic love*. Rev. ed. Grand Rapids, Mich.: Fleming H. Revell, 2002.

Harley, Willard F. *His needs, her needs: building an affair-proof marriage*. 15th anniversary ed. Grand Rapids, Mich.: Fleming H. Revell, 2004.

Henslin, Earl R. *The way out of the wilderness: learn how Bible heroes with feet of clay are models for your recovery*. Nashville: T. Nelson, 1991.

Hospice Foundation of America. "End of-life care resources for professionals, patients and families ." Grief, What is Grief?. hospicefoundation.org (accessed January 4, 2012).

Hughes, Barbara. *Devotions for ministry wives: encouragement from those who've been there*. Grand Rapids, Mich.: Zondervan, 2002.

Hunter, Brenda. *In the company of women: deepening our relationships with the important women in our lives—mothers, daughters, sisters, friends & mentors*. Sisters, Or.: Multnomah Books, 1994.

Hyman, Mark. *The UltraMind solution: fix your broken brain by healing your body first : the simple way to defeat depression, overcome anxiety, and sharpen your mind*. New York: Scribner, 2009.

Integrated Publishing. "Medical Reference and Training Manuals." Facts About the Recovery Room. http://armymedical.tpub.com (accessed December 29, 2011).

Jakes, T. D.. *Let it go: forgive so you can be forgiven*. New York: Atria Books, 2012.

Jakes, T. D. *Maximize the moment: God's action plan for your life*. New York: G.P. Putnam's Sons, 1999.

Jakes, T. D. *Reposition yourself: living life without limits*. New York: Atria Books, 2007.

Jamieson, Janet T., and Philip D. Jamieson. "Sermons, Illustrations and Leadership Resources for Church Pastors." Using Pastoral Housing Strategically. preaching.com (accessed January 1, 2012).

Jeremiah, David. *The coming economic Armageddon: what Bible prophecy warns about the new global economy*. New York: FaithWords, 2010.

Johnson, Barbara. *Mama Get The Hammer! There's A Fly On Papa's Head!*. Dallas-London-Vancouver-Melbourne: Word Publishing, 1994.

Johnson, Wm. Robert. "Statistics on Terrorism." Statistics on Terrorism. http://johnstonarchive.net (accessed December 29, 2011).

Jones, G. Curtis. *1000 illustrations for preaching and teaching*. Nashville, Tenn.: Broadman Press, 1986.

Kay, Ellie. *The debt diet: an easy-to-follow plan to shed debt & trim spending*. Minneapolis, Minn.: Bethany House, 2005.

Kimbuende, Eric, Usha Ranji, and Alina Salganicoff . "Home - KaiserEDU.org, Health Policy Education from the Henry J. Kaiser Family Foundation." Prescription Drug Costs, Calculations Using National Health Expenditures Data from Centers for Medicare and Medicaid Services . http://kaiserEDU.org (accessed December 28, 2011).

Korem, Danny. *Streetwise parents, foolproof kids*. Colorado Springs, Colo.: NavPress, 1992.

LaHaye, Tim F. *Why you act the way you do*. 2nd, printing, Living books ed. Wheaton, Ill.: Tyndale House Publishers, 19881984.

Langberg, Diane. *Counsel for pastors' wives*. Grand Rapids, MI: Ministry Resources Library, 1988.

Laskey, Jen. "Health Information, Resources, Tools & News Online - EverydayHealth.com." 6 Ways to Reduce Stress and Protect Your Heart. http://everydayhealth.com (accessed December 28, 2011).

love-quotes-and-quotations.com. "Inspirational Love Quotes on Everything from Romance to Sports." Friendship Quotes Collection Sistahs. http://love-quotes-and-quotations.com (accessed January 5, 2012).

MacArthur, John. *Alone with God*. Wheaton, Ill.: Victor Books, 1995.

Merriam-Webster's collegiate dictionary. 11th ed. Springfield, U.S.A: Merriam-Webster, Inc., 2003.

Merrill, Dean. *Clergy couples in crisis: the impact of stress on pastoral marriages*. Carol Stream, Ill, 1985.

Meyer, Joyce. *Battlefield of the Mind*. New York: Warner Faith, 1995.

Meyer, Joyce. *Approval addiction: overcoming your need to please everyone*. New York: Warner Faith, 2005.

Miller, Susan. *After the boxes are unpacked: moving on after moving in*. Colorado Springs, Colo.: Focus on the Family Pub. ;, 1995.

Ministries, Christian Word . *Prayers*. 10 ed. Lexington, KY: Christian Word Ministries.

Ministries, Crown Financial . "Crown Financial Ministries." Getting Out of Debt. http://crown.org (accessed December 29, 2011).

Moore, Beth. *Get out of that pit: straight talk about God's deliverance from a former pit-dweller*. Nashville, TN: Integrity Publishers, 2007.

Moore, Beth. *So long, insecurity: you've been a bad friend to us*. Carol Stream, Ill.: Tyndale House Publishers, 2010.

NIV women's devotional Bible 2: New International version. Grand Rapids, Mich.: Zondervan Pub. House, 1995.

Nickelson, Ronald L.. *Standard Lesson Commentary 2009-2010*. Cincinnati, OH: Standard Publishing Company, 2009.

O'Connor, Karen. *Getting Old Ain't For Wimps*. Eugene, OR: Harvest House Publishers, 2004.

O'Connor, Lindsey . *If Mama Ain't Happy, Ain't Nobody Happy!*. Eugene, OR: Harvest House Publishers, 1996.

Omartian, Stormie. *A book of prayer*. Eugene, Or.: Harvest House Publishers, 2006.

Orman, Suze. *The money class: learn to create your new American dream*. New York: Spiegel & Grau, 2011.

Osbeck, Kenneth W. . *Amazing Grace: 366 inspiring hymn stories for daily devotions*. Grand Rapids, MI: Kregel Publications, 1990.

Osteen, Joel. *Your best life now: 7 steps to living at your full potential*. New York: Warner Books, 2004.

Our Daily Bread, Daily Readings from the Popular Devotional, Volume 2. Grand Rapids, MI: RBC Ministries, 2009.

Ozirney, Linda. "The Torch Leader - Holding Forth the Gospel Light." Fashions for the Pastor's wife. http://torchleader.com (accessed January 1, 2012).

Pannell, Nancy. *Being a minister's wife— and being yourself*. Nashville, Tenn.: Broadman Press, 1993.

Parrish, Archie, and John Parrish. *Best friends: developing an intimate relationship with God*. Waco, Tex.: Word Books, 1987.

Parrott, Les, and Leslie L. Parrott. *Lovetalk starters: 275 questions to get your conversations going*. Grand Rapids, Mich.: Inspirio, 2004.

Parrott, Les, and Leslie L. Parrott. *Your time-starved marriage: how to stay connected at the speed of life*. Grand Rapids, Mich.: Zondervan, 2006.

Parshall, Janet, and Sarah Parshall Perry. *When the fairy dust settles: a mother and her daughter discuss what really matters*. New York: Warner Faith, 2004.

Patterson, Dorothy Kelley, Tim F. LaHaye, and Beverly LaHaye. *A handbook for ministers' wives: sharing the blessings of your marriage, family, and home*. Nashville, Tenn.: Broadman & Holman, 2002.

Peale, Ruth Stafford. *The adventure of being a wife*. Englewood Cliffs, N.J.: Prentice-Hall, 1971.

Pegues, Deborah Smith. *30 days to taming your tongue*. Eugene, Or.: Harvest House Publishers, 2005.

Pentz, Croft M.. *The complete book of zingers*. Wheaton, Ill.: Tyndale House Publishers, 1990.

quotaegarden.com. "The Quote Garden - Quotes, Sayings, Quotations, Verses." Quotes About Excuses. http://quotegarden.com (accessed January 5, 2012).

Riviere, Bill, and Inc Bean. *The L.L. Bean guide to the outdoors*. New York: Random House, 1981.

Rogers, Dr. Adrian. *Adrianisms Volumes 1: The Wit and Wisdom of Adrian Rogers*. Memphis, TN: Love Worth Finding Ministries, 2007.

Rogers, Dr. Adrian. *Adrianisms Volume 2: The Wit and Wisdom of Adrian Rogers*. Memphis, TN: Love Worth Finding Ministries, 2007.

Rosberg, Gary, and Barbara Rosberg. *The great marriage Q & A book.* Colorado: Tyndale House Publishers, 2006.

Russell, A. J.. *God calling: a devotional diary / c edited and with an introduction by A.J. Russell.*. New York: Barnes & Noble, 2007.

Schlessinger, Laura. *The proper care and feeding of husbands.* New York: HarperCollins, 2004.

Shelley, Marshall. *Well-intentioned dragons: ministering to problem people in the church.* Minneapolis: Bethany House Publishers, 1994.

Skills for success. Bristol: Soundview Executive Book Summaries, 1989.

Smith, Hannah Whitall, and Melvin Easterday Dieter. *The Christian's secret of a holy life: the unpublished personal writings of Hannah Whitall Smith.* Grand Rapids, Mich.: Zondervan, 1994.

Smith, M.A., Melinda, and Jeanne Segal, Ph.D.. "Helpguide.org: Expert, ad-free articles help empower you with knowledge, support & hope." Coping With Grief & Loss . http://helpguide.org (accessed December 29, 2011).

Spurgeon, C. H.. *Morning & evening daily readings.* Grand Rapids, Mich.: Christian Classics Ethereal Library, 199.

Staff, Mayo Clinic. "Mayo Clinic." Burns:First Aid. http://mayoclinic.com (accessed December 28, 2011).

Stock, Gregory. *The book of questions.* New York: Workman Pub., 1987.

Sumner, Sarah. "ChristianityToday.org | Coming in Early 2012." The Seven Levels of Lying. http://christianitytoday.org (accessed January 1, 2012).

Swindoll, Charles R.. *Strike The Original Match.* Portland, OR: Multnomah Press, 1980.

ThyLord, Inc.. "good clean christian jokes, christian inspirational quotes, bible christian quotes, hilarious christian jokes". http://christian-Jokes.org (accessed December 28, 2011).

Tubb, Benjamin Robert/A-R Editions, Inc. "Public Domain Music." Popular Hymns of the 19th Century, Joseph Scriven, What A Friend We Have In Jesus. http://pdmusic.org (accessed January 6, 2012).

Tubb, Benjamin Robert/A-R Editions, Inc.. "Public Domain Music." Popular Hymns of the 19th Century, Jeremiah E. Rankin, God Be With You Till We Meet Again. http://pdmusic.org (accessed January 11, 2012).

Tyler, Leslie. "First Lady Exchange - Flash Intro." Shop & Sell 'Sanctified Seconds'—Hats, Clothing, Accessories . http://firstladyexchange.com (accessed January 1, 2012).

Water, Mark. *Bible study made easy*. New Alresford: Hunt & Thorpe, 1998.

White, Pastor Anthony. "Who's Discipling You?." *Epitome Magazine*, August 2009.

Wiersbe, Warren W.. *Wiersbe's expository outlines on the New Testament*. Wheaton, Ill.: Victor Books, 1992.

Williams, Joyce. *She can't even play the piano!: insights for ministry wives*. Kansas City, Mo.: Beacon Hill Press of Kansas City, 2005.

Wilson, P. B.. *Liberated through submission*. Eugene, Ore.: Harvest House, 1990.

Woods, Dr. Jeffrey C. *Getting help: The Complete & Authoritative Guide to Self-Assessment & Treatment of Mental Health Problems*. Oakland, CA: New Harbinger Publications, Inc., 2007.

Wright, H. Norman. *After you say "I do"*. Rev. and expanded. ed. Eugene, Or.: Harvest House Publishers, 1999.

Wright, H. Norman. *Communication: key to your marriage : a practical guide to creating a happy, fulfilling relationship*. Ventura, Calif.: Regal Books, 2000.

Young, Ed. *The 10 commandments of marriage: the do's and don'ts for a lifelong covenant*. Chicago: Moody Publishers, 2003.

www.ingramcontent.com/pod-product-compliance
Lightning Source LLC
Chambersburg PA
CBHW071404090426
42737CB00011B/1348

* 9 7 8 0 9 7 8 9 9 5 3 0 0 *